EU–US Cooperation on Internal Security

This book analyses the cooperation between the European Union and the United States on internal security and counter-terrorism since the 9/11 terrorist attacks.

In particular, four areas of cooperation are examined: customs and supply chain security; judicial cooperation (the mutual legal assistance and extradition agreements); law enforcement cooperation (the Europol–US agreements); and the EU–US agreements for the sharing of air passengers' data (PNR agreements). These cases are analysed through a conceptual framework based on the theories of international regimes, with the data being drawn from an extensive documentary analysis of media sources collected through the 'Nexis' database, official documents, and from 13 semi-structured elite interviews with US and EU officials. The book argues that the EU and the US have established a transatlantic internal security regime based on shared principles, norms, rules, and interests. While at the beginning of this process the EU had a more reactive and passive stance at the later stages both the EU and the US were active in shaping the transatlantic political agenda and negotiations. The book demonstrates how the EU has had a much more proactive role in its relations with the US than has often been assumed in the current literature.

This book will be of much interest to students of EU policy, foreign policy, international security and IR in general.

Dimitrios Anagnostakis is a researcher on international security, terrorism, the European Union, and transatlantic relations. He is a Teaching Fellow at Liverpool Hope University, UK.

Routledge Studies in European Security and Strategy

Series Editors: Sven Biscop
Egmont Royal Institute for International Relations, Belgium
and
Richard Whitman
University of Kent, UK

The aim of this series is to bring together the key experts on European security from the academic and policy worlds, and assess the state of play of the EU as an international security actor. The series explores the EU, and its member states, security policy and practices in a changing global and regional context. While the focus is on the politico-military dimension, security is put in the context of the holistic approach advocated by the EU.

Tactical Nuclear Weapons and Euro-Atlantic Security
The future of NATO
Edited by Paolo Foradori

The EU and Military Operations
A comparative analysis
Katarina Engberg

The EU and Effective Multilateralism
Internal and external reform practices
Edited by Edith Drieskens and Louise van Schaik

EU Foreign Policy and Crisis Management Operations
Power, purpose and domestic politics
Benjamin Pohl

EU Foreign Policy, Transitional Justice and Mediation
Principle, policy and practice
Laura Davis

The European Defence Agency
Arming Europe
Edited by Nikolaos Karampekios and Iraklis Oikonomou

EU Security Policy and Crisis Management
A quest for coherence
Nicole Koenig

The EU, Strategy and Security Policy
Regional and strategic challenges
Edited by Laura Chappell, Jocelyn Mawdsley and Petar Petrov

EU–US Cooperation on Internal Security
Building a transatlantic regime
Dimitrios Anagnostakis

EU–US Cooperation on Internal Security

Building a transatlantic regime

Dimitrios Anagnostakis

LONDON AND NEW YORK

First published 2017
by Routledge
2 Park Square, Milton Park, Abingdon, Oxon OX14 4RN

and by Routledge
711 Third Avenue, New York, NY 10017

Routledge is an imprint of the Taylor & Francis Group, an informa business

© 2017 Dimitrios Anagnostakis

The right of Dimitrios Anagnostakis to be identified as author of this work has been asserted by him in accordance with sections 77 and 78 of the Copyright, Designs and Patents Act 1988.

All rights reserved. No part of this book may be reprinted or reproduced or utilised in any form or by any electronic, mechanical, or other means, now known or hereafter invented, including photocopying and recording, or in any information storage or retrieval system, without permission in writing from the publishers.

Trademark notice: Product or corporate names may be trademarks or registered trademarks, and are used only for identification and explanation without intent to infringe.

British Library Cataloguing-in-Publication Data
A catalogue record for this book is available from the British Library

Library of Congress Cataloging-in-Publication Data
Names: Anagnostakis, Dimitrios, author.
Title: EU–US cooperation on internal security : building a transatlantic regime / Dimitrios Anagnostakis.
Other titles: European Union–United States cooperation on internal security
Description: Abingdon, Oxon ; New York, NY : Routledge, 2017. | Series Routledge studies in European security and strategy | Includes bibliographical references and index.
Identifiers: LCCN 2016038438| ISBN 9781138690165 (hardback : alk. paper) | ISBN 9781315520179 (ebook)
Subjects: LCSH: Internal security–European Union countries. | Internal security–United States. | Security, International–International cooperation. | Terrorism–Prevention–International cooperation. | Judicial assistance–International cooperation. | Law enforcement–International cooperation. | Airlines–Passenger lists–International cooperation. | European Union countries–Foreign relations–United States. | United States–Foreign relations–European Union countries.
Classification: LCC HV8194.A2 A63 2017 | DDC 363.32094–dc23
LC record available at https://lccn.loc.gov/2016038438

ISBN: 978-1-138-69016-5 (hbk)
ISBN: 978-1-315-52017-9 (ebk)

Typeset in Times New Roman
by Wearset Ltd, Boldon, Tyne and Wear

Printed and bound in Great Britain by
TJ International Ltd, Padstow, Cornwall

To my parents Maria and Nikos

Contents

Acknowledgements		viii
List of abbreviations		ix
	Introduction	1
1	Theories of international regimes	21
2	Customs security cooperation between the European Union and the United States	44
3	Judicial cooperation between the European Union and the United States: the mutual legal assistance and extradition agreements	67
4	Transatlantic law enforcement cooperation: the agreements between Europol and the United States	90
5	The passenger name record agreements between the European Union and the United States	115
	Conclusion	148
Index		165

Acknowledgements

I would like first to thank my PhD supervisor Wyn Rees for his help and guidance during the duration of my doctoral studies. His encouragement, patience, and support were immensely helpful. My thanks also go to Alex Danchev, Rory Cormac, Sarah Léonard, and David Gill for their insightful comments and suggestions on the manuscript. They bear no responsibility for any shortcomings in this book.

My thanks are owed to the Alexander S. Onassis Public Benefit Foundation, which provided generous financial assistance for the completion of this project. This research would have been impossible to carry out without the Foundation's help and support.

I would like to thank the officials from the European Union and the United States who shared their knowledge and information with me. Their practitioner perspective is crucial for this book. Although they are not named here, I am grateful for their kindness.

Thanks are also due to Andrew Humphrys and Hannah Ferguson at Routledge for their help in organising the reviews and in addressing various issues related to the publication process. I would also like to thank the anonymous reviewers of this book for their useful comments and constructive criticism.

My thanks also go to all my friends and colleagues in the UK, Greece, and Turkey who contributed to a friendly environment.

I owe special thanks to Melis for her support and patience. Her encouragement and our shared moments kept me motivated for the duration of this project.

Finally, I would like to thank my parents Maria and Nikos for their ceaseless support and sacrifices. I would not have been able to get this far without them. This book is dedicated to them.

Abbreviations

AEO	Authorised Economic Operator
API	Advance Passenger Information
APIS	Advance Passenger Information System
CAPS	Computer-Assisted Aviation Pre-screening System
CBP	Customs and Border Protection Unit
CRS	Computer Reservation Systems
CSI	Container Security Initiative
C-TPAT	Customs-Trade Partnership Against Terrorism
DHS	Department of Homeland Security
EAW	European Arrest Warrant
EC	European Community
EU	European Union
FAA	Federal Aviation Administration
FBI	Federal Bureau of Investigation
JHA	Justice and Home Affairs
JSB	Joint Supervisory Body
MLA	Mutual Legal Assistance
NTA	New Transatlantic Agenda
PNR	Passenger Name Records
TFTP	Terrorist Finance Tracking Programme
US	United States
WCO	World Customs Organization

Introduction

The 9/11 terrorist attacks against the United States (US) had a massive effect on the security policies of both the European Union (EU) and the US, and they worked as a catalyst for EU–US counter-terrorism relations. In a matter of a few years the EU concluded international agreements with the US on customs security, the transfer of air travellers' data, the transfer of financial data, mutual legal assistance and extradition, security research, the sharing of judicial information with Eurojust, and the sharing of criminal intelligence and operational information with the European Police Office (Europol). Apart from the agreements, cooperation between the two actors expanded on a number of policy areas related to internal security, ranging from stolen passports, travel documents' standards, and money counterfeiting, to cyber security, human trafficking, and child pornography.

Such a broad and deep cooperation between the EU and the US on internal security matters had no precedent and was unthinkable in the pre-9/11 period. Indeed, in a conference on EU–US relations in 1996, the US diplomat Earl Anthony Wayne posed the question: 'Does the existence of the Third Pillar actually make any difference at all?' (Wayne, cited in Den Boer 1998: 111). At a time when relations between the EU and the US were institutionalised with the establishment of the New Transatlantic Agenda (NTA) and the creation of the first direct EU–US institutional settings, the prevalent thinking among both US and EU officials and scholars was that as far as transatlantic relations are concerned the third pillar 'cannot deliver' (Den Boer 1998: 112; Cullen 1998: 108; Wayne 1998: 7). Tellingly, in an edited book (Gardner and Stefanova: 2001) published in 2001 (before the 9/11 terrorist attacks) on the transatlantic security challenges and the future agenda of EU–US relations, there was no mention of justice and home affairs issues. Rather, the focus of the book was on NATO and on its relation with European Security and Defence Policy as well as on the transatlantic cooperation regarding the Balkans, Russia, and the Middle East peace process.

The main research aim of this book is to explore the way the EU and the US have negotiated international agreements in the policy field of internal security. This analysis is important for a number of reasons. First, it touches upon the broader issue of international cooperation in the fight against terrorism. While

2 Introduction

Pillar (2001) has included diplomacy in his list of counter-terrorism instruments, he has been sceptical about multilateral efforts to combat terrorism and he has highlighted that 'the counterterrorist diplomacy that matters most is bilateral' (Pillar 2001: 75). The patterns of international counter-terrorism cooperation differ, however, across the various counter-terrorism elements (Romaniuk 2010: 4). While there have been numerous multilateral initiatives for the countering of terrorist financing under the auspices of the United Nations and the Financial Action Task Force, no similar multilateral efforts have emerged with regard to intelligence and law enforcement where bilateralism and ad hoc cooperation have been the preferred modes of cooperation for states. States have also disagreed on the definition of terrorism, and this has arguably impeded international counter-terrorism cooperation, especially in the pre-9/11 period (Romaniuk 2010: 33). Diverging threat perceptions and interests and different historical experiences have similarly been cited as impediments to multilateral counter-terrorism cooperation (Pillar 2001). This work touches upon these issues by looking at four cases of EU–US internal security cooperation, the initial impetus for which has been the fight against terrorism. The questions that emerge concern the degree to which the EU and the US differ in their respective approaches to counter-terrorism and the extent to which such differences had an impact on the EU–US relationship and negotiations.

A second broad theme that is linked to the previous theme is the way global standards for counter-terrorism and internal security emerge. On the one hand, Svendsen (2008, 2011), who has focused on the area of intelligence cooperation for counter-terrorism, has argued that global standards and norms and best practices related to intelligence liaison and cooperation have started to emerge. These norms have been promoted and diffused through networks or epistemic communities of intelligence officials. On the other hand, Romaniuk (2010) has emphasised that multilateral counter-terrorism cooperation has been a strongly political rather than technocratic process in which power and competition have a crucial role. Multilateralism has been used strategically as a tool by states to advance their interests in a process akin to forum-shopping, where actors either try to impose their preferred set of rules or resist imposition from other actors.

Similarly, this book examines the way the rules of the EU–US agreements were negotiated. These agreements were examples of a regional (transatlantic) or 'minilateral' mode of cooperation rather than of a global counter-terrorism initiative. Their importance lay not only in the context of transatlantic security but in that the EU and the US have emerged as two of the most significant counter-terrorism actors globally, which have the potential to shape the global standards in this field. In other words, the successful solving of any differences between the EU and the US on specific counter-terrorism measures can open the way for the two sides to exert more effective global leadership in this area and to influence the political agenda and outcomes of the relevant international organisations. Other states may subsequently imitate similar measures and policies or alternatively be pressured to comply with them. Indeed, in the cases of Passenger Name Records (PNR) transfers and customs security the EU and the US have expressed their willingness to coordinate their positions and actions in the relevant bodies of the International Civil Aviation Organization (ICAO) and World Customs Organization (WCO).

Finally, a central theme to which this book directly relates is the nature of the EU–US relationship. Since the establishment of the first European Coal and Steel Community in 1957 the US has traditionally been supportive of EU integration. Among the reasons for this support was the US desire to contain the Soviet threat, to strengthen the liberal and democratic values and institutions in Europe, and to incorporate West Germany into the European Community institutions in order to avoid any German revanchist tendencies. In the field of trade and economy, disputes and 'trade wars' with the US have erupted several times since the establishment of the Common Market on issues ranging from import tariffs for bananas and subsidies for aerospace companies, to restrictions for beef imports, rules for airline companies, and genetically modified organism (GMO) food products (Lundestad 2003: 262). Significant friction in EU–US relations was also caused by the US Helms–Burton Act, which provided for sanctions against companies (including European ones) that traded with Cuba, as well as by the similar D'Amato Act concerning Iran and Libya. While Europeans strongly condemned and criticised these unilateral and extraterritorial instances of US policy there was no rupture in EU–US relations given the centrality and the strategic importance that both sides accorded to the EU–US relationship (Lundestad 2003: 263).

In the above mentioned disputes, the US has employed various policies and tactics as a response to EU trade and commercial diplomacy. In particular, Devuyst (2001: 283) has mentioned three policy tracks through which the US has tried to produce favourable outcomes for American interests: 'the "pre-emptive intervention track" ... the "exploitation of European weakness track" ... and the "support for unification track"'. Part of these policy tracks has also been the intensive lobbying of the US Mission to the EU in the Commission, the European Parliament, other EU bodies and institutions, the member states, think tanks, and the private sector (Winand 2001).

Cooperation between the EU and the US on internal security matters was established mainly after the 9/11 attacks as a novel field of EU–US relations and thus a central question that has emerged concerns the way the EU and the US have handled their relationship in this new policy field. From the EU perspective, the main issue is how to deal with or manage US power. From the US perspective, the central questions concern the added value that the EU provides and the issue of what is the most efficient way of dealing with the EU, which is perceived as a confusingly complex entity (Schnabel and Rocca 2005: 100). These issues have been a constant feature of EU–US relations, especially as far as trade and commercial relations are concerned (Smith 2005). In the post-9/11 period the same issues have emerged with regard to the EU–US relations on third-pillar matters. The trade and commercial disputes of the 1990s were followed by disagreements over the use of commercial data for security purposes, over data protection in law enforcement and judicial cooperation, and over the unilateral and extraterritorial nature of certain US security measures (Suda 2013). A question therefore emerges regarding the way the EU managed these new instances of US pressure on internal security issues, especially given that on these issues the EU was not as strong or unified as it was in the field of trade and economy.

In the 1990s, the growing interdependence between the transatlantic economies and the increase of the EU and European Community (EC) competencies were accompanied by trade conflicts and friction. Similarly, in the post-9/11 period, the security interdependence between the EU and the US – as demonstrated by the 9/11 hijackers' links with Europe and the rapid growth and development of the third pillar of the EU were accompanied by tensions, which were followed, however, by cooperation and the conclusion of international agreements. Therefore, the central research question of this book is the following: why and how were the EU–US agreements on internal security issues negotiated and what do the EU–US negotiations reveal about the nature of the EU–US relationship. The conceptual framework that is used to answer this question is based on the theories of international regimes.

The surprising finding of this research is that, contrary to the literature on EU–US counter-terrorism relations that has mostly depicted the EU as a 'pushover' led by the US, the EU–US internal security relationship can be better described as a partnership based on common interests. Rather than being passive and accepting all the rules imposed by the US, the EU managed to exercise significant agency in its relations with the US. For example, the start of the negotiations for a mutual legal assistance and extradition agreement was an EU initiative.

Moreover, this research shows that simplistic distinctions or polarisations that depict Europeans as being focused exclusively on data protection and human rights and Americans as being concerned only about security miss the fact that Europeans and Americans were themselves divided over the issue of transatlantic internal security cooperation. While the EU officials from the Council of the EU and the Directorate-General for Home Affairs have shared, to a great extent, similar views with their American counterparts on internal security matters, the European Parliament has frequently voiced its disagreement with US policies. Therefore, a peculiar alliance has emerged among certain European and American officials who have sided against the maximalist positions of the European Parliament. Similarly, regarding the issue of 100 per cent scanning for sea-bound containers, the US administration and EU officials worked together to dissuade the US Congress from insisting on the implementation of the 100 per cent scanning rule.

An additional interesting finding of this research concerns the ambivalent stance of the US towards the EU. This has been largely missed in the literature, which has often assumed that the US would almost automatically have an interest in working with the EU. Whether the US would negotiate an agreement with the EU or not was, however, itself a product of bargaining. For example, in the mutual legal assistance and extradition agreements and in the mutual recognition agreement for the EU and US business-to-government customs security programmes, the EU had to persuade the US that working with Brussels would provide the added value that Washington sought. The EU officials highlighted in their talks with Americans the efficiency-related gains that the US would benefit from by negotiating with the EU rather than separately with each member state.

Finally, this book shows that EU consistency and the relationship between the Commission, the member states, and the European Parliament were important factors in transatlantic relations, for two reasons. First, ensuring the consistency of EU counter-terrorism policies and measures was central to the Commission's calculations on how to showcase the value of the EU to the Americans. The Commission made a significant effort every time to frame the issues under discussion as issues that are better addressed at an EU level rather than at a bilateral level between member states and the US. When the European Parliament intervened, the Commission was concerned that this intervention would make the Americans lose patience with the EU and defect from the negotiations. Second, the EU's internal consistency (or lack of it) affected its bargaining power in the negotiations with the US. In the case of the PNR agreements, for example, several European states revealed in private talks with the Americans that if the EU–US negotiations failed then they would not initiate legal proceedings against airlines as the EU negotiators were highlighting to their American counterparts.

Therefore, apart from the focus on EU–US internal security agreements this research also touches upon a number of different debates and broader themes, including the nature of the EU–US relationship, the tactics that the two sides use to advance their interests, and the effect of EU integration and consistency on the foreign policies of the EU.

Defining internal security

The focus of this book is on the issue-area of internal security. This issue-area comprises the policies and measures that states and regional and international organisations adopt and employ to combat and address internal security threats. The internal security threats can range from organised crime, terrorism, and drug trafficking to cyber-crime, human trafficking, and illegal immigration (Mitsilegas *et al.* 2003: 2; Rees 2006: 6). Regarding the EU, in 2010 the Council of the EU, in the EU's first internal security strategy, identified 'terrorism, serious and organised crime, drug trafficking, cyber-crime, trafficking in human beings, sexual exploitation of minors and child pornography, economic crime and corruption, trafficking in arms, and cross-border crime' (Council of the EU 2010: 2) as significant challenges to the internal security of the union and its member states. The tools that the Council suggested for addressing the above threats included judicial cooperation (for instance, the mutual recognition of judicial decisions and joint investigations), the sharing of information (for example, the establishment of a passengers' data sharing system), customs cooperation, and border controls and the integrated management of external borders. Similarly, the communication from the Commission in 2010 (European Commission 2010) regarding the implementation of the EU's internal security strategy identified terrorism, organised crime, cyber-crime, natural and man-made disasters, and the management of external borders as the main internal security challenges of the EU; the Commission called, among others, for the establishment of an EU PNR system, the expansion of risk-management techniques for customs controls in member states, and the intensification of judicial and law enforcement cooperation.

The above internal security threats and measures were also highlighted in US strategic documents. For instance, in the US 'Strategy to Combat Transnational Organized Crime' (US National Security Staff 2011), the US highlighted, among others, the threats of drug and human trafficking and the measures and tools of intelligence sharing, targeting the financing of organised crime, and strengthening judicial and law enforcement cooperation with third partners and international organisations, such as Europol and Interpol. Additionally, the US 'National Strategy for Homeland Security' (US Homeland Security Council 2007) emphasised the threats of terrorism and natural and man-made disasters and focused on tools such as border controls, customs security measures, and international cooperation.

Given the above, the definition of internal security that is used in this book is that internal security is a policy area comprising police and law enforcement measures, judicial tools, intelligence, border and transportation security, and critical infrastructure and civil protection measures. The above tools and measures are used for addressing internal security challenges, which include terrorism, organised crime, drug trafficking, illegal immigration, human trafficking, and cyber-crime. In this sense, internal security overlaps with the concept of homeland security, which is preferred in the US and comprises 'intelligence, justice and law enforcement, border and transportation security, infrastructure protection, counter-CBRN (Chemical Biological Radiological and Nuclear) measures, detection, early warning, antiterrorism research, and emergency preparedness and response' (Dalgaard-Nielsen 2006: 3). Both concepts are broad in terms of the scope of the threats and challenges they seek to address.

Transatlantic internal security and counter-terrorism cooperation

Traditionally, the EU–US relationship has been examined in the literature only as far as EU–US trade and economic relations are concerned, given that only in this field did the two sides manage to make significant progress in the 1990s (Grieco 1990; Featherstone and Ginsberg 1996; Peterson 1996; Smith 1998, 2001; Devuyst 2001). Prominent topics that were discussed were the EU–US trade disputes, the resolution of these disputes, the bargaining power of the two sides, and the tactics they used. This work contributes to the literature on EU–US relations by examining through a regime-theory perspective the same issues of bargaining, negotiation, and conflict resolution as they emerged in a novel area of transatlantic cooperation, that of internal security.

The EU–US internal security agreements that were signed after the 9/11 attacks prompted the emergence of a body of literature that mapped the various ways in which the EU and the US interacted on internal security and counter-terrorism (Pawlak 2009a, 2009b; Occhipinti 2010; Kaunert 2010; Kaunert and Léonard 2011; Rees 2011; Ripoll Servent and MacKenzie 2012; Kaunert *et al.* 2012; Porter and Bendiek 2012; Suda 2013; Ilbiz *et al.* 2015; Anagnostakis 2016). It is in mainly to this literature that this book seeks to make a contribution by analysing the transatlantic relationship through a regime-theory perspective. The majority of the research has focused on the Passenger Name Record agreements, with relatively less focus on the mutual legal assistance and extradition agreements and the Europol agreements, and with no in-depth detailed research at all having been conducted on EU–US customs security relations. Therefore, to have a more detailed account of the paths to cooperation that the EU and the US followed on internal security issues the inclusion of other case studies is necessary. The examination of a number of different cases gives a more complex picture of the EU and its relationship with the US. Similarly, the application of a regime-theory perspective allows the examination of various aspects of the EU–US relationship and the factors that played a role in the unfolding of EU–US internal security cooperation. While part of the literature has portrayed the EU as adopting a reactive and passive position, this book demonstrates that this was only part of the story and that there have been examples where the EU demonstrated initiative and shaped the political agenda.

The main debates in this literature have concerned the nature of the EU–US counter-terrorism relationship and the influence of the US on the EU with regard to counter-terrorism policies and measures. Regarding the first topic, a central question has been whether the EU has been bullied into accepting US demands or, in Occhipinti's (2010) words, whether the EU could be better described as a 'partner' or as a 'pushover' regarding its relations with the US. These two categories are not, however, necessarily dichotomous. This book shows that, depending on the case under question, there were examples of the EU actively shaping the transatlantic agenda and negotiations, as well as examples where the US imposed its views on Europeans. Pawlak (2007, 2009a, 2009b) and Argomaniz (2009) have highlighted the reactive nature of the EU in the case of the PNR agreements, where the EU was responding each time to US initiatives and pressures. According to these two authors, the EU–US PNR talks and negotiations represented, during their initial stage, a case of unilateral imposition of rules from the US to the EU. Crucial in this imposition was the power asymmetry between the EU and the US.

On the other hand, Kaunert and Léonard (2011) and Occhipinti (2010) have argued that the EU has been a partner of the US rather than a 'pushover' and that it has shown a considerable degree of agency in its relations with the US. Moreover, Kaunert (2010) and MacKenzie (2012) have transferred the theoretical framework of actorness from the area of EU foreign policy and EU environmental policy respectively to the field of EU counter-terrorism. While the two authors have used different sets of actorness criteria and different examples, their central research question has been the same: that is the investigation of the EU's and Europol's international actorness. Kaunert (2010) and MacKenzie (2012)

8 Introduction

have also reached the same conclusions, noting that the EU and Europol could indeed be considered as international actors in the area of counter-terrorism in the post-9/11 period, having had a significant degree of autonomy in their relations with the US.

The actorness approach, while useful in giving a picture of the nature of the EU in the area of counter-terrorism and internal security, does not answer the question of why, for example, concessions were made by the US towards Europol, as Kaunert has argued, or how and under what conditions the Europol–US deals were negotiated. It cannot, in other words, provide answers to the research question of this book. Additionally, the work on actorness and Europol–US relations is less centred on Europol–US cooperation itself and on transatlantic relations and more focused on the nature of the EU and on testing whether the EU fits the theoretical criteria of international actorness. Regime theory, as it is applied in this book, allows a more detailed examination of the bargaining process that preceded the conclusion of the agreements, gives a more holistic picture of transatlantic relations in the area of internal security, and is more fit to answer the question of how the EU and the US negotiated and concluded agreements in this policy field.

Despite their different views on the nature of the EU–US relationship, Pawlak (2009a, 2009b), Argomaniz (2009), Kaunert (2009), Occhipinti (2010; 2013), and Kaunert *et al.* (2012) have come to the conclusion that there has been a convergence of the EU and the US on certain counter-terrorism principles and approaches. To explain this convergence, Occhipinti (2010) has emphasised the role of common interests, which have led to the conclusion of several EU–US agreements in the fields of judicial and law enforcement cooperation, and border and transport security. This convergence was also based on a common transatlantic belief in the utility of the counter-terrorism measures and tools that have been the focus of the EU–US agreements as well as on a realisation that the two sides faced common threats. From a similar perspective, Kaunert (2009) has shown that the EU and the US shared the willingness to cooperate with each other and to achieve joint gains.

Argomaniz (2009), Pawlak (2009a, 2009b) and Kaunert *et al.* (2012) have also come to the above conclusion, shared by Kaunert (2009) and Occhipinti (2010) – that there has been a convergence between the EU and the US on counter-terrorism – though their explanations have been based mainly on a constructivist conceptual framework. In particular, Argomaniz (2009) has argued that the EU–US interactions in the case of PNR included not only the elements of bargaining and cost-benefit calculations but also processes of social learning that made the EU move closer to the US positions regarding the value and importance of passengers' data sharing. Similarly, Kaunert *et al.* (2012) have emphasised how the social interactions between the US and the EU have shaped the latter's interests and its willingness to cooperate and work with Washington on counter-terrorism. While the analyses mentioned above have shed light on the mechanism through which the two sides have re-constituted their interests under the context of the logic of appropriateness, Pawlak (2007, 2009a, 2009b) has focused more

Introduction 9

on the environment that has allowed such interactions to take place. Pawlak has adopted a networks perspective, tracing the emergence of transatlantic professional networks that have brought together EU and US 'securocrats' or, in other words, the two sides' security-oriented officials (Pawlak 2007, 2009a). Similar to the sociological institutionalist analyses mentioned previously, Pawlak has argued that the informal contacts and cooperation and the personal relationships built over time in a networked environment have contributed to and facilitated the convergence of the two sides' views on PNR sharing.

The above debate on processes of socialisation among the EU and US officials has been closely related to another topic that this literature has examined, that is the influence of the US on the EU regarding counter-terrorism policies and measures. The EU, having proposed a PNR system and having legislated customs security provisions similar to the US ones, has followed the American example in the cases of PNR and customs security respectively. Additionally, in the case of the US Terrorist Finance Tracking Program (TFTP) there have been suggestions in the EU about developing a similar EU-based system. The above examples have prompted several scholars to argue from a sociological perspective that the social interactions between EU and US officials have ultimately changed the perceptions of Europeans about the social appropriateness of the US counter-terrorism plans. While Kaunert *et al.* (2012) and Argomaniz (2009) have approached the subject through a constructivist and sociological-institutionalism perspective respectively, Pawlak (2009a) has adopted a policy-networks framework, focusing more on the networked environment that has allowed the flourishing of social contacts and interactions. The common point of agreement of these scholars was that the European Union was influenced and convinced by the US about the social appropriateness of PNR exchanges in the fight against terrorism and in this sense the two sides' norms in the area of border and transport security have been converging. Porter and Bendiek (2012) have come to the same conclusion, though they based their analysis in the conceptual framework of security communities.

Though this book starts from a different conceptual background, it confirms the findings of the scholars mentioned previously: that the EU has indeed been convinced about the importance of, for instance, PNR sharing and the risk-management approaches to customs security. EU officials calculated that having, for example, a PNR system could serve the practical interests of the union in the fight against terrorism and more broadly in countering organised crime. In this sense, the findings of this research are close to Occhipinti's (2010), Kaunert's (2009) and Kaunert and Léonard's (2011) argument about the existence of common interests and the willingness of the two parties to overcome their political or legal differences. Occhipinti (2010) dealt with EU–US internal security cooperation in one chapter only, and did not look extensively at the issue of how transatlantic differences were overcome, while this book provides a deeper analysis of each area of cooperation.

Regarding the preference and interest formation among actors, social interaction and mutual self-reflection is only one of the ways that learning and, as a result, a change in means and/or interests can take place. As it is shown in the next chapter, learning processes can also occur through cost-benefit calculations when the political, social, and security environment changes, or when actors imitate and 'borrow' policies and measures adopted elsewhere without necessarily any social interaction taking place. The above mechanisms need not be mutually exclusive.

Finally, the literature mentioned previously has focused predominantly on the case of PNR agreements. In the policy field of transport and border security, an additional case was that of EU–US customs security cooperation, which has attracted less scholarly attention than PNR. EU–US customs security was examined only very briefly in Occhipinti (2010), in Kaunert and Léonard (2011), and in Grillot *et al.* (2010). The reason for this is that the EU–US negotiations for the 2004 customs security agreement were much less confrontational and controversial than the PNR negotiations, given that the former touched predominantly on technical issues. At the same time, the issue of data protection, which created friction in transatlantic relations, was almost irrelevant for the area of customs. The above do not mean, however, that this case should be ignored when examining EU–US relations. The examination in this book of the field of customs security adds to the existing literature on EU–US border and transport security cooperation by focusing on how the EU and the US managed their relationship in an area other than the PNR transfers.

The conceptual framework: theories of international regimes

To answer the research question of how the EU and the US cooperate on internal security matters this work employs a conceptual framework based on theories of international regimes. The latter emerged as a distinct field of enquiry in international relations scholarship in the late 1970s and early 1980s with the aim of exploring the questions of why and how states cooperate and the impact of international regimes in global politics.

Theories of international regimes have been applied mainly to the areas of international environmental cooperation and international political economy. Scholars have pointed out that environmental and economic and trade problems have given rise to trans-boundary externalities (Young 1994: 23) and instrumental and situational interdependence respectively (Keohane 1984: 122–123). Trans-boundary externalities occur when the actions that take place in the jurisdiction of one state have a direct impact on the welfare of another state (Young 1994: 23). Environmental trans-boundary externalities create in turn the need for international environmental cooperation and for the establishment of governance systems such as international regimes. Similarly, in the case of the global economy, Keohane has talked about instrumental interdependence, where 'actors may be interested in the welfare of others only insofar as the others can take action that affects them' (Keohane 1984: 122), and about situational interdependence, where 'actors may be interested in the welfare of others not only for instrumental reasons, but because improvements in others' welfare improve their own, and vice versa, whatever the other actor does' (Keohane 1984: 123). These types of interdependence create, according to Keohane, the demand for international regimes.

In the case of the EU and the US the political rhetoric of actors after the 9/11 attacks has emphasised the existence of similar patterns of trans-boundary externalities and interdependence in the area of security. The EU and the US officials noted that the security policies that were adopted in European countries could affect the welfare of American citizens (Federal News Service 2006). Moreover, well-planned policies may not bring the desired results due to outside influences and interferences. In a situation where trans-boundary externalities are present, a state's policies and strategies against terrorism may be less effective; these policies are affected by external actors and by the policies of other states. It has been often highlighted by policymakers that transnational terrorism cannot be fought effectively by purely national means and that national internal security policies are closely linked with each other (CNN 2001; Federal News Service 2006).

Both this political rhetoric and the work of Young (1994) and Keohane (1984) on externalities and interdependence are based on a conceptualisation of international relations that emphasises the existence of common and mutual interests as the basis of cooperation in a given policy area. This conceptualisation is linked with the interest-based or liberal school of international regimes (Keohane 1982, 1984). Therefore, one theoretical strand of the broader family of theories of international regimes appears to be well fitted for explaining the emergence of EU–US cooperation on internal security. This signifies that theories of international regimes can provide an analytically useful conceptual framework for accounting for transatlantic negotiations and cooperation in this policy area.

Indeed, these theories have previously been useful tools in explaining and analysing cooperation between international actors in the fields of international security and counter-terrorism as well as in understanding European Community–US relations (Nye 1987; Smith 1987; Grieco 1990; Rittberger 1990; Romaniuk 2010). In particular, Nye has applied regime theory to the US–Soviet security relationship, looking at how the two actors started to change their ideas and views on nuclear weapons and nuclear strategy and how this learning process led gradually to the establishment of a security regime. Nye's approach belongs to the knowledge-based school of regime formation, given that it emphasised the role of learning, knowledge, and ideas. Rittberger has similarly analysed cooperation between East and West from a regime-theory perspective looking, for example, at the emergence of an East–West security regime that was based on the negotiations for the reduction of conventional forces in Europe and the establishment of Confidence and Security-Building Measures (CSBM). More recently, Hasenclever *et al.* (2000) have analysed the same topic of conventional arms control in Europe through their model of contextualised rationalist regime theory. Regarding counter-terrorism, Romaniuk (2010) and Rees (2006) have applied regime theory to analyse global counter-terrorism cooperation and the transatlantic counter-terrorism relationship respectively. Romaniuk has posed the question of why and under what conditions states choose to cooperate multilaterally in the fight against terrorism. Using the theories of international regimes as his conceptual background he has shown how global counter-terrorism is a contested and deeply politicised process where actors seek either to impose their standards or to resist such attempts at imposition by other actors.

The external relations of the EU with third countries have also been analysed through an 'external governance' perspective, which investigates the way EU rules are adopted in third countries as well as the factors that increase the likelihood of such adoption (Lavenex and Schimmelfennig 2009, 2013 Wolff 2009, 2012). This conceptual framework focuses predominantly on the EU, presuming that only the EU will seek to project its rules and norms onto third countries through a one-way process. In other words, the conceivable outcomes are either that the country under question will adopt the relevant EU rules or that it will not. In at least two of the cases that this book examines, however, it was the US that unilaterally imposed certain rules that affected the EU, which led the two sides to a process of negotiation. In these cases, the US rather than the EU sought initially to project its rules on other countries. Additionally, the external governance literature is focused mostly on how EU-originated rules are adopted domestically by other countries rather than on how rules are negotiated and incorporated in international agreements. This negotiations-oriented perspective is better captured by the theories of international regimes.

The conceptual model used in this book combines the power-based, interest-based, and the weak cognitivist approaches to regime formation. More details about the theories of international regimes and their operationalisation in this research follows in the second chapter of the book.

Methodology

The aim of this book is to examine the EU–US internal security relationship through an analysis of four cases of EU–US internal security cooperation in the aftermath of the 9/11 attacks: EU–US customs security cooperation; the mutual legal assistance and extradition agreements; the Europol–US agreements; and the PNR agreements. The intensification of the contacts between the EU and the US on a broad array of internal security issues and the conclusion of several international agreements in the same field is conceptualised as an emergence of a nascent regional regime. The four cases that are examined in this book and the issues of why and how the EU and the US negotiated a number of agreements in the field of internal security are therefore analysed and explored through a conceptual framework based on the theories of international regimes.

The research methods used for this research include documentary analysis and the conduct of semi-structured elite interviews. In particular, this book's data sources include EU documents, which are publicly available on the websites of the relevant EU institutions or agencies, and the speeches, articles, book chapters, and memoirs of EU and US officials and practitioners. Data was also collected from various news sources using the LexisNexis search engine and from semi-structured elite interviews. In total, six US officials and nine EU officials were interviewed in 13 interviews (in two of the interviews two officials were present) conducted during two trips to the US and four trips to Brussels. Finally, the US State Department diplomatic cables leaked by WikiLeaks were searched according to keywords related to the cases examined in this book.

The research logic that is followed in this research is that of structured, focused comparison (George and Bennett 2005: 67). A set of specific research questions that reflect the main objective of this book is asked and guides data collection in each case. This allows the comparison of the findings of each case in the conclusion of the book. The research is also focused, in the sense that only certain aspects of the cases examined are analysed, as explained in more detail in the second chapter.

The universe of possible cases is not very big given that the EU and the US do not have a long history of cooperating in the field of internal security. In particular the EU and the US have signed agreements on customs security, the transfer of air travellers' data, the transfer of financial data, mutual legal assistance and extradition, security research, the sharing of judicial information with Eurojust, and the sharing of criminal intelligence and operational information with Europol. There are other areas of transatlantic internal security cooperation (such as the fight against human trafficking and the identification of stolen passports), though cooperation in these fields has not resulted in the negotiation and signing of international agreements and therefore they are outside the scope of this research. In other words, to better understand how the two sides cooperate on internal security matters what is crucial is to include cases where there was substantial cooperation between the two sides resulting in the negotiation and conclusion of agreements.

Inevitably, there are some cases which are not examined here (for example, the EU–US TFTP agreements or the Eurojust–US agreement) given the inherent limitations of the scope of this book. To compensate for this limitation, the four cases selected for examination in this research reflect variation – in terms of the time in which the agreements were negotiated and signed, and the EU authority that signed the agreements. They also span across various sub-areas of internal security (border and transport security, data protection, customs security, law enforcement, judicial cooperation, and intelligence sharing). A possible criticism that may be raised here is that a case of non-agreement is not included. However, there are no examples of the EU and the US negotiating an internal security agreement and, finally, failing to reach a compromise and conclusion. Moreover, the purpose of this theory-driven research is to understand and analyse the EU–US relationship rather than to test specific theories. In the latter case variance in the final outcome of the negotiations (conclusion of an agreement) would indeed be more necessary.

Finally, one limitation of this study concerns the low number of interviews. The response rate to the letters requesting interviews was not high (28 per cent for the EU officials and 23 per cent for the US officials) given that the topics examined touch upon a number of sensitive security issues. This limitation has been partially addressed by using publicly available speeches, articles, and quotations of EU and US officials.

Background: EU–US internal security and counter-terrorism cooperation before the 9/11 attacks

The fight against organised crime and terrorism emerged as a policy area for EU–US relations only after the EU acquired competencies in this field with the establishment of Justice and Home Affairs (JHA) as the third pillar of the European Union after the Maastricht Treaty. The EU–US relationship in this period had three main features. On the one hand, the US was interested in working with the EU on internal security matters, which had become an important area in the post-Cold War security environment. On the other hand, Washington was frustrated by the slow progress of Europeanisation and integration in third-pillar issues and by the consequent EU rebuff of the US proposals for more intense cooperation on counter-terrorism and on the fight against organised crime and drug trafficking. This European rebuff was not only related to the slow progress of integration on the third pillar but also to the opposition of certain member states to linking the EU with the US and to institutionalising the EU–US relationship in justice and home affairs matters (Gardner 1997: 57). Finally, and stemming from the above, the US stance regarding the value of the EU as a partner was often ambivalent, with voices inside the US administration and bureaucracy doubting the significance of working with the EU as opposed to enhancing bilateral links with member states.

During the 1990s, the US took a great interest in EU integration, especially as far as third-pillar matters were concerned. During that period, Washington was in favour of and supported the Europeanisation of the fight against terrorism, drugs, and organised crime and it was watching carefully the 1996 intergovernmental conference of member states, which resulted in the signing of the Amsterdam Treaty. Regarding the second pillar and the common foreign and security policy, the Americans were concerned about the emergence of a distinct European defence architecture that could be placed outside the NATO framework and their influence. On the contrary, the integration of third-pillar issues did not present any similar challenges for the US, given that NATO was focused predominantly on military security rather than on the so-called 'global challenges' of transnational crime, drug trafficking, and terrorism. The US perceived that it would benefit from the Europeanisation of the area of justice and home affairs, which could establish a European 'one-stop' point for the Americans with regard to law enforcement cooperation and information sharing. At the same time, however, the US continued to rely on the bilateral links that it had established with European member states.

The internationalisation of US law enforcement and the US interest in the EU's third-pillar integration stemmed from the enhanced emphasis that Washington placed on the fight against drugs and organised crime. The end of the

Cold War with the collapse of the Soviet Union moved the transnational challenges of organised crime and drug trafficking to the top of the political and security agenda (Rees and Mahncke 2004: 4). The collapse of the communist regimes in Eastern Europe created an area of instability where crime could flourish. The proliferation of nuclear materials from Russia and the former Soviet republics presented an additional danger for the US, especially with regard to the scenario where terrorist groups acquired such materials. There was an increasing connection between terrorist groups and organised crime networks; the former could rely on crime and drug trafficking to finance their operations and activities.

Regarding intra-European JHA cooperation in the 1990s, it remained problematic. The Europeanisation of the justice and home affairs area has touched upon a number of sensitive issues, such as border controls and criminal law approximation, which have traditionally been linked to the sovereignty of modern states (Mitsilegas *et al.* 2003). Therefore, despite the acknowledgement of the transnational character of the 1990s threats, member states have been reluctant to cede part of their sovereignty in internal security matters. In practice, this was demonstrated by the slow ratification of the Europol Convention, the difficulties of implementing Tampere's proposals regarding the mutual recognition of judicial decisions, the disagreements regarding the future role of Eurojust, and the lack of any progress on the European Arrest Warrant (EAW). In addition to sovereignty-related sensitivities there were substantial differences among the European legal and criminal law systems, which made cooperation difficult (Mitsilegas *et al.* 2003). While the UK and Ireland have a common law tradition based on judicial precedence and on previous court cases, continental Europe has a civil law system based on codified legal regulations. Moreover, European countries differed on the definitions of crimes (for example, terrorism), on whether an offence was placed under criminal law or under civil or administrative law (for example, fraud or corruption), and on their national judicial structures and bodies; similar differences could be seen in the organisation, scope, and remit of national police forces. Finally, the intergovernmental decision-making in the third pillar, where decisions in the Council were taken under the consensus rule, meant that progress in this area was very slow.

Overview of the book

The second chapter of the book introduces the theoretical framework that is used in this project and which is based on the theories of international regimes. It discusses the regime-theory literature with a focus on the concept of international regimes and the issue of regime formation. It presents the three main schools of regime theory (the power-based, the interest-based, and the knowledge-based) as well as the theoretical models that have sought to bring these schools together and have included more than one variable. On the basis of the above discussion, this chapter proposes for the analysis of the EU–US security relationship a multivariate regime-formation model based on the social factors of power, interests, and knowledge, as well as on contextual factors. This model differs from previous regime-formation models mainly in that the interaction effects between the three social forces are articulated more explicitly.

The theories of international regimes and the theoretical model presented in the second chapter are applied to four empirical cases in order to analyse how EU–US internal security cooperation has emerged. The third chapter starts by examining how customs security was conceptualised in the EU and the US before and after the 9/11 attacks. It then proceeds to an empirical investigation of three sub-cases related to transatlantic customs security: (1) the Container Security Initiative (CSI) and the 2004 EU–US agreement, (2) the 2012 EU–US decision for the mutual recognition of the two actors' business-to-government customs security programmes, and (3) the US rule on 100 per cent container scanning. The talks and negotiations for the two agreements and the 100 per cent rule are conceptualised as a regime-formation process through which the EU and the US have established principles and rules for their cooperation on customs security matters. The aim in the analysis of the above sub-cases is to reveal the factors that have influenced the two sides' cooperation and negotiations.

The fourth chapter focuses on how the EU and the US negotiated and concluded the 2003 EU–US mutual legal assistance and extradition agreements. This chapter starts by presenting the context for transatlantic judicial cooperation, showing that before the 9/11 attacks the issue of transatlantic judicial cooperation against transnational threats such as organised crime, drug trafficking, and terrorism was mainly framed as a bilateral problem that the US had to address in its relations with the EU member states. It continues with the agenda formation for the two agreements showing how the issue of EU–US judicial cooperation came to the forefront of the political agenda after the 9/11 attacks. The main part of the chapter uses regime theory to investigate empirically the negotiations for the two agreements and to reveal the forces that shaped these negotiations. The focus is on three issues that created friction between the two sides and on how the differences on these issues were solved. These three problematic areas included human rights (death penalty and special courts/ military tribunals), data protection, and the European Arrest Warrant.

The fifth chapter looks at the two Europol–US agreements signed in 2001 and 2002 examining how Europol and the US negotiated and concluded these agreements and how they solved any differences that emerged. The first section of the chapter introduces the historical context of the relations between Europol and the US, looking first at the internationalisation of law enforcement in the 1990s and the relations between the two sides until 2000 when talks started for the conclusion of a strategic agreement. Then the chapter focuses on the negotiations for the two agreements. More space is devoted to the negotiations for a personal data agreement, where a number of difficulties emerged given the differences between the EU and the US on the protection of personal data. This chapter looks at how these differences were handled from a regime-theory perspective.

The last empirical case examined focuses on the talks and negotiations for the three Passenger Name Record agreements (2004, 2007, and 2012). Similarly to the Europol–US agreements and the MLA agreement, the issue of personal data protection created friction between the two sides during their PNR negotiations. The first section starts with the context showing that before the 9/11 attacks the use of PNRs for law enforcement purposes was not considered an option for either the EU or the US. In the immediate aftermath of the 9/11 attacks the concept of smart borders and the utility of PNRs for security purposes acquired dominant status only in the US. This section continues by showing how the issue of PNR transfers entered the arena of EU–US relations and became the subject of EU–US negotiations. The second section of the chapter is divided into three parts, which analyse the negotiations for the three PNR agreements from a regime-theory perspective. As with the other empirical chapters, the emphasis is on the forces that shaped the two sides' negotiations, on how differences were solved, and on the tactics that each actor used to influence its counterpart.

Finally, the conclusion of the book starts with a discussion and a comparison of the main findings of the four empirical chapters. The next section of the conclusion expands on these findings, discussing the lessons and implications for EU–US relations. Finally, the last section of the conclusion suggests three areas for further research: (1) the effectiveness of EU–US counter-terrorism and internal security cooperation; (2) whether and how the EU and the US coordinate their actions and work together in international forums and international organisations for the establishment of global internal security and counter-terrorism standards; and (3) the role of private actors (such as airlines or shipping companies) in the area of internal security and the interaction and relationship between economic regimes and security regimes.

References

Anagnostakis, D. (2016) 'Securing the Transatlantic Maritime Supply Chains from Counterterrorism: EU–US Cooperation and the Emergence of a Transatlantic Customs Security Regime', *Studies in Conflict & Terrorism*, 39(5), pp. 451–471.

Argomaniz, J. (2009) 'When the EU is the "Norm-taker": The Passenger Name Records Agreement and the EU's Internalization of US Border Security Norms', *Journal of European Integration*, 31(1), pp. 119–136.

CNN (2001), 'Anti-terror effort focuses on international cooperation, safety', 20 September 2001.

Council of the EU (2010) 'Draft Internal Security Strategy for the European Union: "Towards a European Security Model"', 5842/2/10, 23 February 2010.

Cullen, D. (1998) 'Transatlantic Relations in the Fields of Justice and Home Affairs –Can the EU Really Deliver?', in J. Monar (ed.) *The New Transatlantic Agenda and the Future of EU–US Relations*. London: Kluwer Law International, pp. 79–108.

Dalgaard-Nielsen, A. (2006) 'Transatlantic homeland security: why, what, and how?', in Dalgaard-Nielsen, A. and Hamilton, D. (eds) (2006) *Transatlantic Homeland Security: protecting society in the age of catastrophic terrorism*. Abingdon: Routledge, pp. 1–17.

Den Boer, M. (1998) 'Defying a Global Challenge: Reflections About a Joint EU–US Venture Against Transnational Organised Crime', in J. Monar (ed.) *The New Transatlantic Agenda and the Future of EU–US Relations*. London: Kluwer Law International, pp. 109–126.

Devuyst, Y. (2001) 'European Unity in Transatlantic Commercial Diplomacy', in É. Philippart and P. Winand (eds) *Ever Closer Partnership: Policy-Making in US–EU Relations*. Brussels: P.I.E.-Peter Lang, pp. 283–312.

European Commission (2010) 'The EU Internal Security Strategy in Action: Five steps towards a more secure Europe', COM (2010) 673, 22 November 2010.

Featherstone, K. and Ginsberg, R. (1996) *The United States and the European Union in the 1990s: partners in transition*. London: Macmillan Press.

Federal News Service (2006) 'Remarks by Homeland Security Secretary Michael Chertoff at the Federalist Society for Law and Public Policy's Annual National Lawyers Convention', 17 November 2006.

Gardner, A.L. (1997) *A New Era in US–EU Relations? The Clinton Administration and the New Transatlantic Agenda*. Aldershot: Ashgate.

Gardner, H. and Stefanova, R. (eds) (2001) *The New Transatlantic Agenda: Facing the Challenges of Global Governance*. Aldershot: Ashgate.

George, A.L. and Bennett, A. (2005). *Case studies and theory development in the social sciences*. Cambridge, Massachusetts: The MIT Press.

Grieco, J. (1990) *Cooperation among Nations: Europe, America, and Non-Tariff Barriers to Trade*. Ithaca: Cornell University Press.

Grillot, S., Cruise, R. and D'Erman, V. (2010) *Protecting Our Ports: Domestic and International Politics of Containerized Freight Security*. Aldershot: Ashgate.

Hasenclever, A., Mayer, P. and Rittberger, V. (2000) 'Integrating Theories of International Regimes', *Review of International Studies*, 26(1), pp. 3–33.

Ilbiz, E., Kaunert, C. and Anagnostakis, D. (2015) 'The counterterrorism agreements of Europol with third countries: Data protection and power asymmetry', *Terrorism and Political Violence*, 4 November 2015, pp. 1–18.

Kaunert, C. (2009) 'The External Dimension of EU Counter-Terrorism Relations: Competences, Interests, and Institutions', *Terrorism and Political Violence*, 22(1), pp. 41–61.

Kaunert, C. (2010) 'Europol and EU Counterterrorism: International Security Actorness in the External Dimension', *Studies in Conflict & Terrorism*, 33, pp. 652–671.

Kaunert, C. and Léonard, S. (2011) 'The external dimension of counter-terrorism co-operation', in C. Kaunert (ed.) *European Internal Security: Towards Supranational Governance in the Area of Freedom, Security and Justice*. Manchester: Manchester University Press, pp. 90–120.

Kaunert, C., Léonard, S. and MacKenzie, A. (2012) 'The social construction of an EU interest in counter-terrorism: US influence and internal struggles in the cases of PNR and SWIFT', *European Security*, 21(4), pp. 474–496.

Keohane, R. (1982) 'The demand for international regimes', *International Organization*, 36(02), pp. 325–355.

Keohane, R. (1984) *After hegemony: cooperation and discord in the world political economy*. Princeton, NJ: Princeton University Press

Lavenex, S. and Schimmelfennig, F. (2009) 'EU rules beyond EU borders: theorizing external governance in European politics', *Journal of European Public Policy*, 16(6), pp. 791–812.

Lavenex, S. and Schimmelfennig, F. (eds) (2013) *Democracy Promotion in the EU's Neighbourhood: From Leverage to Governance?* Abingdon: Routledge.

Lundestad, G. (2003) *The United States and Western Europe since 1945: From Empire by Invitation to Transatlantic Drift*. Oxford: Oxford University Press.

MacKenzie, A. (2012) 'The external dimension of European homeland security', in C. Kaunert, S. Léonard and P. Pawlak (eds) *European Homeland Security: A European strategy in the making?* Abingdon: Routledge, pp. 95–110.

Mitsilegas, V., Monar, J. and Rees, W. (2003) *The European Union and Internal Security: Guardian of the People?* Basingstoke: Palgrave Macmillan.

Nye, J. (1987) 'Nuclear Learning and US-Soviet regime', *International Organization*, 41(3), pp. 371–402.

Occhipinti, J. (2010) 'Partner or Pushover? EU Relations with the US on Internal Security', in D. Hamilton (ed.) *Shoulder to Shoulder: Forging a Strategic US–EU Partnership*. Washington, DC: Brookings Institution Press, pp. 121–138.

Occhipinti, J. (2013) 'Availability by Stealth? EU Information-sharing in Transatlantic Perspective', in C. Kaunert and S. Léonard (eds) *European Security, Terrorism and Intelligence*. Basingstoke: Palgrave Macmillan, pp. 143–184.

Pawlak, P. (2007) 'From Hierarchy to Networks: Transatlantic Governance of Homeland Security', *Journal of Global Change and Governance*, 1(1), pp. 1–22.

Pawlak, P. (2009a) 'Network Politics in Transatlantic Homeland Security Cooperation', *Perspectives on European Politics and Society*, 10(4), pp. 560–581.

Pawlak, P. (2009b) *Made in the USA? The Influence of the US on the EU's Data Protection Regime Liberty and Security in Europe*. Brussels: Centre for European Policy Studies (CEPS).

Peterson, J. (1996) *Europe and America: The Prospects for Partnership*. Abingdon: Routledge.

Pillar, P. (2001) *Terrorism and US foreign policy*. Washington, DC: Brookings Institution Press.

Porter, A. and Bendiek, A. (2012) 'Counterterrorism cooperation in the transatlantic security community', *European Security*, 21(4), pp. 497–517.

Rees, W. (2006) *Transatlantic Counter-Terrorism Cooperation: The New Imperative*. Abingdon: Routledge.

Rees, W. (2011) *The US–EU security relationship: the tensions between a European and a global agenda*. Basingstoke: Palgrave Macmillan.

Rees, W. and Mahncke, D. (2004) 'Introduction', in D. Mahncke, W. Rees and W. Thompson (eds) *Redefining Transatlantic Security Relations: The Challenge of Change*. Manchester: Manchester University Press, pp. 1–14.

Ripoll Servent, A. and MacKenzie, A. (2012) 'The European Parliament as a "Norm Taker"? EU–US Relations after the SWIFT Agreement', *European Foreign Affairs Review*, 17(2), pp. 71–86.

Rittberger, V. (ed.) (1990) *International regimes in East–West politics*. London: Pinter Publishers.

Romaniuk, P. (2010) *Multilateral Counter-Terrorism*. Abingdon: Routledge.

Schnabel, R. and Rocca, F. (2007) *The Next Superpower? The Rise of Europe and Its Challenge to the United States*. Lanham, Maryland: Rowman and Littlefield Publishers.

Smith, R.K. (1987) 'Explaining the non-proliferation regime: anomalies for contemporary international relations theory', *International Organization*, 41(02), pp. 253–281.

Smith, M. (1998) 'Competitive cooperation and EU–US relations: can the EU be a strategic partner for the US in the world political economy?', *Journal of European Public Policy*, 5(4), pp. 561–577.

Smith, M. (2001) 'The European Union's commercial policy: between coherence and fragmentation', *Journal of European Public Policy*, 8(5), pp. 787–802.

Smith, M. (2005) 'Taming the Elephant? The European Union and the Management of American Power', *Perspectives on European Politics and Society*, 6(1), pp. 129–154.

Suda, Y. (2013) 'Transatlantic Politics of Data Transfer: Extraterritoriality, Counter-Extraterritoriality and Counter-Terrorism', *Journal of Common Market Studies*, 51(4), pp. 772–788.

Svendsen, A. (2008) 'The globalization of intelligence since 9/11: frameworks and operational parameters', *Cambridge Review of International Affairs*, 21(1), pp. 129–144.

Svendsen, A. (2011) 'On "a Continuum with Expansion"? Intelligence Cooperation in Europe in the Early Twenty-first Century', *Journal of Contemporary European Research*, 7(4), pp. 520–538.

US Homeland Security Council (2007) 'National Strategy for Homeland Security', 5 October 2007.

US National Security Staff (2011) 'Strategy to Combat Transnational Organized Crime', 25 July 2011.

Wayne, E.A. (1998) 'The Potential of the New Transatlantic Partnership: An American Perspective', in J. Monar (ed.) *The New Transatlantic Agenda and the Future of EU–US Relations*. London: Kluwer Law International, pp. 3–12.

Winand, P. (2001) 'The US Mission to the EU in "Brussels DC", the European Commission Delegation in Washington DC and the New Transatlantic Agenda', in É. Philippart and P. Winand (eds) *Ever Closer Partnership: Policy-Making in US–EU Relations*. Brussels: PIE-Peter Lang, pp. 107–155.

Wolff, S. (2009) 'The Mediterranean Dimension of EU Counter-terrorism', *Journal of European Integration*, 31(1), pp. 137–156.

Wolff, S. (2012). *The Mediterranean dimension of the European Union's internal security*. Basingstoke: Palgrave Macmillan.

Young, O. (1994) *International Governance: Protecting the Environment in a Stateless Society*. Ithaca: Cornell University Press.

1 Theories of international regimes

Introduction

This chapter introduces the theoretical framework that is used in this book, which is based on the theories of international regimes. One of the main issues of regime theory is regime formation, or in other words how international institutions, agreements, and governance systems are negotiated and concluded (Young 2005: 92–95). Regime theory has been previously used in analysing international agreements on environmental problems (Dimitrov 2003; Andresen *et al.* 2013), economic and trade issues, technological issues and telecommunications (Ruggie 1975; Cogburn 2003; Raustiala and Victor 2004; Park 2009), security issues and counter-terrorism, and human rights. In transatlantic relations, in particular, Grieco (1990) has previously looked at US–EC trade relations from a realist standpoint, while Rees (2006) has focused more on the topic of regime maintenance and persistence by looking at how the EU and the US used and adapted previously established avenues of cooperation for counter-terrorism purposes after the 9/11 attacks. Therefore, theories of international regimes can provide a fruitful conceptual background for analysing the cooperation and negotiations between the EU and the US, and thus for answering the main research question of this book of how and why the two sides negotiated agreements in the area of internal security.

Regime theory emerged in the late 1970s and 1980s as a response to the growing economic interdependence between states (Krasner 1983a). The central question that regime theory sought to answer was how states could cooperate and reap joint benefits under conditions of international anarchy (Stein 1983; Keohane 1983). In other words, the intellectual puzzle that the early researchers of regime theory focused on was why states cooperated and created institutions in the area of trade and economy despite the absence of a central authority that could enforce such institutions (Kindleberger 1973; Keohane 1984; Webb and Krasner 1989). The first focus of regime theory was on regime formation, or in other words on the conditions that were necessary for the creation of international institutions as well as on the maintenance of regimes, with three theoretical schools emerging: a realist, a liberal, and a knowledge-based school (Hasenclever *et al.* 1997: 1–2).

The regime theory literature expanded significantly in the 1980s and 1990s. Regime theorists dealt with a number of theoretical issues related to the definition of regimes, regime formation, regime maintenance, and regime effectiveness (Levy et al. 1995: 1–2). Regime effectiveness was an especially important issue in the sense that it dealt with the question of whether regimes made any difference in global politics, with theorists coming from the realist school being more sceptical than scholars from the liberal and cognitive schools (Hasenclever et al. 1997: 2).

Empirically, the case studies that were selected by scholars for the testing of regime theories concerned mainly the areas of international environmental protection and international trade and economics. Other issue-areas included telecommunications (Cowhey 1990; Krasner 1991) and human rights (Krasner 1993). The reason that the early focus of regime theorists was on these areas was that regime theory emerged initially as a liberal challenge to traditional realist approaches. These realist theories could, arguably, not account for instances of cooperation in low-politics areas such as the ones mentioned previously and they had a predominantly military-oriented and conflict-oriented view of global politics. The realist school of regime theory emerged in an effort to reply to this criticism, while at the same time there were several scholars who employed regime theories for the analysis of security issues, thus broadening the scope of these theories.

The concept of international regimes

This section presents the theoretical debate on the definition and operationalisation of international regimes. It also addresses the criticisms that have been made of the concept of regimes and presents the definition that is used for this book. International regimes are defined here as international institutions in a given issue-area comprised of explicit rules on which actors have agreed. The starting point for identifying whether a regime exists or not in an issue-area is the presence of explicit rules in the form of international agreements.

The first definitions of regimes came from Ruggie (1975) and Keohane and Nye (1977), who defined regimes as 'a set of mutual expectations, rules and regulations, plans, organizational energies and financial commitments, which have been accepted by a group of states' (Ruggie 1975: 570); and as 'sets of governing arrangements that affect relationships of interdependence ... [and] networks of rules, norms, and procedures that regularize behaviour and control its effects' (Keohane and Nye 1977: 19) respectively. The most famous definition of regimes however came from Krasner (1983b), in what was named the 'consensus definition' of regimes: 'regimes can be defined as sets of implicit or explicit principles, norms, rules, and decision-making procedures around which actors' expectations converge in a given area of international relations' (Krasner 1983b: 1). Krasner's definition has been one of the most widely used definitions and even two decades after its emergence researchers continue to employ it (Jägerskog 2001; Leonard 2005) for the analysis of instances of international cooperation.

The enduring success of Krasner's definition was due to the fact that it moved beyond a strictly legal and formalistic analysis of international treaties and international organisations, which was led by scholars coming from the field of international law. Krasner's reference to implicit rules and norms opened up opportunities for researchers to examine cooperation that was not necessarily framed under a formal organisation or treaty. Additionally, the consensus definition constituted a break with the predominant realist structural analyses which focused on conflict rather than on cooperation. Despite the subsequent emergence of various regime definitions, all the conceptualisations of regimes have shared one crucial characteristic that was implied by Krasner's consensus definition: international regimes are not to be equated with international organisations. Regimes can be accompanied by international organisations that have agency, personnel, and a permanent structure, though this is not necessary.

The main weakness of the consensus definition, however, was that it presented researchers with two problems of operationalisation. The first one was the difficulty of assessing whether and when the actors' expectations about the rules or norms of a regime converge. In other words, what was the threshold at which one could assert that the relevant actors converged around certain principles and rules? Related to the above concern was that, while the reference on implicit rules and norms is useful in expanding regime theory's scope of enquiry, it created similar difficulties in identifying these implicit rules in practice. It was mainly due to the above reasons that researchers have challenged the consensus definition as being too elastic (Young 1986) and the regime concept in general as being woolly, given that 'people mean different things when they use it' (Strange 1983: 343).

Following Krasner's definition, and given the criticisms previously mentioned, a number of alternative definitions and conceptualisations of regimes emerged in the literature. In particular, Keohane proposed a formal conceptualisation according to which regimes 'are institutions with explicit rules, agreed upon by governments, that pertain to particular sets of issues in international relations' (Keohane 1989: 4). The advantage of this definition is that it addresses the elasticity found in the consensus definition by focusing on explicit rules and regulations that can be found in international treaties or other public texts. While in this way implicit regimes are moved out of regime's theory scope there are significant gains to be derived with regard to the clarity of the concept of international regimes.

A number of scholars (Zacher 1987: 114; Young 1989: 13–15) have challenged this contract-oriented definition, as well as the original consensus definition, arguing that the issue of implementation was crucial in conceptualising regimes. Otherwise, researchers could end up focusing on dead-letter regimes, the provisions of which were not followed in practice by states. Therefore, according to this behaviour-oriented approach the presence of regimes in an issue-area can be identified on the basis of the observed behaviour of actors: 'observable regularities in the behaviour' (Young 1989: 15) of actors and

24 Theories of international regimes

affirmative statements (supportive of certain rights and obligations) by the most powerful actors (Zacher 1987: 114) were considered reliable indicators of the existence of 'regime injunctions' (ibid.) in an issue-area.

At the same time, a cognitive approach to defining a regime emerged, which focused on the shared understandings and the intersubjective meanings shared by the members of a given regime. In particular, Kratochwil and Ruggie (1986) defined regimes as 'governing arrangements constructed by states to coordinate their expectations and organize aspects of international behaviour in various issue-areas' (Kratochwil and Ruggie 1986: 759) and as comprising 'a normative element, state practice, and organizational roles' (ibid.). Building on Krasner's consensus definition, which emphasised convergent expectations as the basis of international regimes, Kratochwil and Ruggie argued that regimes are inherently characterised by a high degree of intersubjectivity, and they added that 'we know regimes by their principled and shared understandings of desirable and acceptable forms of social behaviour' (Kratochwil and Ruggie 1986: 764). In other words, Kratochwil and Ruggie opted for an interpretive epistemological approach to researching international regimes that departed from the positivist mainstream analysis of regimes.

Both the behavioural and the cognitive approaches had weaknesses, however. The behavioural approach, while it avoided focusing on dead-letter arrangements, over-emphasised the importance of regularities in behaviour at the expense of identifying the exact rules that guide actors' behaviour in a given issue-area. This approach thus gave rise to the question of whether 'state behaviour is, in fact, rule-governed' (Haggard and Simmons 1987: 494). The cognitive approach, on its part, shared the same disadvantage of Krasner's definition in that it lacked a clear threshold at which one can assert that actors' expectations have converged.

Finally, following the above definitions, a revised consensus definition of regimes emerged in the 1990s, which bridged Keohane's formal definition with the behavioural approaches and included two requirements. According to this new definition, the starting point for identifying a regime was the presence of explicit rules in an issue-area (Rittberger 1993: 10–11; Keohane 1993: 28). Following this, the actors should recognise the rules as valid and refer to them affirmatively (Rittberger 1993: 10–11; Keohane 1993: 28). While these two elements were sufficient for calling an international arrangement a regime researchers could also seek to identify a smaller group of arrangements in which there was a third component of 'rule-consistent behaviour' (Rittberger 1993: 11).

Keohane's definition is used in this book, according to which international regimes are institutions that have been established in an issue-area and are comprised of explicit rules that actors have agreed on (Keohane 1993: 28–29). While this definition rules out the presence of implicit regimes, the parsimony of regime conceptualisation is strengthened. Security regimes in particular are systems of rules 'regulating certain aspects of security relationships' between actors (Müller 1993: 361). Security regimes do not encompass the whole array of security relationships among states and international organisations but they rather emerge in certain sectors and 'narrower sub-areas of security policy' (Müller 1993: 361; Rittberger 1990: 1). In accordance with Keohane's definition when applied into the field of security, security regimes are 'sets of rules' in the area of security 'that prescribe behavioural roles, constrain activity, and shape expectations' (Keohane 1989: 3). Security regimes are therefore identified by the presence of international agreements related to security matters that specify rules and regulations for the relevant actors (Keohane 1993: 28).

As shown in the introduction, this book looks at four cases of international agreements that have been signed between the EU and the US in the area of internal security: (1) the 2004 customs security agreement and the 2012 mutual recognition decision, (2) the mutual legal assistance (MLA) and extradition agreements, (3) the Europol–US agreements, and (4) the PNR agreements. These agreements established rules for the regulation of the interactions between the US, the EU, and the EU member states in the area of internal security. Therefore, and according to the definitions provided in the previous paragraph, through the conclusion of the agreements examined in this book the EU and the US have established a regional transatlantic internal security regime. This regime is defined as a nascent transatlantic institution in the field of internal security comprised of the EU, the EU member states, and the US, the behaviour of which is guided by the explicit rules contained in the EU–US internal security agreements.

The focus of this book on the negotiated explicit rules could be open to the criticism that the EU–US internal security regime has been a dead-letter regime. However, the empirical evidence on the two sides' cooperation does not support this claim, given that the EU and the US have complied with the rules of the concluded agreements. In particular, an EU–US joint-review in 2013 found that the two sides have complied with the rules of the 2012 PNR agreement. Similarly, in the area of customs security, the EU and the US have started implementing the mutual recognition of the two sides' business-to-government security programmes as well as the provisions of the 2004 agreement related to the expansion of the Container Security Initiative into European ports. Regarding the Europol–US agreements and the EU–US legal assistance and extradition agreements, both the EU and the US have made extensive use of the new tools and regulations that these agreements introduced. The above suggest that the EU–US agreements on internal security do not amount to a 'dead-letter' regime. In other words, the danger associated with a formal definition of regimes that international agreements might not be complied with has not been present in the cases examined in this book.

This section has examined the issue of the conceptualisation and definition of international regimes. The EU–US relationship on internal security is conceptualised as a regional internal security regime, or in other words as a nascent transatlantic institution in the field of internal security. The rules of this regime were incorporated into the relevant EU–US agreements. The next section will discuss the topic of regime formation or how theories of international regimes have explained and approached the emergence of regimes.

Regime formation

This section touches upon the issue of regime formation as it was approached by the three main schools of regime theory. These power-based, interest-based, and knowledge-based schools focus on the social factors of power, interests, and knowledge respectively to explain how and when states and other actors cooperate to create international institutions. Additionally, contextual factors and exogenous events have been cited, especially from the researchers from the interest-based and knowledge-based schools, as important factors that influence regime formation. The main argument of this section is that the power-based, interest-based, and weak cognitivist schools of regime formation overlap and there is, as a result, a potential for creating a synthetic model based on these three approaches.

Based on the regime formation theories, this section presents four hypotheses related to EU–US negotiations and cooperation:

1 The EU and the US will seek to impose their preferences through sanctions and coercion. The two actors are expected to change their behaviour and stance due to considerations of political costs.
2 The EU and the US will initiate negotiations voluntarily to realise joint benefits, the concluded agreements will reflect both sides' concerns, and the two actors will seek to influence each other through side payments and compensations. The two actors are expected to adjust to each other's preferences due to considerations of mutual benefits to be gained.
3 The EU and the US will start negotiations spontaneously, driven by shared principles and beliefs regarding the suitable response to internal security problems. The EU and the US are expected to change their course of action under the influence of new knowledge.
4 Contextual factors will trigger the emergence of an issue at the international political agenda. Contextual factors will enhance or diminish the strategic position of the negotiating actors. Domestic and national events will influence the regime formation process.

The above hypotheses are combined together into a multivariate model of institutional bargaining according to which all three social forces of power, interests, and knowledge – as well as political context – may play a role in the EU–US negotiations. In other words, this section argues in favour of a synthetic approach to regime formation which rejects single-factor explanations and which has been established as the most prominent path to analysing the emergence of regimes (Hasenclever *et al.* 1997; Leonard 2005; Andresen *et al.* 2013).

The power-based school

The power-based school of regime formation is based on the realist paradigm of international relations theory, which has emphasised the importance of the relative distribution of power in the international system. In particular, the main approaches that have emerged are the hegemonic stability theory (Kindleberger 1973; Snidal 1985), Krasner's (1991, 1993) power-oriented approach, and Grieco's (1988, 1990) modern realist perspective.

The theory of hegemonic stability has been the first realist approach to international regimes to emerge. In particular, Kindleberger (1973) has argued that the maintenance and stability of the international economic system has been based on the presence of a hegemon. The latter, with its preponderance in material resources, has provided stability to the members of the regime in the form of a public or collective good (Hasenclever *et al.* 1997: 88).

Hegemonic stability theory was related to two propositions regarding regime formation. No regime could emerge without the presence of a hegemon, which was defined as an actor that held a preponderance of material resources in an issue-area (Hasenclever *et al.* 1997: 90). Additionally, the maintenance of a given regime was directly connected to the presence of the hegemon that established it. In other words, when the power of the hegemon declined then regimes declined too (Hasenclever *et al.* 1997: 91). The above hypotheses have, however, been disproved in a number of empirical studies (Keohane 1984; Rittberger and Zürn 1991; Young and Osherenko 1993; Levy *et al.* 1995; Young 1994: 88, 1998; Leonard 2005) and as a result hegemonic stability theory in its original form cannot be considered tenable (Hasenclever *et al.* 1997: 91). In the place of this theory, two alternative realist accounts have subsequently emerged.

International regimes have been predominantly analysed from a liberal perspective, which emerged in the 1980s with Keohane's seminal work 'After Hegemony' (Keohane 1984) as a theoretical challenge to hegemonic stability theory. Realism counter-attacked in the early 1990s with the work of Krasner (1991, 1993) and Grieco (1988, 1990). In particular, these authors highlighted the importance of state power (Grieco 1990: 4; Krasner 1993: 139–140) and emphasised that states are driven by calculations of relative gains rather than absolute gains, as liberals argued (Grieco 1990: 20; Krasner 1991: 365). According to Grieco (1990: 44), states are 'defensive positionalists', meaning that they seek to retain their relative position in the international system. International cooperation is difficult given states' fear that the relative gains from cooperative arrangements 'may advantage partners' that could thus be transformed into 'domineering' friends (Grieco 1990: 45). Grieco (1990: 47, 231) acknowledged, however, that the provision of side payments could mitigate the concerns of disadvantaged states about relative gains by restoring the 'pre-cooperation balances of capabilities'.

Regimes are created by the most powerful actors, which seek in this way to enhance their interests (Krasner 1991: 362, 1993: 140); and regime formation is distributional in the sense that 'gains for one actor mean losses for another' (Krasner 1993: 140). To resolve these distributional conflicts and to compel other states to comply with their preferred set of rules powerful actors use threats, penalties, and sanctions (Krasner 1991: 363) and engage in unilateral action (Grieco 1990: 231; Krasner 1991: 343). Additionally, a powerful state is usually less in need of an agreement and therefore it can threaten to defect from cooperation in order to ensure the compliance of other states (Krasner 1991: 343; Hasenclever et al. 1997: 106–107).

However, similarly to hegemonic stability theory, several cases have disconfirmed Krasner's and Grieco's assertion that regime formation was an exercise in distributive bargaining where power played a dominant role (Young 1994, 1998; Leonard 2005). Young (1994), for example, has shown that in international environmental cooperation the parties were engaged in integrative bargaining and that power in the sense of having a preponderance of material resources could not always be translated automatically into bargaining leverage. These criticisms were acknowledged by Krasner, who conceded that there are some international issues that were better explained by liberal approaches (Krasner 1993: 140). The latter could offer better insights on issues related to market failures, while realism is stronger in explaining issues related to distributional conflicts (Krasner 1993: 140).

Additionally, Grieco's reference to side payments and 'equitable achievements of gains' (Grieco 1990: 47) overlapped with Young's interest-based approach, which emphasised the equitability of outcomes and the use of side payments in integrative bargaining in order to satisfy the needs of all parties (Young and Osherenko 1993: 169–170; Young 1994: 109). Similarly, Young did not wholly reject the role of power. While he argued that imposition and coercion was a rare phenomenon in multilateral negotiations he conceded that powerful actors might increase their leverage during integrative bargaining by offering rewards to other parties akin to Grieco's side payments (Young 1994: 90).

The above suggest that there is potential for a synthesis between the power-based and interest-based schools of regime formation and that rather than seeking to explain cases of international cooperation based exclusively on one factor it is more fruitful to explore possible interaction effects between these factors. The next section will present the interest-based approach to regime formation, where a similar argument will be made regarding the research potential of a multivariate model.

The interest-based school

The interest-based school of international regimes has been the mainstream approach to analysing the emergence, maintenance, and effectiveness of international regimes. This section presents Keohane's functional theory and Oran Young's theory of institutional bargaining.

Robert Keohane's functional theory emerged in the 1980s as a direct criticism of the realist theory of hegemonic stability (Keohane 1982, 1984). According to Keohane, hegemonic stability theory could not account for cases where the decline of the hegemon that established a given regime was not followed by a subsequent decline in that regime. For Keohane, the emergence of regimes was explained by the functions that these regimes provided to their members

(Keohane 1984: 81–82). In particular, even when states knew that they could reap joint benefits by acting together, the lack of information about the intentions of the other parties inhibited cooperation. This situation resembled the prisoner's dilemma in game theory, where the fear of being cheated impeded the two actors from realising common gains (Keohane 1984: 68). Regimes removed this uncertainty and they reduced the information and transaction costs related to the negotiation and conclusion of agreements (Keohane 1984: 88). In other words, international regimes facilitated cooperation. According to Keohane, cooperation took place through the adjustment of actors to each other's preferences (mutual adjustment) (Keohane 1984: 52).

While Keohane provided a thick account of why states seek to establish regimes, he did not elaborate on how these regimes were negotiated in the first place and on the stage that preceded regime formation. In particular, if regimes are established to facilitate states' cooperation and the conclusion of international agreements in a given issue-area then the question emerges of how regimes, which are themselves international agreements, originate initially in the absence of the conditions that, according to Keohane, enable cooperation (Hasenclever *et al.* 1997: 43–44). Keohane implicitly acknowledged this gap when he noted that his theory covers the 'demand' aspect of regimes and that hegemonic stability theory may indeed offer some useful insights regarding the 'supply' aspect (Keohane 1984: 209; Hasenclever *et al.* 1997: 38). This, again, reinforces the argument made previously about the potential complementarity between power-based and interest-based approaches.

Oran Young developed his model of institutional bargaining partly as an attempt to account for the supply aspect of regime establishment, which, as mentioned previously, constituted a gap in the interest-based theories of international regimes. Initially, Young (1989) distinguished between three different types of regimes depending on the dominant social factor that influenced regime creation: power-based 'imposed' regimes, interest-based 'negotiated' regimes, and knowledge-based 'spontaneous' regimes. Subsequently, however, he dropped this distinction, arguing that the vast majority of regimes emerge through a process of negotiations and bargaining (Young 1994, 1998) and that instances of mere imposition or purely spontaneous regimes are rare (Young and Osherenko 1993).

While Young placed his model on the liberal family of regime theories several characteristics of this model overlap with the other two regime theory schools. At the same time, Young criticised the interest-based accounts, arguing that these accounts tend to downplay the fact that the negotiating parties often resort to bargaining tactics (Young 1994: 91). He also noted that regime-formation models based on game theory cannot capture the fact that the negotiating parties may face internal divisions (two-level games) (ibid.) and that the identity of the participants in negotiations is not fixed but rather fluid and can be an issue of negotiations for itself (ibid.: 94).

Regarding the other approaches to regime formation, Young is equally critical. His main argument against the realist school is that structural power may

30 Theories of international regimes

not always be translated into bargaining leverage and that there are several other alternative sources of negotiating leverage. In particular, there are actors that, despite their inability to impose their preferences onto other actors, hold blocking or veto powers due to their strategic position in a given issue-area (Young 1994: 89, 125–128). The constitutive principles of international society (for example, the principle of sovereignty) (ibid.: 121), specific ideas related to the problem at stake (ibid.: 124), and lack of domestic political consensus may all limit the ability or the willingness of strong actors to exercise structural power. Similarly, powerful actors cannot easily control how problems and issues are framed for discussion in the agenda-setting stage or the identity of the participating parties in negotiations (ibid.: 123). Negotiations are generally integrative rather than distributive, negotiators seek to establish solutions that are perceived as acceptable and equitable by all parties, and powerful actors want to avoid being perceived as a 'bully' (ibid.: 126–127, 130–134). Finally, weak states can potentially enhance their leverage in negotiations and achieve significant results through the effective use of superior bargaining skills or by making a plea about their inability to implement certain provisions into the domestic context (the 'strength of weakness') (ibid.: 129, 132). While Young does not dismiss the role of power as irrelevant to processes of regime formation he notes that power is exercised in the form of rewards and side payments rather than in the form of coercion and imposition (ibid.: 90). Finally, with regard to the cognitive approaches to regime formation, Young highlights the fact that knowledge is frequently used in a tactical way to advance actors' interests and positions and that knowledge should be expected to play a greater and more independent role during the agenda-setting stage of regime formation rather than during the actual negotiations (ibid.: 97–98).

Given the above criticisms, Young presents his own model of regime formation that focuses on the bargaining that precedes the conclusion of agreements. Moreover, Young indirectly addresses two criticisms of regime theory in general: the lack of attention to the role that domestic actors and factors may play and the treatment of states as unitary actors. Young's model is also indirectly a synthetic model where interaction effects may take place between the social factors that influence bargaining. For example, he argues that the equitability of the concluded deals, which is an interest-based factor (Young and Osherenko 1993: 249), is necessary for regime formation to succeed. At the same time, however, he mentions at several points in his book on the model of institutional bargaining (Young 1994: 90, 135–136) that powerful actors can – through rewards and side payments – create attractive deals 'which already constitute a move in the direction of equity' (Young 1994: 133). The above interaction between power and interest factors that Young mentions is similar to Grieco's reference to side payments and 'equitable achievements of gains' (Grieco 1990: 47).

Having first criticised the previous approaches to regime formation, Young presents an alternative model of regime establishment. In particular, he argues that negotiations usually take place under the tacit understanding that the final agreement should be acceptable by all parties (consensus rule) and that the participants in these negotiations are not always fixed and their number may vary (Young 1994: 99). The solutions adopted in the negotiations are generally accepted by all parties as equitable. Bargaining is not distributive, as realists argue, but rather integrative or mixed-motive, where actors try to establish mutually beneficial deals (ibid.: 100). States are complex entities comprising of various interest groups and transnational linkages may be built between such groups (ibid.: 103–104). Negotiations do not take place in a vacuum but they are linked with broader political, social, and economic events that can both inhibit and facilitate the conclusion of a deal (ibid.: 105). Exogenous shocks or crises can increase the likelihood that negotiations will be concluded successfully as well as the introduction of salient solutions and the incorporation of compliance and monitoring mechanisms into the agreements (ibid.: 110–114). Finally, Young (ibid.: 114) argues that entrepreneurial leadership is crucial in institutional bargaining processes. Entrepreneurial leadership is defined as the efforts made by certain negotiators to popularise the issues under question and to devise salient solutions and deals that are acceptable to all parties (Young 1991: 294, 1994: 114).

This section presented the interest-based approaches to regime formation, highlighting the prospects for synthesis and interaction between the power-based and interest-based models. The next section presents the knowledge-based approaches to regime formation.

The knowledge-based school

The knowledge-based theories of international regimes focused on the role of knowledge, ideas, and normative beliefs to explain the processes of international regime formation. While the realist and liberal approaches did not problematize the origin of states' interests and preferences, assuming that they were exogenously given, scholars from the cognitive school argued that the identification of interests and the formation of preferences are based and shaped by knowledge and ideas in the form of causal and normative beliefs (Goldstein and Keohane 1993: 3). While, according to functional explanations, actors' interdependence in a given issue-area created a demand for the establishment of regimes for the knowledge-based approach, it is new knowledge that influences the demand for regimes (Hasenclever *et al.* 1997: 139). Additionally, cognitivists emphasised the role of scientific advice for policymakers who faced increasing uncertainty regarding the choices that they should take and the options they have. In the same vein as the interest-based approaches, in which a minimum of common interests between states is a prerequisite for cooperation, the knowledge-based theories consider a minimum of shared meanings and understandings regarding the problem at stake necessary for the emergence of international arrangements.

The knowledge-based approaches can be divided into two categories. While weak cognitivism treats the identities of the parties involved in regime establishment as stable, strong cognitivism, which is based on sociological explanations, emphasises the iterative processes of mutual identity formation that take place among the relevant actors. Strong cognitivism is not compatible with the other currents of regime theory, given its radically different ontological underpinnings.

Starting from the weak cognitivist approach, Goldstein and Keohane, in their work on the role of ideas in foreign policymaking, emphasised the importance of world views and principled and causal beliefs, which can influence policymaking and policy outcomes in three ways (Goldstein and Keohane 1993). In particular, the above types of ideas can serve as road maps for decision-makers in uncertain situations and environments or in crisis times: interests and preferences may be shaped by principled beliefs and the means to realise these interests may be influenced by causal beliefs (Goldstein and Keohane 1993: 13–17; Hasenclever *et al.* 1997: 143–144). Moreover, when actors have to choose among various policy options and their preferences diverge, ideas can serve as focal points. In this way 'shared cultural, normative, religious, ethnic, or causal beliefs' play a coordinating role enabling actors' cooperation (Goldstein and Keohane 1993: 18). Finally, ideas can be influential and shape political outcomes through the political institutions into which they are embedded (ibid.: 20).

Keohane and Goldstein's framework managed to address the gap of the realist and liberal theories of regimes, which did not enquire into the origins of interests and preferences. In the case of roadmaps, ideas shape actors' interests and preferences and in this way an additional link is added in the chain that connects preferences with outcomes. Additionally, ideas can mediate between preferences and outcomes in the form of focal points. The above weak cognitivist approach is not incompatible with the power-based and interest-based theories given that it does not challenge the rationalist premises on which these theories are based. Therefore, there is significant scope for integrating this knowledge-based framework with the realist and liberal accounts of regime formation in order to have a fuller picture of the way regimes emerge. Goldstein and Keohane do not, however, enquire into the question of how and from where ideas and knowledge are born and how they find their way into policymakers' minds. This gap is addressed by the literature on epistemic communities, which will be mentioned subsequently.

The role of knowledge in regime formation was also the focus of Joseph Nye (1987) who emphasised the importance of international learning in generating consensual knowledge. Similar to Goldstein and Keohane (1993), Nye (1987: 372) argued that interests are not static but rather subject to change. New knowledge about causal effects in a given issue-area and new beliefs about the world may change the way national interests are defined through a process of 'complex learning' ibid.: 380). Alternatively, when new knowledge changes the means that actors use to achieve their ends the learning is 'simple' (ibid.). These learning processes among international actors generate consensual, shared, and convergent knowledge in an issue-area, which can subsequently lead to the formation of an international regime (ibid.: 392).

However, this approach lacks a clear understanding of how regimes are negotiated after knowledge has become consensual. In this sense, Young is right in pointing out that the focus on consensual knowledge and learning appears to be based 'on a spontaneous process that has no engine to drive it' (Young 1994: 96). Moreover, the consensual knowledge framework has not touched in a systematic way on the issue of how knowledge is generated and disseminated to policymakers. The latter issue was the focus of the literature on epistemic communities.

The literature on epistemic communities (Haas 1989, 1992a, 1992b, 1993; Adler 1992; Adler and Haas 1992) sought to address the issue of how shared understandings and knowledge are accepted by policymakers and thus influence the process of regime formation. Similar to the cognitivist approaches mentioned previously, this literature emphasised that policymakers frequently face uncertainty regarding the choices they should make and therefore they seek the advice of epistemic communities (Haas 1989: 380, 1992a: 188). The latter are defined as networks of 'professionals with recognized expertise and competence in a particular domain and an authoritative claim to policy-relevant knowledge within that domain or issue-area' (Haas 1992b: 3). Epistemic communities share a common understanding about a given problem as well as a common notion of what constitutes an appropriate technical solution to this problem (Hasenclever *et al.* 1997: 149). The knowledge disseminated by the members of the epistemic community shapes actors' perceptions and interests 'making them prone to choose one set of norms and rules rather than another' (ibid.: 151).

The above knowledge-based approaches enhanced and expanded the research agenda related to international regimes. The presence of consensual knowledge or shared understandings alone is not however a sufficient factor for the emergence of regimes (Young and Osherenko 1993: 237). Additionally, Haas and Adler acknowledged that knowledge can play a role in regime formation even if it is not shared by all the relevant parties; this can happen when an epistemic community influences the policymakers of a single country or organisation, which subsequently exerts influence to other parties (Adler and Haas 1992: 379). For example, in Haas' 'modified follow-the-leader' regime pattern an epistemic community is present and influential only in the hegemonic country that establishes the regime: 'the regime would still be created through the intercession of the hegemon but its substance would reflect epistemic consensus' (Haas 1993: 187–188). Moreover, there is an overlap between Adler and Hass's transnational epistemic communities and Young's transnational alliances of 'scientific and environmental communities' (Young 1994: 104). Similar to the power-based and interest-based theories, the weak cognitivist approaches therefore present ample scope for integration with the approaches from the other schools of regime theory.

The strong cognitivist approaches to international regimes differ from the weak knowledge-based theories as well as from the power-based and interest-based frameworks in that they reject the rationalist ontology and positivist epistemology that all the other theories and approaches share. States and international actors are conceptualised not as utilitarian and rational calculators but rather as social actors and role-players (Wendt 1992). In other words, norms and rules are not selected on the basis of a logic of consequentiality but rather on the basis of a logic of social appropriateness. What is appropriate is determined by normative structures and by political and social institutions under the framework of which actors' cooperation takes place (Hasenclerver *et al.* 1997: 157). International regimes are socially constructed through socialisation processes where actors' identities are redefined and become mutually constitutive (Wendt 1992). This conceptualisation of regime formation is based on an ontology of regimes that differs from the ontology on which rationalist approaches are based. For strong cognitivists, regimes, which are based on social practices, have an inherent intersubjective element and, therefore, they should be researched through an interpretive epistemology.

The central question of this book is how and why the EU and the US concluded international agreements in the area of internal security. A rationalist model focused on the negotiations, the interests, and the structural constraints of the two parties can be useful in answering this question and in providing insights into the EU–US relationship at this nascent regime-building stage. Wendt (1992), for example, acknowledged that rationalist perspectives can indeed provide insights into the behaviour of actors before the establishment of rule-based cooperation and that constructivist accounts can be more useful at later stages when institutions have proliferated and actors have started formulating collective identities (Hasenclever *et al.* 1997: 186–187). In other words, if someone sought to examine the long-term influence of the established EU–US regime on the two sides' interactions and cooperation or the question of how cooperation is possible at all (the normative underpinnings of cooperation) then strong cognitivist theories could indeed provide a fruitful framework of analysis. The selection of a research framework should be ultimately dependent on the research question examined (Wendt 1992: 423).

Additionally, and in contrast to the weak knowledge-based approaches, the strong knowledge-based theories cannot be integrated with realist and liberal accounts into a unified model given their different ontologies regarding the conceptualisation of regimes and the behaviour of actors and, as a result, their different epistemologies. There is, however, scope for juxtaposing and assessing the explanatory value of positivist and interpretive approaches especially with regard to the issue of regime robustness and maintenance (Hasenclever *et al.* 1997: 221).

Synthetic and multivariate models

In parallel with single-factor analyses of international regimes, several authors (Young and Osherenko 1993; Haas 1993; Young 1998; Hasenclever *et al.* 2000; Leonard 2005; Andresen *et al.* 2013) argued in favour of theoretical frameworks which incorporated more than one variable. In this section, the four frameworks of Young and Osherenko (1993), Haas (1993), Young (1998), and Hasenclever *et al.* (2000) are presented. These frameworks constitute the most systematic attempts in regime theory literature to create conceptual frameworks that include all three social factors of power, knowledge, and interests.

Young and Osherenko (1993) were the first scholars who argued in favour of a multivariate model of regime formation. Testing various hypotheses in a number of environmental case studies they found that single-factor accounts of regime establishment had very little explanatory value. For this reason, they proposed a model according to which the social forces of power, interests, and knowledge 'feed into a process of institutional bargaining', and, at the same time, the cross-cutting factors of leadership and context direct or channel the operation of these forces in the case studies under question (Young and Osherenko 1993: 240). In particular, leadership could take three forms. Structural leaders are negotiators who translate power in the sense of material resources into bargaining leverage during the negotiations with other parties (Young 1991; Young and Osherenko 1993: 232). Entrepreneurial leaders use their negotiating skills in order to devise innovative deals that overcome impediments to cooperation and to enhance integrative bargaining among the relevant parties (Young 1991: 294; Young and Osherenko 1993: 232). Finally, intellectual leaders disseminate knowledge to policymakers and negotiators in order to change the perceptions of the latter regarding the issue or problem under question.

While Young and Osherenko recognised the importance of interaction effects between the three main social factors related to regime formation they did not delve deeply into these effects. For example, they mentioned briefly that knowledge can shape the way actors understand and define their interests and that an entrepreneurial leader may at the same time be also a structural leader. Regarding the enquiry into the link between knowledge and interests this task was taken by Goldstein and Keohane (1993) as mentioned previously in this chapter.

A similar multivariate model was proposed and tested subsequently by Young (1998) who included the additional variable of the regime formation stage. In particular, Young (1998: 21) divided the regime-formation process into three stages (agenda formation, negotiation, and operationalisation) and he hypothesised that the role of the social forces of power, interests, and knowledge varies among these stages. Indeed the results from Young's case studies confirmed his hypotheses that the role of knowledge is more important in the agenda formation stage, the role of interests in the stage of negotiations, and the role of power in the implementation (operationalisation) stage (ibid.: 169–171).

Haas, on his part, rather than creating a unified model of regime establishment proposed four different patterns of regime creation: the realist 'follow-the-leader' pattern, the liberal institutionalist bargaining pattern, the 'epistemically informed bargaining' pattern, and the 'modified follow-the-leader' pattern. (Haas 1993: 174). The first two patterns are the typical realist and liberal cases of hegemonic imposition and institutional bargaining respectively (ibid.: 180–187). Haas, however, sought to expand these approaches by adding elements from the literature on epistemic communities and he therefore proposed two additional regime patterns: the 'modified follow-the-leader' pattern and the 'epistemically informed bargaining' pattern (ibid.: 187–190).

The first represents a synthesis of the realist and cognitivist schools while the latter is a synthesis of the liberal and cognitivist perspectives. In particular, in

36 Theories of international regimes

the modified follow-the-leader pattern the regime is still established by a hegemonic power but the substance and content of the regime 'would reflect epistemic consensus' (Haas 1993: 187–188). The conditions for this pattern to emerge are power concentration in one dominant state, uncertainty, and the presence and influence of an epistemic community in that dominant state (ibid.: 187). On the contrary, the epistemically informed bargaining does not require any initiative from a strong state; the regime is formed through a process akin to the liberal institutional bargaining, though with the addition that the interests and preferences of actors reflect the beliefs of the national epistemic communities (ibid.: 188–189). The enabling conditions related to this pattern are the consolidation of the influence of epistemic communities in the relevant countries and the fragmentation of power in the issue-area under question (diffuse power) (ibid.: 188, 191). At the same time, shocks or crises related to the issue-area under question may create a pressure for governments to take action, facilitating thus the start of the process of regime negotiation and formation (ibid.: 188).

One significant and original contribution of Haas was that he showed through an empirical application of his patterns that the regime-formation path of a single regime can include various regime patterns rather than only one pattern (Haas 1993: 191). This conceptualisation allows a more flexible and deeper examination of the regime establishment process. At the same time, Haas made a reference to the conditions that are conducive for each regime pattern; an issue that was not addressed in detail by Young and Osherenko (1993).

Finally, Hasenclever *et al.* (2000) presented their own model of regime formation, which is based on a rationalist integration of realist and liberal theories and on a subsequent synthesis of the rationalist approaches with the weak cognitivist perspectives. At the same time, they argued that a synthesis between the rationalist and the strong cognitivist (constructivist) approaches is not feasible given their diametrically opposed ontologies regarding regimes and actors' behaviour (Hasenclever *et al.* 2000: 31–32).

Hasenclever *et al.* (2000: 13) noted that the realist and interest-based theories start with different assumptions regarding the context under which cooperation takes place. For neo-liberals, states are interested only in absolute gains and their biggest fear is that they may be cheated by other actors. Bargaining is therefore integrative and regimes are established for the realisation of common gains. For realists, states are interested in relative gains, their biggest fear being that the other parties may end up better off from cooperation. Bargaining is distributive as a result with actors using threats and coercion to compel the other parties into submission. Given the above, Hasenclever *et al.* (ibid.) created a synthetic model of a 'contextualized rationalist theory' of regimes, according to which when relative gains are important for actors then it is expected that the realist hypotheses will hold true while when absolute gains are important then it is expected that the interest-based hypotheses will be true. However, they did not expand on the factors that enhance or diminish an actor's concerns about relative and absolute gains.

Regarding the role of the weak cognitivist theories, they noted that the knowledge-based and the rationalist (realist and neo-liberal) arguments can work together addressing different 'links in a single causal chain' (Hasenclever *et al.* 2000: 26). In particular, knowledge and ideas can shape interests, which subsequently explain outcomes. The previously mentioned approaches related to epistemic communities, consensual knowledge, and road maps all fit into this type of model where weakly cognitivist variables are 'causally prior ... to the rationalist ones' (ibid.). Alternatively, ideas and knowledge can intervene between interests and outcomes in the form of focal points which help actors coordinate their positions (ibid.: 28).

This section presented the synthetic models to regime formation as well as the approaches that incorporated various elements from the three regime theory schools. Based on these models and approaches, the next section presents the conceptual framework used in this book.

Operationalisation: a multivariate model of regime formation for analysing the EU–US negotiations

This book conceptualises the EU–US regime-formation process as a bargaining process in which interests, power, and knowledge may play a role and may also interact with each other. The starting point for this conceptualisation is Oran Young's model of institutional bargaining. Similar to this model, the process of regime formation is conceptualised in this book as a bargaining process through which the rules of the regime are established. Cases of purely imposed or purely spontaneous regimes are rare and the vast majority of regimes emerge through a process of negotiations. Applying this approach to the EU–US internal security relationship, the negotiations between the EU and the US for the agreements examined in this book are conceptualised as a bargaining process for the establishment of a transatlantic internal security regime.

The next step for devising a regime-formation model is identifying the factors that feed into this model. While Young (1994) focused mostly on interest-based factors, Young and Osherenko (1993), Haas (1993), and Hasenclever *et al.* (2000) emphasised that power and knowledge can be as important as interests in the regime-formation process. The latter approach is adopted for the conceptual framework of this book given that it allows a deeper examination of the EU–US relationship. Therefore, it is hypothesised in this book that the EU–US regime-formation process is shaped and influenced by the social forces of power, interests, and knowledge.

According to the power-based theories, the EU and the US will seek to impose their preferences through sanctions and coercion and the negotiators are expected to exercise structural leadership (distributional bargaining). The two actors are expected to change their behaviour and stance due to considerations of political costs. The exercise of structural leadership and the role of power are expected to be more prominent in distributional issues and in topics on which the EU and the US preferences diverge. Distributive issues are issues for which winners and losers can be easily identified and for which the losses of one party amount to gains for the other party and vice versa. These issues are traditionally the focus of realists who argue that in the negotiations for relatively assessed goods and for distributive issues the bargaining will be distributive, it will involve the use of tactics such as threats and coercion, and the role of power will be prominent.

According to the interest-based theories, the EU and the US will initiate negotiations voluntarily to realise joint benefits, and the concluded agreements will reflect both sides' concerns. The negotiators are expected to influence each other through side payments and compensations and thus reach equitable solutions (entrepreneurial leadership). The two actors will change their stance due to considerations of expected benefits. Mutual adjustment and integrative bargaining are expected to be the characteristics of the two sides' negotiations, and power will not be translated easily into bargaining leverage. The above characteristics will be more prominent in integrative issues and topics; integrative issues are issues for which mutual benefits from a deal can be easily identified. These issues have been examined by theorists coming from the interest-based school, which focused on absolutely assessed goods and on regime formation in the context of a minimum level of common interests. In the negotiations for integrative issues and for issues in which it is difficult to determine in advance the costs and benefits of the various proposed deals and solutions, bargaining will be integrative; in integrative bargaining actors try to devise mutually beneficial solutions and deals (a win-win solution).

According to the knowledge-based theories, the EU and the US are expected to start negotiations spontaneously driven by their shared principles and causal beliefs regarding the internal security problems they face. Consensual knowledge regarding the suitable response to these problems is expected to be the catalyst and driver of the EU–US cooperation. The EU and the US are expected to change their interests or/and their means to pursue these interests as well as their stance under the influence of new knowledge. Negotiators and policy-makers are expected to disseminate during the negotiations new knowledge and ideas and to devise focal points that help the EU and the US to overcome bargaining impediments (intellectual leadership). The role of ideas and knowledge is expected to be bigger during the agenda-formation stage and in highly technical issue-areas.

Young and Osherenko (1993) and Young (1991) have argued that the social forces of power, interests, and knowledge shape the regime-formation process in the form of structural, entrepreneurial, and intellectual leadership respectively. This is, however, a restrictive approach given that power, interests, and knowledge can influence regime formation in other ways too. For example, a change in the broader global political environment can induce an actor to adopt certain ideas and change its interests as a result without necessarily being persuaded by an intellectual leader. Therefore, in the framework used for this book the three types of leadership represent only one of the ways that the social factors of power, interests, and knowledge can a play a role in regime formation.

Two additional issues related to regime formation that can provide analytical insights in the cases examined in this book and that are taken into account in the framework proposed here are the conditions that are conducive for a social factor to play a greater role in regime formation, which were examined in detail by Hasenclever *et al.* (2000), and the possible interaction effects between the three social forces. Regarding the first issue, as shown previously, power-based approaches are expected to have stronger explanatory value in differences over distributive issues while the interest-based patterns of regime formation are expected to have stronger explanatory value in integrative issues. Moreover, the role of knowledge is expected to be more prominent in technical areas.

Concerning the second issue, the authors mentioned in the previous section addressed the interaction effects between the three social forces only implicitly and passingly. The interaction effects that are included in the framework of this book and are expected to be present in the EU–US negotiations are the following: Power can be used for devising equitable results (power-interests interaction), ideas can be used tactically for the advance of certain interests and positions (interests-knowledge interaction), power can be used for the imposition of rules which reflect certain ideas (power-knowledge interaction), and knowledge can shape the way interests are defined and/or means are chosen (knowledge-interests interaction).

In addition to the above, the political and social context is added in the conceptual framework of this book as an additional factor that can influence the regime-formation process. Apart from the three social forces of power, interests, and knowledge, regime theorists also looked into the role of context (contextual factors) and exogenous events for regime formation though the examination of the role of these factors was not always explicitly articulated. In particular, Young and Osherenko (1993) noted that contextual factors channel the operation of the three social forces in the bargaining process. Additionally, Young and Osherenko (1993) and Young (1998) highlighted that the broader global political environment and global and national political events and developments can be crucial in triggering the emergence of a regime or facilitating its conclusion. Similarly, Goldstein and Keohane (1993), starting from a knowledge-based perspective, stressed that when external political or other crises erupt then policymakers are more likely to change their beliefs and ideas and, thus, their interests. On the contrary, the synthetic model of Hasenclever *et al.* (2001) did not make any mention of contextual factors. Moreover, a number of interest-based factors, such as those highlighted by Young (1994), are anyway related to the issue of political context. For example, Young (1994) has mentioned that the political characteristics of an issue-area can potentially enhance the strategic position and the bargaining power of an actor in a manner disproportionate to this actor's structural (material) power. The inclusion of contextual factors allows a more detailed examination of the regime-formation process and for this reason they are included in the model used for this book.

Finally, the distinction of Young (1998) regarding the stages of regime formation is adopted here. In particular, the emergence of a regime can be divided into the stages of agenda setting or agenda formation, negotiation, and implementation or operationalisation. This book focuses on the stages of agenda setting and negotiation, the implementation stage being out of the scope of this research. While this distinction can be useful for analytical purposes the actual boundaries between the three stages are not always rigid. For example, the agenda for the negotiations can be subject to bargaining and negotiations for itself.

The model presented in Table 1.1 differs from previous regime-formation models in several respects. First, the interaction effects between the three social forces are articulated more explicitly. Second, this model starts from the basic premise of Young's model of institutional bargaining (Young 1994) that regime formation is ultimately a negotiated process; at the same time, it departs from Young's interest-based model in that it assigns equal weight to the other two social forces of power and knowledge. Third, with its inclusion of political context as a fourth factor, this model differs from the model of Hasenclever *et al.* (2001), which ignored contextual factors.

Table 1.1 A multivariate model of regime formation for analysing the EU–US negotiations

Social factors	Evidence in favour	More likely	Interaction effects
Power	Use of threats and coercion	In distributive issues	Power is used for devising equitable results (power-interests)
	Change of stance due to political costs		
Interests	Use of side payments and compensations	In integrative issues	Power is used for imposing rules that reflect certain ideas (power-knowledge)
	Change of stance due to expected gains and benefits		
Knowledge	Promotion of ideas and new knowledge	In technical areas and issues	Knowledge is used tactically for supporting certain interests (interests-knowledge)
	Change of stance due to new knowledge regarding the issue under question	After external crises and shocks	Knowledge shapes actors' interests (knowledge-interests)
		At the agenda-setting stage of regime formation	
Political context and exogenous events	Contextual factors trigger the emergence of an issue at the international political agenda		
	Contextual factors enhance or diminish the strategic position of the negotiating actors		
	Domestic and national events influence the regime-formation process		

Multivariate models, such as the one presented previously, are not without potential weaknesses. In the trade-off between analytical simplicity and explanatory value these models lean towards the latter end of the spectrum. The inclusion of various factors from different theoretical schools can create problems related to the coherency of the model. The fact, however, that the number of cases examined in this book is small means that the research priority is on examining these cases as much in detail as possible and multivariate approaches are appropriate and useful in this regard (Pennings *et al.* 2006: 136). Another criticism one could raise concerns the potential incommensurability of the various schools described previously. Indeed, it is difficult to combine the strong cognitivist school with the other rationalist approaches to regime formation. This chapter has shown, however, that the other approaches (power-based, interest-based, and the weak cognitivist school) examined can indeed be synthesised in a unified model.

To sum up, this chapter has surveyed the regime theory literature and more particularly the literature on regime formation. A regime formation framework and model has been presented for the analysis of the EU–US internal security relationship. The following chapters will answer the main research question of this book of how the EU and the US have cooperated on internal security matters by looking at four cases of transatlantic internal security cooperation through a multivariate regime formation model.

References

Adler, E. (1992) 'The emergence of cooperation: national epistemic communities and the international evolution of the idea of nuclear arms control', *International Organization*, 46(1), pp. 101–145.

Adler, E. and Haas, P. (1992) 'Conclusion: Epistemic Communities, World Order, and the Creation of a Reflective Research Program', *International Organization*, 46(1), pp. 367–390.

Andresen, S., Rosendal, K. and Skjærseth, J.B. (2013) 'Why Negotiate a Legally Binding Mercury Convention?', *International Environmental Agreements: Politics, Law and Economics*, 13(4), pp. 425–440.

Cogburn, D. (2003) 'Governing global information and communications policy: Emergent regime formation and the impact on Africa', *Telecommunications Policy*, 27, pp. 135–153.

Cowhey, P. (1990) 'The International Telecommunications Regime: The Political Roots of Regimes for High Technology', *International Organization*, 44(2), pp. 169–199.

Dimitrov, R. (2003) 'Knowledge, Power, and Interests in Environmental Regime Formation', *International Studies Quarterly*, 47, pp. 123–150.

Goldstein, J. and Keohane, R. (1993) 'Ideas and Foreign Policy: An Analytical Framework', in J. Goldstein and R. Keohane (eds) *Ideas and Foreign Policy: Beliefs, Institutions, and Political Change*. Ithaca: Cornell University Press, pp. 3–30.

Grieco, J. (1988) 'Anarchy and the Limits of Cooperation: A Realist Critique of the Newest Liberal Institutionalism', *International Organization*, 42(3), pp. 485–507.

Grieco, J. (1990) *Cooperation among Nations: Europe, America, and Non-Tariff Barriers to Trade*. Ithaca: Cornell University Press.

Haas, P. (1989) 'Do Regimes Matter? Epistemic Communities and Mediterranean Pollution Control', *International Organization*, 43(3), pp. 377–403.

Haas, P. (1992a) 'Banning chlorofluorocarbons: epistemic community efforts to protect stratospheric ozone', *International Organization*, 46(1), pp. 187–224.

Haas, P. (1992b) 'Introduction: epistemic communities and international policy coordination', *International Organization*, 46(1), pp. 1–35.

Haas, P. (1993) 'Epistemic Communities and the Dynamics of International Environmental Cooperation', in V. Rittberger (ed.) *Regime Theory and International Relations*. Oxford: Oxford University Press, pp. 168–201.

Haggard, S. and Simmons, B. (1987) 'Theories of International Regimes', *International Organization*, 41(3), pp. 491–517.

Hasenclever, A., Mayer, P. and Rittberger, V. (1997) *Theories of international regimes*. Cambridge: Cambridge University Press.

Hasenclever, A., Mayer, P. and Rittberger, V. (2000) 'Integrating Theories of International Regimes', *Review of International Studies*, 26(1), pp. 3–33.

Jägerskog, A. (2001) *The Jordan River Basin: Explaining Interstate Water Cooperation Through Regime Theory*. London: Water Issues Study Group, School of Oriental and African Studies (SOAS).

Keohane, R. (1982) 'The demand for international regimes', *International Organization*, 36(02), pp. 325–355.

Keohane, R. (1983) 'The demand for international regimes', in S. Krasner (ed.) *International Regimes*. Ithaca: Cornell University Press, pp. 141–172.

Keohane, R. (1984) *After hegemony: cooperation and discord in the world political economy*. Princeton, NJ: Princeton University Press.

Keohane, R. (1989) *International institutions and state power*. Boulder: Westview Press.

Keohane, R. (1993) 'The Analysis of International Regimes: Towards a European-American Research Programme', in V. Rittberger (ed.) *Regime Theory and International Relations*. Oxford: Clarendon Press, pp. 23–48.

Keohane, R. and Nye, J. (1977) *Power and Interdependence* (Second Edition ed.). Boston: Harper Collins Publishers.

Kindleberger, C. (1973) *The World in Depression 1929–1939*. London: Allen Lane.

Krasner, S. (1983a) 'Preface', in S. Krasner (ed.) *International Regimes*. Ithaca: Cornell University Press.

Krasner, S. (1983b) 'Structural causes and regime consequences: regimes as intervening variables', in S. Krasner (ed.) *International Regimes*. Ithaca: Cornell University Press, pp. 1–22.

Krasner, S. (1991) 'Global Communications and National Power: Life on the Pareto Frontier', *World Politics*, 43(03), pp. 336–366.

Krasner, S. (1993) 'Sovereignty, Regimes, and Human Rights', in V. Rittberger (ed.) *Regime Theory and International Relations*. Oxford: Oxford University Press, pp. 139–167.

Kratochwil, F. and Ruggie, J.G. (1986) 'International Organization: A State of the Art on an Art of the State', *International Organization*, 40(4), pp. 753–775.

Leonard, E. (2005) *The Onset of Global Governance: International Relations Theory and the International Criminal Court*. Aldershot: Ashgate.

Levy, M., Young, O. and Zürn, M. (1995) 'The Study of International Regimes', *European Journal of International Relations*, 1(3), pp. 267–330.

Müller, H. (1993) 'The Internalization of Principles, Norms, and Rules by Governments: The Case of Security Regimes', in V. Rittberger (ed.) *Regime Theory and International Relations*. Oxford: Oxford University Press, pp. 361–388.

Nye, J. (1987) 'Nuclear Learning and US–Soviet regime', *International Organization*, 41(3), pp. 371–402.

Park, Y.J. (2009) 'Regime formation and consequence: The case of internet security in the East–Asia "Four Tigers"', *Government Information Quarterly*, 26, pp. 398–406.

Pennings, P., Keman, H. and Kleinnijenhuis, J. (2006) *Doing Research in Political Science: An Introduction to Comparative Methods and Statistics*. London: Sage.

Raustiala, K. and Victor, D. (2004) 'The Regime Complex for Plant Genetic Resources', *International Organization*, 58(2), pp. 277–309.

Rees, W. (2006) *Transatlantic Counter-Terrorism Cooperation: The New Imperative*. Abingdon: Routledge.

Rittberger, V. (1990) 'Editor's Introduction', in V. Rittberger (ed.) *International regimes in East–West politics*. London: Pinter Publishers, pp. 1–8.

Rittberger, V. (1993) 'Research on International Regimes in Germany: The Adaptive Internalization of an American Social Science Concept', in V. Rittberger (ed.) *Regime Theory and International Relations*. Oxford: Clarendon Press, pp. 3–22.

Rittberger, V. and Zürn, M. (1991) 'Regime Theory: Findings from the Study of East–West Regimes', *Cooperation and Conflict*, 26(4), pp. 165–183.

Ruggie, J.G. (1975) 'International Responses to Technology: Concepts and Trends', *International Organization*, 29(3), pp. 557–583.

Snidal, D. (1985) 'The limits of hegemonic stability theory', *International Organization*, 39(4), pp. 579–614.

Stein, A. (1983) 'Coordination and Collaboration: Regimes in an Anarchic World', in S. Krasner (ed.) *International Regimes*. Ithaca: Cornell University Press, pp. 115–140.

Strange, S. (1983) 'Cave! hic dragones: a critique of regime analysis', in S. Krasner (ed.) *International Regimes*. Ithaca: Cornell University Press, pp. 337–354.

Webb, M., and Krasner, S. (1989) 'Hegemonic stability theory: an empirical assessment', *Review of International Studies* (15), pp. 183–198.

Wendt, A. (1992) 'Anarchy is what States Make of it: The Social Construction of Power Politics', *International Organization*, 46(2), pp. 391–425.

Young, O. (1986) 'International Regimes: Towards a New Theory of Institutions', *World Politics*, 39(1), pp. 104–122.

Young, O. (1989) *International Cooperation: Building Regimes for Natural Resources and the Environment*. Ithaca: Cornell University Press.

Young, O. (1991) 'Political Leadership and Regime Formation: On the Development of Institutions in International Society', *International Organization*, 45(3), pp. 281–308.

Young, O. (1994) *International Governance: Protecting the Environment in a Stateless Society*. Ithaca: Cornell University Press.

Young, O. (1998) *Creating Regimes: Arctic Accords and International Governance*. Ithaca: Cornell University Press.

Young, O. (2005) 'Regime theory and the quest for global governance', in A. Ba and M. Hoffmann (eds) *Contending Perspectives on Global Governance*. Abingdon: Routledge, pp. 88–109.

Young, O. and Osherenko, G. (1993) 'Testing Theories of Regime Formation: Findings from a Large Collaborative Research Project', in V. Rittberger (ed.) *Regime Theory and International Relations*. Oxford: Oxford University Press, pp. 223–250.

Zacher, M. (1987) 'Trade Gaps, Analytical Gaps: Regime Analysis and International Commodity Trade Regulation', *International Organization*, 41(2), pp. 173–202.

2 Customs security cooperation between the European Union and the United States[1]

The EU and the US economies account for almost a third of world trade flows (European Commission 2016). A large part of this trade is conducted through the transatlantic shipping line with maritime cargo vessels; in particular, in 2001 the container traffic between Europe and the US amounted to 5.1 million containers while in 2006 this number rose to 6.1 million containers (Wilson and Benson 2009: 15). Less than 2 per cent of these containers were inspected for security purposes (US Senate 2003). This was one of the customs security gaps that officials from both the EU and the US identified after the 9/11 attacks; in general, for these officials the global supply chains started being viewed as especially vulnerable to terrorist exploitation.

This chapter examines three sub-cases related to the customs security measures that emerged in the EU–US political and security agenda: the Container Security Initiative (CSI), the Mutual Recognition Decision, and the 100 per cent scanning rule. In the first two the EU and the US came to an agreement in 2004 and 2012 respectively while the latter was an initiative of the US Congress in 2007 that was never implemented.

Apart from transatlantic security, the sub-cases of this chapter touch also upon the economic and trade relationship of the EU and the US. Given the large volume of containerised transatlantic trade, customs security measures related to cargos could potentially impede this trade. Such was the case, for example, of the 100 per cent rule that, according to the EU, would, if implemented, affect the EU–US trade negatively and would be very costly in terms of investments.

In other words, the case that this chapter examines had important implications for both the security and the economy of the US and the EU. Failure of the two parties to agree on common security standards for international supply chains would increase the costs for companies and as a result for transatlantic trade. Moreover, overemphasising the security aspects of customs controls would similarly harm transatlantic trade and economy. Therefore, the new customs security measures needed to be accompanied with trade facilitation elements, and the EU and the US needed to agree on these elements to avoid establishing different systems of rules with which companies had to comply.

This chapter looks at how the two sides negotiated the two agreements and handled the case of the 100 per cent rule through a regime theory perspective; in this way it addresses this book's central research question of how the EU and the US cooperated on internal security matters. The talks and negotiations for the two agreements and the 100 per cent rule are conceptualised as a regime-formation process in which the EU and the US established rules for their cooperation on customs security matters.

This chapter shows that in both Europe and the US before the 9/11 attacks the security aspects of customs functions and international supply chains were not pronounced, and therefore there was no attempt to establish a regime. The 9/11 attacks were an external crisis that changed political priorities and initiated a learning process on both sides of the Atlantic, highlighting thus the importance of political context for processes of regime formation.

The US, being a recent victim of terrorist attacks, moved first to set the agenda of the new customs security rules. The EU shared the security objectives of the US and did not have any objection to the actual content of the rules – in this sense the relationship of the two sides could be characterised as a partnership. However, the EU objected to the bilateralist approach that Washington was pursuing.

Regarding the issue of the mutual recognition of the two sides' business-to-government programmes, this was an initiative taken by the EU. The latter had an active role shaping the agenda and pointing out to the US the economic and security benefits that a mutual-recognition agreement would entail. Finally, the 100 per cent issue emerged through a legislative act by Congress, which mandated that all US-bound containers should be scanned before their arrival in US ports. Both the EU Commission and the US administration disagreed with this measure, which parted from the customs security principles that the two sides embraced.

The first section presents the context of customs security in Europe and the US. Then, this chapter examines the 2004 agreement, the Mutual Recognition Agreement, and the 100 per cent scanning issue.

The context

This section examines how customs security was conceptualised before and after the 9/11 attacks. It is argued in this section that prior to the 9/11 attacks customs authorities in both the EU and the US were mainly focused on revenue collection and on anti-narcotics and anti-smuggling operations. The security and especially the counter-terrorism aspects of customs functions were not emphasised, with the result that no comprehensive measures for the protection of supply chains were in place in either the US or the EU. Given that the terrorist threat against containers was not identified as a problem by either side no regime was formed prior to 9/11. The 9/11 attacks prompted a change in the threat perceptions in both the EU and the US, where the supply chains were not only seen as a vital element of global trade but also as a potential liability with regard to terrorist attacks. This highlights the role of external events and exogenous shocks for the process of regime formation.

Customs security before the 9/11 attacks

Before the 9/11 attacks the anti-terrorism aspect of customs security was not considered a high-priority area; rather, the efforts of customs authorities were focused on counter-narcotics and anti-smuggling activities. The threat from the terrorist use of the international supply chains did not loom large given that there was no precedent for such an attack (Bowman 2007: 199). The terrorist attacks against the marine transportation system had mainly been of the cruise/ferry vessel-bombing or cruise/ferry vessel-hijacking kind (Booth and Altenbrun 2002: 3–5).

As a result, only a miniscule percentage of containers were inspected, less than 2 per cent of cargo containers (US Senate 2003), and little advance information on the content of cargos was available when shipments were arriving at US ports (Bowman 2007: 198). The cargo vessels were required to file vessel manifests concerning the content of the cargo only 48 hours before the arrival of the vessels at a US port (Bowman 2007: 200); and the decision on whether a shipment was legitimate was taken only on the basis of the requisite documentation. This approach was not very reliable, since the documents-related requirements were nominal; the shippers, for example, were not required to identify the originator or the recipient of the shipments, or to itemise the contents of the cargo (US Senate 2003). Additionally, the rationale behind cargo inspections was the collection of customs duties, and in the balance between trade facilitation and trade security the emphasis was clearly on the trade facilitation aspect of customs (Interview US 2012c).

The gaps in customs and container security were first identified in the 2000 'Report of the Interagency Commission on Crime and Security in US Seaports' (US Interagency Commission on Crime and Security in US Seaports 2000). The latter painted a bleak picture with regard to customs and container security controls:

> Criminals can bypass the federal clearance and inspection process through underreporting, misreporting, or not reporting at all. Information on ships' manifests is often wrong or incomplete ... and sometimes deficient for the purposes of import risk assessment.
>
> (Ibid.: 7, 16)

These security gaps were considered an important issue with regard only to organised crime and drug trafficking; the report focused on these threats and noted that 'there is no indication that US seaports are currently being targeted by terrorists' (ibid.: 5). In conclusion, the prevalent characteristic of supply chain security at that period was the 'almost complete absence of any security oversight in the loading and transporting of a box from its point of origin to its final destination' (US Senate 2003). After the 9/11 attacks, the 9/11 Commission Report highlighted this absence of security controls in the customs and cargo sector and urged the government to take drastic action in order to reduce the vulnerabilities in this area (US National Commission on Terrorist Attacks Upon the United States 2004: 391–393).

Similar to the US, before 9/11 the use of the international supply chains for terrorist purposes was not considered as a threat by either the EU or the member states. Rather, the focus was on the fight against customs fraud and customs law infringements and on the smuggling of prohibited goods (such as drugs, arms, counterfeit goods, and endangered species) (European Commission 2003b: 40). This focus could be seen, for example, in the 1997 'Naples II Convention on Customs Cooperation' (Council of the EU 1997); in this document the threats that were emphasised included the 'illicit traffic in drugs and psychotropic substances, weapons, munitions, explosive materials, cultural goods, dangerous and toxic waste, nuclear material or materials or equipment intended for the manufacture of atomic, biological and/or chemical weapons' (ibid.).

Given that neither the EU nor the US viewed the terrorist exploitation of supply chains as a high-risk threat, no initiatives were taken by either side towards transatlantic cooperation in this field. The result of this lack of political prioritisation was that a customs security regime formation process did not start prior to 9/11. This confirms that broader social and political factors can influence whether an issue will be framed as a problem that needs consideration and demands action. While the EU and the US signed an agreement in 1997 on mutual assistance in customs matters, this agreement concerned only issues related to the breach of customs legislation and the establishment of 'smooth trade relations' between the two parties; no reference at all was made in the text to supply chain security issues.

Customs security after the 9/11 attacks: the US and EU threat perceptions

The 9/11 attacks changed the priorities and the threat perceptions of both the US and the EU. Concerning the US, the shock of the 9/11 attacks prompted a change in the American threat perceptions with regard to customs. The international supply chains of goods were seen not only as an essential part of US trade but also as a potential security liability in the sense that terrorists could exploit the maritime trade system and use it as a means for their plans (Interview US 2012c). A number of US government officials expressed the opinion that the most likely targets for terrorists in the post-September 11 period were ports and container vessels and that vigilance was urgently needed in this area (US Senate 2003). This view was strengthened by information pointing towards the existence of ties between al-Qaeda and the shipping industry.

Prior to 9/11 there were no comprehensive systems in place for customs security. The coupling of the US reliance on containers for overseas trade with the lack of effective customs controls created an insecure environment where a number of threats could materialise. First, the containers that arrived at US ports could contain conventional explosive devices or materials related to weapons of mass destruction that could be used for terrorist attacks (such as chemical, biological, radiological, and nuclear agents). Additionally, the international supply chain could be used for the smuggling of persons (terrorist organisations' operatives) into US territory. In other words, the maritime shipping lines could be used by terrorists as a logistical means for the transfer of explosive materials or operatives into the US homeland (Allen 2008: 177–178).

Second, US-bound sea containers could conceal explosive devices programmed to set off or remotely detonated when the vessels containing the containers arrived at US ports (Allen 2008: 178). The destruction that would be caused would be particularly high in the special case of a terrorist nuclear attack against a US seaport. Alternatively, terrorists could use a cargo ship's legitimate load (such as chemicals, petroleum, and liquefied natural gas) as the means to conduct an attack.

Third, significant costs and disruption would be caused not only in the case of an actual attack but also in the case of a credible threat of an explosive device incident. In a simulation conducted by the Department of Homeland Security (DHS), two Radiological Dispersal Devices were supposed to have been discovered in containers in the ports of California and Georgia (Allen 2008: 178). As part of its response to the incident the DHS simulated the temporary shutdown of all US seaports in order that a thorough search could be conducted, and the economic losses that would have resulted from these closures were estimated at $66 billion. All US-bound cargo traffic would slow, the inter-modal container system along with millions of tons of goods would come to a standstill, and the economic costs of the shutdown would probably be larger than the direct costs associated with the destruction caused by the bomb itself (Simon and Knake 2006: 192).

Similar threat perceptions were prevalent in the EU after the 9/11 attacks (Interview EU 2012b; Interview EU 2012e). In parallel with the US, there was a realisation in the EU that there were immense shortcomings with regard to container security; this was due to the simple reason that hitherto customs and supply chain logistics were not framed as security issues at all (Interview EU 2012b). In the words of the then EU Commissioner for the Internal Market, Taxation and Customs Union, Frits Bolkenstein,

> The terrifying events on September 11 made the logistical world realise that the supply chain is vulnerable and a possible target to be used for terrorist activities such as the transport of Weapons of Mass Destruction and explosives
>
> (Bolkenstein, cited in RAPID 2003)

The above US and EU threat perceptions were reflected in their strategic documents and policy papers. In December 2002 the US Coast Guard adopted its 'Maritime Strategy for Homeland Security', which sought to link the US 'National Strategy for Homeland Security' (US Office of Homeland Security 2002) and the US 'National Security Strategy' (The White House 2002) into the maritime domain (US Coast Guard 2002: 1). In accordance with the spirit of the

US 'National Security Strategy', the emphasis on the Coast Guard's homeland security strategy was on 'identifying and intercepting threats well before they reach US shores' (US Coast Guard 2002: i). The threat emanating from a possible exploitation of the US marine transportation system for terrorist purposes was highlighted, and one of the US strategic objectives that was mentioned in the document was for the US Coast Guard to thwart this threat 'as far from our shores as possible' (US Coast Guard 2002: 18).

The EU's policy and strategic documents similarly reflected the new threat perceptions. For instance, in the 'Communication from the Commission to the Council, the European Parliament, the European Economic and Social Committee and the Committee of the Regions on Enhancing Maritime Transport Security' (European Commission 2003a) it was highlighted that any ship could be used as means for terrorist attacks and that such threats made a focus on maritime security necessary. In a similar vein, the Council resolution of 2003 on a strategy for customs cooperation (Council of the EU 2003) and the Commission's analysis on the role of customs in the integrated management of external borders (European Commission 2003b) identified terrorist and organised crime attacks against supply chains as one of the main threats to EU's safety and security.

The Container Security Initiative (CSI) and the 2004 EU–US agreement

After 9/11 the perceptions of the two sides regarding the role of customs changed; the new security environment, together with a new set of perceived threats, prompted the EU and the US to give an anti-terrorist mission and role to customs with the security aspect of customs functions being heavily emphasised. The US moved first with regard to customs security measures, thus initiating the process of regime formation, and the EU followed, imitating to a certain extent the US practices in this field. In other words, initially the role of the EU was highly reactive. This section presents the negotiations for the 2004 customs security agreement.

The post-9/11 US customs security measures

In the immediate aftermath of the 9/11 attacks the role of knowledge was prominent in two senses. First, as a result of the changed threat perceptions mentioned previously, customs functions in the US were reconceptualised in terms of the new emergency stemming from the fight against terrorism. The new security environment, together with a new set of perceived threats, prompted the US to give an anti-terrorist mission and role to customs (Interview US 2012c). Second, apart from this reconceptualization, the US security officials and practitioners also converged around the concept of 'smart borders'; these officials and practitioners held the professional belief that the application of this new idea about border controls in the customs area was the best solution to the customs security gaps identified (*US Customs Today* 2002a, 2002b).

This indicates that a learning process took place where the US redefined its interests under the influence of new knowledge about the country's security environment and about the optimal US response. New knowledge about causal effects in a given issue-area and new beliefs about the world may change the way national interests are defined. At the heart of this process was a US group of security professionals, experts and policymakers that included officials from the US Customs Service and from other organisations, such as the US Coast Guard and the Border Patrol unit; policymakers from the Bush administration; and members of the academic and scientific community (Interview US 2012c). In the face of the new threat environment this group acted as a reducer of uncertainty for the US administration. First, it promoted the idea of treating the area of customs as a predominantly anti-terrorist and security-oriented space, and, second, it incorporated customs functions into the broader homeland security plan of creating smart borders.

As a response to the problem of customs security vulnerabilities mentioned previously the US Customs and Border Protection Unit (CBP) established a plan based on five pillars: (1) the use of advance information, (2) the use of automated risk targeting, (3) the use of sophisticated detection technology at ports of entry, (4) the Container Security Initiative (CSI), and (5) the launch and expansion of C-TPAT (Customs-Trade Partnership Against Terrorism) (*US Customs and Border Protection Today* 2005). The main architect of this plan was the US Commissioner for Customs, Robert Bonner, who moved counter-terrorism to the centre of CBP's mission and activities:

> Beyond its immediate effects, the terrorist attacks will no doubt have a great impact on the work of Customs and its mission for many years to come.... For the foreseeable future, our top priority is and must be counter-terrorism in all its forms.
> (Bonner, cited in *US Customs Today* 2001)

This five pillar system was part of the broader US homeland security strategy and in particular of the US plan for the establishment of 'smart borders', which appeared in the first US strategy for homeland security in 2002 (US Office of Homeland Security 2002: 22). In the latter it was envisioned that the 'border of the future' would be a continuum framed by land, sea, and air and built upon concentric circles of defence (ibid.). In this layered approach to border controls the first line of defence would be overseas (US Department of Homeland Security Strategic Plan 2004: 14). When people or goods passed through the various layers, the relevant US security bodies would screen and filter these people and goods with the help of risk management techniques.

The application of the smart borders concepts into the customs area meant in practice that the US customs security functions would be 'exported' and take place abroad; in other words, functions like the collection of information regarding the content of cargos and the screening and inspection of containers would take place overseas rather than at the US ports of arrival (Interview US

2012c). According to Commissioner Bonner, there was a need for US Customs to 'push the border outward to better protect against the international terrorist threat' (Bonner, cited in *US Customs Today* 2003). In a similar vein, he stressed that '[the US] can no longer afford to think of the border merely as a physical line separating one nation from another' and that 'the ultimate goals of pushing the border outward are to allow US Customs more time to react to potential threats, to stop threats before they reach [the US], and to expedite the flow of commerce across [the American] borders' (Bonner, cited in *US Customs Today* 2003).

The Container Security Initiative and the 24-hour rule

The Container Security Initiative, together with the 24-hour advance vessel manifest rule (24-hour rule), were two of the measures that were introduced by the US Customs for the implementation of the smart borders plan into the customs area. Through these measures the US initiated a customs security regime formation process; the US, being recent victims of terrorist attacks, moved first, thus shaping the security agenda. With these initiatives, the US officials exercised all forms of leadership (intellectual, structural, and entrepreneurial). The role of knowledge was evident in the fact that the customs security rules that the US was exporting were based on the idea and conceptual framework of smart borders (Interview US 2012c); in this sense the US officials were trying to shape the intellectual capital of its partners and allies. At the same time, the unilateral imposition of the extraterritorial 24-hour rule, accompanied by penalties for non-complying actors, was an exercise in structural leadership where the US officials deployed threats in order to ensure that third countries complied with its preferred rule. Finally, entrepreneurial leadership was evident in the promotion of the CSI programme, which depended on the consent and active involvement of third countries; the US made an effort to popularise and draw attention to CSI and it also offered a number of side payments and benefits to the countries that would participate in the programme (Interview US 2012c).

The CSI was initiated in January 2002 and it concerned the foreign ports from which shippers exported goods to the US. CSI had the following elements: (1) shippers would provide advance information about the content of the containers before the cargo vessel left the port of origin; (2) US Customs would establish risk criteria and risk indicators for the identification of the containers that posed the greater risk; (3) containers would be pre-screened at the ports of origin (rather than at the US ports of arrival) on the basis of the cargo information given in advance and on the basis of the risk criteria mentioned previously; and (4) technology would facilitate the scanning of high-risk containers and the development and use of 'smart' containers[2] (*US Customs Today* 2002c).

For the implementation of CSI, the US Customs planned to sign agreements first with the ports and governments that were sending the highest volume of cargo traffic to the US (*US Customs Today* 2002c). These ports (also called mega-ports) were Hong Kong (China), Shanghai (China), Singapore, Kaohsiung

(Taiwan), Rotterdam (Netherlands), Pusan (South Korea), Bremerhaven (Germany), Tokyo (Japan), Genoa (Italy), and Yantian (China). The benefit that the US offered to these ports was that the containers that originated from the CSI ports would have expedited clearance through US customs when they arrived in the US (*US Customs Today* 2002c). In other words, the US tried to achieve the compliance of other states through the provision of compensations and rewards.

Additionally, US Customs officials would be placed in these ports in order to pre-screen the containers (The White House Bulletin 2002), in case the US customs agents thought that a container needed further inspection they would instruct local customs authorities to conduct a physical or other inspection. This was a highly significant aspect of the CSI programme because it touched upon the sensitive issue of state sovereignty (The National Business Review 2002). Through this feature of CSI, the US was asking that a country cede part of its sovereignty by allowing US customs officials to be stationed on its soil.

The 24-hour rule, which was related to the CSI, emerged with the Maritime Transportation Security Act of 2002 (US Congress 2002). In the latter it was highlighted that information about inbound containers should be provided in advance, that is before the arrival of cargos at the US ports. In particular, on October 2002 the US Customs issued the 24-hour rule according to which 'customs must receive the vessel's cargo manifest (declaration) from the carrier 24 hours before the related cargo is laden aboard the vessel at the foreign ports', otherwise US customs could issue a 'No-Load' directive instructing the relevant shipper not to load the containers into the vessel (US Federal Register 2002).

This rule was essential for the implementation of CSI, since the latter was based on the advance provision of cargo information and such provision was made mandatory with the 24-hour rule. However, the 24-hour rule concerned all US inbound shipments and it was not limited to the ports that participated in CSI. Similar to the CSI, the 24-hour rule raised the issue of state sovereignty but it also had economic implications (Interview EU 2013). First, with the threat of issuing a no-load directive to non-compliant shippers the US interfered extraterritorially into a foreign port's jurisdiction and functions regarding the containers and the vessels that were stationed in that port. Second, the 24-hour rule could potentially create costs for shippers and companies that participated in global trade (The National Business Review 2002): for instance, the 24-hour rule meant in practice that companies would bring their containers to the ports at an earlier stage and this increased storage costs and the risk of cargo damage (especially for perishable goods) or theft.

Agenda formation and the EU–US negotiations

The new US system for customs security had an international element. The 24-hour rule became compulsory for third parties through US legislation in October 2002. The CSI, which was initiated on January 2002, was however a voluntary programme, and the US depended on cooperation with third countries on this issue given that the CSI included the stationing of US Customs officials on the soil of third parties. Therefore, the US approached a number of EU member states in order to gain their approval for the CSI, stimulating in this way the demand for a customs security regime; the ultimate aim of the US was to sign with these member states 'declarations of understandings' which would incorporate these countries' ports into the CSI. It was through these two movements, on the one hand the unilateral legislation of the 24-hour rule and on the other hand the entrepreneurial 'promotion' of the CSI, that customs security emerged in the EU–US agenda. Both initiatives were based on and backed by the intellectual underpinnings of the smart-borders concept, pointing to the existence of interaction effects between the social factors of power, interests, and knowledge.

During this agenda-formation stage, the US adopted an approach based on bilateralism and on approaching individual member states rather than the EU institutions. In its interactions with member states the US acted as a 'champion' of the CSI, drawing attention to the problem of supply-chain security and, at the same time, shaping the way this problem was framed for discussion. The entrepreneurial leadership of the US officials was indeed successful, and by September 2002 five European ports (Rotterdam, Antwerp, Hamburg, Bremerhaven, and Le Havre) signed memorandums of understandings regarding CSI with the US. By January 2003 Spain, Britain, and Italy followed (EUobserver 2003a).

The reason for this bilateralist approach lay in the fact that there was a genuine atmosphere of urgency at that time, and the US officials believed that starting negotiations with the EU, which was perceived as a slow moving and cumbersome organisation, would take too much time (Interview US 2012a, 2012b). Approaching member states was perceived as more expedient. The US Customs spokesman justified the US approach saying that CSI was an issue of national security and therefore Washington did not 'have the luxury of time' (*New York Times* 2002). Similarly, in conversation between the US ambassador to Netherlands and the Director of the Department of Homeland Security, the former said: 'I've got the port, I've got the government, give me a day or two and we'll make it happen' (*New York Times* 2002).

On their part, the countries that signed memorandums with the US were motivated by economic and trade concerns; in other words, the entrepreneurial efforts of the US officials were successful. In particular, these countries were afraid that if their ports were not part of CSI then the ports would be perceived as less safe compared to ports with CSI status (*Journal of Commerce* 2002). The shippers would choose the safer option of moving their goods through CSI ports and this would result in economic losses for the ports that were not part of the US programme. For example, when the UK port of Felixstowe was included in CSI, the UK lobbied the US to station US customs agents at the ports of Liverpool, Southampton, and London Thamesport too. Similarly, France with the port of Le Havre joined CSI only after Germany, Belgium, and Netherlands signed memorandums with the US; France 'panicked' that Le Havre may lose trade to these countries' ports (The National Business Review 2002). Therefore, the response of the member states to the US initiative was generally positive.

The US initiatives generated mixed feelings in the EU. On the one hand, the European Union accepted and approved the ideas that formed the basis of the US customs security measures (Interview EU 2012b, 2012e). These ideas and principles included the advance provision of cargo information and the establishment of risk management techniques for the pre-screening of containers. On the other hand, the EU had strong disagreements with the US preference for concluding separate deals with European states. The EU position was that for both legal and efficiency related reasons an EU–US agreement was necessary.

With regard to the first issue, the EU did not have any objection to the actual content of the US measures (Interview EU 2012b, 2012e); from the perspective of the EU officials, the US initiatives 'made sense' in the context of the post-9/11 security environment (Interview EU 2012b). This EU acceptance of the US customs security programme, rather than resulting from a process of mere US imposition, points towards a process of imitation. Indeed, the EU reforms regarding EU's own customs security system were largely based on the US five-pillar plan for customs security that was mentioned previously (Interview EU 2012b; Interview EU 2012e). The EU saw the value in the US supply chain security programme and benefited from the experience of the US, which moved first on this area (Interview EU 2012b, 2012c, 2012d).

Concerning the second issue, the fact that the EU embraced the US principles on customs security did not lead automatically to the emergence of an EU–US regime given that the US favoured concluding deals with individual member states rather than with the EU. This initial difference confirms Young's remark that in processes of regime formation the identity of participants is often fluid and is itself a matter of negotiations.

The EU opposed the bilateral deals of the US and proposed instead the negotiation and conclusion of an EU–US agreement on customs security that would include the expansion of CSI at all EU ports. The EU argument against US bilateralism was that the EU's common internal market and common customs area were affected by the US memorandums with member states. The containers that were shipped from EU's CSI ports would have preferential treatment in the US ports compared to the cargo shipments coming from the EU's non-CSI ports; this in turn gave an advantage to certain EU ports and it created, as a result, distortions in the function of the EU internal market (Interview EU 2012b; *Journal of Commerce* 2003; Associated Press Worldstream 2003).

The main aim of the EU was therefore to transform the bilateral approach that the US was following to an EU–US regime-formation process. Exploratory talks between the EU and the US started on July 2002 and during these talks, as well as during the subsequent negotiations, the EU had a strong strategic position, stemming from the fact that customs issues were part of the first pillar of the EU. In practice, and in terms of the regime-formation process, this meant two things. First, on first-pillar issues the EU had strong competencies and the European Court of Justice played a greater role; for customs agreements with third countries in particular it was the EU that had the competency to negotiate and conclude such agreements. In other words, the bilateral approach of the US clashed with the EU *acquis* and the fact that member states did not have the competency to negotiate customs agreements. Second, and more broadly, the EU's first pillar was predominantly a trade and economy related area where the EU was strong, and where, as a result, the relationship between the EU and the US was not as asymmetric as in the area of law enforcement, for example (Interview EU 2013).

The EU used a number of tactics in order to make the US accept an EU-wide solution regarding CSI and customs security. First, the EU initiated legal action against the member states that joined CSI and signed memorandums with the US (EUobserver 2002, 2003b). Through this action the EU wanted to ensure and safeguard the Union's political coherency and consistency; this in turn would send a signal to the US about the EU's concerns and about the real possibility that the European Court of Justice could render the bilateral deals illegal (Interview EU 2012b). Second, the EU framed the EU–US clash not only in terms of competencies and legality but also in terms of efficiency; the argument that the EU officials were advancing in their talks with their US counterparts was that the US aims could be achieved in a more efficient way at an EU level (Interview EU 2012b; *Journal of Commerce* 2003). An EU-wide agreement would ensure that there were the same risk assessment and screening criteria at all EU ports, and this in turn would be beneficial from both a security and an industry perspective (*Journal of Commerce* 2003). In other words, the EU officials did not only use threats (structural leadership) but also pointed to common benefits (entrepreneurial leadership).

The US officials realised gradually that the EU Commission had competencies for issues related to CSI and that they could not bypass the Commission on that matter as they had tried to do initially (Interview US 2012c): highlighting that even strong actors cannot fully control the issue of the participants in regime-formation negotiations. Additionally, the EU's legal action against member states played a role in changing the US stance. Indeed, a US Customs spokesman admitted that the EU's legal action 'could slow the agency's [US Customs] plans to expand the CSI to more European ports by deterring countries from completing security agreements with the US' (Aviation Week's Homeland Security and Defense 2003). In other words, the US changed its position under the threat of political costs that would otherwise occur. The EU managed therefore to transform the bilateral approach of the US into a regime-formation process that included on the one hand the US and on the other hand the EU.

After the US accepted the EU as its main interlocutor on customs security and CSI issues the Council of the EU gave a negotiation mandate to the Commission and negotiations between the two sides started on March 2003. The negotiations were concluded very quickly (in November 2003) given that no differences emerged on the content of the agreement (Interview EU 2012b). The EU agreed on the content of the CSI. More broadly, the EU and the US agreed on the guiding principles for customs security: multi-layered risk management, trade facilitation, and international cooperation (Interview EU 2012b). These principles were already put into practice in the US (with the CSI and the 24-hour rule). Similarly, the EU initiated customs reforms and projects that were based on the principles mentioned previously and that were similar to the projects emerged in the US.

The agreement between the EU and the US was finally signed on 28 April 2004 (Council of the EU 2004). The scope of the deal was not limited to issues related to the CSI and it went beyond what was previously agreed in the US–member states CSI memorandums; rather, the EU aimed and managed to include in the scope of the agreement broader issues related to customs security (Interview EU 2012b). Such issues included the exchange of best practices in the field of customs security and the establishment of minimum standards for risk-management programmes, for the identification of high-risk shipments, for the screening of high-risk cargos, and for industry-partnership programmes (Council of the EU 2004). Such widening of the scope of the agreement was met positively by the US given that the issues on which the two sides decided to cooperate fitted into the American five-pillar plan for customs security. At the same time, this EU expansion of the two sides' agenda for cooperation gives a picture of the EU that is different from the picture often portrayed in the literature of the EU as a passive actor unable to influence the transatlantic security agenda.

To sum up, this section showed that while initially the EU had a reactive stance with regard to the US, subsequently the EU showed significant initiative. The 2004 customs security agreement moved beyond the US Container Security Initiative, establishing EU–US cooperation on customs security matters in general. This agreement reflected the convergence of the EU and the US on three customs security principles: multi-layered risk management, trade facilitation, and international cooperation. The next section presents the EU–US Mutual Recognition agreement for the two sides' business-to-government customs security programmes.

The EU–US Mutual Recognition Agreement

Part of the US five-pillar plan for customs security was the launch and expansion of the C-TPAT (Customs-Trade Partnership Against Terrorism) programme. The C-TPAT programme was based on the idea that the private sector should be taken into account in the establishment and implementation of security measures given that private actors and companies – for example, importers, shippers and customs brokers – played a great role in the international supply chains system (Frittelli 2005: 22). The involvement of the private sector in supply chain security was especially crucial in the context of the customs security gaps that were identified after the 9/11 attacks (Interview US 2012c). The involvement of private actors in the process of regime formation in general was also acknowledged in the literature on international regimes by authors such as Young (1994, 1998) and Haas (1993).

The US C-TPAT programme was launched in 2001 and was authorised in 2006 with the Security and Accountability for Every Port Act of 2006 (US Congress 2006). Through this programme, US-based companies that were involved in importing goods from overseas could voluntarily adopt a number of security measures. In return, US Customs would offer these companies a number of benefits, such as faster security clearances and less security inspections. The similar concept of Authorised Economic Operator (AEO) was adopted by the World Customs Organization (WCO) in the organisation's 2005 'SAFE Framework of Standards to Secure and Facilitate Global Trade'. Finally, the EU, inspired by both the American C-TPAT and the WCO standards, initiated in 2005 its own Authorised Economic Operator programme (Interview EU 2012b).

In the above context, a particular issue that the WCO highlighted was that of the mutual recognition of the various AEO systems. In other words, the WCO stressed that customs authorities and governments should recognise each other's systems and security measures regarding AEOs as equivalent and therefore grant the same benefits as those AEOs. This process of mutual recognition would be especially beneficial for the industry given that companies could benefit from a broadened array of trade facilitation measures (Interview EU 2013).

Taking into account WCO's SAFE Framework, the EU proposed to the US in 2005 the start of talks for the mutual recognition of the two sides' programmes for authorised companies (Council of the EU 2005: 10; Interview EU 2012b, 2012e). In this way, the EU officials exercised a form of entrepreneurial leadership popularising and drawing attention to the issue of mutual recognition. At the same time, the EU promoted and favoured a particular form of this recognition process, framing the problem as an EU–US issue rather than as an issue to be dealt by member states separately with the US. The EU was pointing to the benefits that mutual recognition would bring to both the EU and the US.

The EU initiative for the mutual recognition of the European AEO and the American C-TPAT showed again an EU that took the lead in the EU–US regime-formation process. This itself was a significant development given the frequent portrayal of the EU in the literature as an actor being led by the US on security issues. However, it was only in 2007 that the US agreed to engage in talks with Europeans about the feasibility of EU–US mutual recognition; the two sides decided in January 2007 to create a working group on mutual recognition. The aim of the group was the creation of a roadmap towards recognition and the drafting of proposals and suggestions for an EU–US agreement on mutual recognition (EU–US Joint Customs Cooperation Committee 2007). Despite the creation of this group, US support for such an agreement remained lukewarm at least until 2008 and early 2009 (Interview EU 2012b, 2012e).

The main reason behind the US reluctance and the main block to the further development of the EU–US customs security regime was, again, the initial American insistence on working with member states rather than with the EU as a whole. The US preferred to recognise the business-to-government programmes of only certain countries: for example, Germany, France, and the UK (Interview EU 2012e). The US was reluctant to recognise the AEO programmes of the new Eastern European member states whose customs security measures it did not fully trust (Inside US Trade 2007; Interview EU 2012e). Additionally, the US insisted that there was no point in having substantial discussions with the EU on the issue of mutual recognition until the EU's AEO programme was implemented and fully functional and until the EU ensured that the AEO scheme was applied equally in all member states (*Shipping Digest* 2007; Inside US Trade 2007). While the EU's AEO plan was launched in 2005, by 2007 not all EU member states had implemented the relevant regulations (*Journal of Commerce* 2007). The US was therefore reluctant to agree to a set date for the conclusion of the EU–US mutual recognition process until the EU's AEO system was fully operational in all EU member states (Inside US Trade 2007).

For the EU Commission, however, a bilateral approach was a 'red line' and it could not, therefore, be accepted (Interview EU 2012e). Similar to the CSI, the selective recognition of the AEOs of only some countries would create trade distortions for the EU internal market, given that the AEOs of those countries would be in an advantageous position compared with other AEOs. Additionally, US bilateralism clashed with the EU competencies on customs. As an EU official noted with regard to mutual recognition,

> [T]hose countries that wish to sign mutual recognition agreements with only some EU member states will be disappointed: owing to the legal structure of the EU, the mutual recognition of AEO and/or security measures can only be agreed at EU-level and not with individual Member States.
> (Aigner 2010: 54)

The breakthrough came with the start of the implementation of the EU's AEO scheme on 1 January 2008. This satisfied the US demand that the EU's AEO should be operational before the EU–US recognition process started. As a result, the two sides agreed in March 2008 on a 'Roadmap towards Mutual Recognition of Trade Partnership Programs' (EU–US Joint Customs Cooperation Committee 2009). This document was crucial as it 'set the way out forward' for mutual recognition by identifying the steps that the EU and the US had to take to achieve this aim (Interview EU 2012e). The recognition roadmap included a number of technical, operational, legal, and evaluation areas of action that needed completion for recognition to be achieved; such areas included, for example, the data elements that customs authorities would exchange and the proper legal framework for the implementation of recognition (EU–US Joint Customs Cooperation Committee 2009).

The Mutual Recognition Agreement was finally signed on 4 May 2012 and full implementation started on 31 January 2013. The initiative for this agreement came from the EU, which in this way played an important role in shaping the agenda of the EU–US customs security cooperation. More importantly, the mutual recognition decision served as a catalyst for change in the American C-TPAT programme and this, in turn, points towards a process where the US was influenced by the EU and adopted EU standards internally. Indeed, as one US official admitted, the influence from and the imitation of each other's ideas and programmes on homeland security is more mutual than normally assumed (Interview US 2012c).

In particular, when the C-TPAT was established it covered only companies that imported goods from overseas to the US; in other words, C-TPAT covered US importers. On the contrary, the EU's AEO programme had both an imports and an exports aspect. When the mutual recognition process started an important element in the EU–US talks was that of the reciprocity of the final agreement (Interview EU 2012e); for the final mutual recognition decision to be reciprocal the US had to expand C-TPAT to exporters and, indeed, such an expansion was included in the EU–US recognition road map. Following the adoption of the road map, the US Customs and Border Protection Unit started planning the expansion of C-TPAT to exporters in 2013 (Advisory Committee on Commercial Operations to US CBP 2013).

The mutual recognition case was also an example of the interaction effects between European integration and the regime formation processes of the EU with the US. Indeed, the refusal of the US to enter into substantive talks with the EU on mutual recognition until the EU's authorised operators plan was fully functional in all member states points towards the existence of such interaction effects. According to the EU officials interviewed, US bilateralism could be neutralised if the EU member states stood loyal to the EU policies (Interview EU 2012a; Interview EU 2013). The more consistent and coherent the EU was internally the more credible it appeared to the US, and the EU's credibility, in turn, affected the US calculations (Interview US 2012d).

In conclusion, the case of the Mutual Recognition Agreement shows a number of important insights for the EU–US relationship. This agreement was an EU initiative, which was met initially with scepticism by the US and, as with the 2004 agreement, the US stance was ambivalent. The expansion of the EU's AEO programme in all member states of the EU convinced the US about the benefits of the agreement. The Mutual Recognition Agreement triggered also a change in the domestic US C-TPAT programme, highlighting the significant influence of the EU.

The 100 per cent scanning rule

This section presents the 100 per cent scanning issue, which emerged through an initiative of the US Congress as an example of how political contextual factors can influence the regime-formation process. EU officials were opposed to this measure and tried to dissuade US officials from implementing it through a combination of threats (structural leadership) and a persuasion campaign (intellectual leadership).

In 2006, the US Congress passed the Security and Accountability for Every Port Act (US Congress 2006). Among others, the act instructed the US Department of Homeland Security to test the feasibility of scanning all US-bound containers in foreign ports for nuclear and radiological materials. This test was initiated in December 2006 with the Secure Freight Initiative (SFI) that was implemented in three ports (Southampton in the UK, Port Qasim in Pakistan, and Puerto Cortes in Honduras). In early 2007, however, the new Democratic

Congress passed the 9/11 Commission Act (US Congress 2007), which, among others, amended the 2006 Safe Port Act. The Congress legislated that by 2012 all US-bound cargo should be scanned with radiological and nuclear detection equipment at overseas ports; otherwise, the shipping vessels would be prohibited from entering the US.

The 100 per cent scanning requirement was another extraterritorial and unilateral measure along the lines of the 24-hour rule. The 100 per cent scanning legislation, however, did not have the full support of the US administration and the Department of Homeland Security; rather, it was a politically motivated Congress initiative (Interview EU 2012b, 2012e; Interview US 2012b, 2012c). In particular the new Democratic Congress wanted to demonstrate through its first act (the 9/11 Commission Act) that it was as committed to the security of the US as the Republican administration (Grillot *et al.* 2010:36). Additionally, the 9/11 Commission Act served the purpose of criticising the Republican Bush administration for shortcomings in the area of homeland security (Interview EU 2012b, 2012e).

The EU was fiercely opposed to such a measure for a number of reasons; in particular, the Commission conducted three technical studies in which the impact of the 100 per cent rule was examined with regard to trade, maritime transport, and security (European Commission 2010). These studies formed the basis of the EU officials' intellectual campaign in which they tried to persuade their US counterparts about the huge costs and disadvantages that 100 per cent scanning would have. First, according to these studies, the 100 per cent scanning rule would have huge investment and operational costs for European countries (European Commission 2010: 8). European ports would have to spend money on new equipment and technology, on changing their procedures and regulations, and on expanding their facilities. Regarding operational costs, the implementation of the 100 per cent rule would require an increase in port personnel, while maintenance and energy consumption costs would increase too (European Commission 2010: 8). Second, according to the EU, the 100 per cent scanning rule would disrupt EU–US maritime transport and trade given that the direct and indirect transport costs of containers would increase (European Commission 2010: 9). Additionally, there would be trade distortions in the EU internal market since small ports would not be able to invest in the necessary equipment and, therefore, they would lose the US-related part of their business. Third, the 100 per cent rule would affect other sectors of the economy too; the increased transport costs would be transferred to the prices of the final products affecting consumers' purchasing capacity. Finally, according to the EU reports, the 100 per cent rule would not improve security (European Commission 2010: 11). Especially for the EU, implementation of the 100 per cent legislation would incur huge opportunity costs given that scarce resources and personnel in European customs authorities would be diverted from their projects into trying to implement the US legislation (Interview EU 2012e).

More broadly, the US measure departed from the principle of multi-layered risk management, according to which containers would be screened on the basis of risk criteria and only the high-risk containers would be scanned. This principle formed the basis of the US approach to customs as shown previously. It was a principle that was shared by both the EU and the international community in general, especially through the initiatives of the World Customs Organization (Interview EU 2012e). The 100 per cent rule, however, created the possibility of having globally diverging and incompatible standards for customs security, which in turn would cause trade disruptions and losses.

The EU officials used the above arguments as the basis for an intellectual campaign that aimed to influence the US Congress and to promote the alternative customs security model of risk management. In particular, the EU Commission sent its reports and studies regarding the 100 per cent rule to the Department of Homeland Security in order that the latter would present these studies to the US Congress (Interview EU 2013). Indeed, in a Senate Hearing on the 100 per cent rule (US Senate 2008) the US administration presented the EU's view on the issue, along with the views of the WCO and of the industry; the US officials themselves expressed in this hearing their concern about the feasibility of the rule. At the same time, the EU officials exercised intellectual leadership on a second front, arguing against the 100 per cent rule in the context of the WCO (Interview 2012e).

Apart from the above action, EU officials also exercised a form of structural leadership, threatening the US in two areas. First, the EU made clear that the possibility of initiating legal action against the US in the context of the World Trade Organisation was open (Interview EU 2012e): according to the EU Commissioner for Taxation and Customs, Kovács, the 100 per cent rule 'might pave the way for an EU complaint with the World Trade Organization that the US has violated the international rules of free and fair trade' (Associated Press 2007b). Second, the EU left open the possibility of demanding from the US reciprocal measures on customs security for which the US was not ready (Caldwell 2008: 19). According to Commissioner Kovács, 'following the logic of international trade, if any major player introduces measures unilaterally, it could be followed by reciprocal measures' (European Report 2007).

The EU threats of legal action against a US security measure give a picture of an EU as a more assertive actor than normally assumed in the literature. This assertiveness was related to the fact that the EU had a strong strategic position in the area of trade and economy, and therefore the Union could capitalise on this area of strength to bring bargaining leverage into the talks with the US. Additionally, the strategic position of the EU was strengthened by the fact that the shipping industry opposed the 100 per cent rule and started pressuring the US Congress to change its stance. For example, in April 2007 two business groups (US Chamber of Commerce and Business Europe) that represented the vast majority of the companies involved in transatlantic trade wrote to the US Senate calling for the removal of the 100 per cent scanning legislation (Associated Press 2007a).

The 100 per cent rule was never implemented. The relevant legislation gave the Department of Homeland Security the authority to extend the July 2012 deadline set by the 9/11 Commission Act for the start of the programme. By 2012 the leadership of the Department of Homeland Security made clear that it did not intend to implement the 100 per cent rule and it extended the deadline by two years (Interview EU 2013); rather, the US officials remained committed to the previous approach based on the principle of risk management (Interview US 2012b; Interview US 2012c). This approach was a core element of the US National Strategy for Global Supply Chain Security, published in 2012, in which there was no mention of the 100 per cent scanning requirement.

According to an EU official, one of the consequences of the 100 per cent scanning issue was that, despite being initiated by the legislators and not by the administration, it isolated the US, it undermined the US position in the international discussions about customs security, and it made the Americans move gradually towards more cooperative policies and attitudes (Interview EU 2012e). This isolation and the huge international reaction to the Congress's measures showed the US that unilateral policies that were shaped and implemented without prior consultation with US allies could be costly in terms of Washington's relations with its partners (Interview EU 2012e).

The 100 per cent issue case shows how initiatives relevant for EU–US regime formation could stem from the domestic level. Additionally, the effort of the EU officials to influence the Congress and to exercise intellectual leadership towards the US legislature shows how during the process of regime formation actors worked at both the executive and the domestic/legislative level; similar processes can be seen in the PNR case in this book, where the US was lobbying the European Parliament in an effort to influence the parliamentarians' vote on the third EU–US PNR agreement.

Conclusion

This chapter analysed the emergence of the EU–US customs security cooperation, addressing thus the main research question of this book about the way the EU and the US have cooperated on internal security matters. The customs security principles around which the EU and the US have converged are three: multi-layered risk management, international cooperation, and trade facilitation. These principles were incorporated into the 2011 EU–US joint statement on supply chain security and into the EU–US 2004 agreement. The transatlantic customs security norms that were established included the obligation of the two parties to share and exchange best practices and information, to develop common security standards, and to coordinate their positions in international fora. More specific rules also started to emerge, such as the rules related to the implementation of the mutual recognition decision. Finally, the decision-making procedures of this regime included the Joint Customs Cooperation Committee (JCCC), the Transport Security Cooperation Group, and the customs security working groups established through the EU–US agreements.

This chapter highlighted the importance of external crises and shocks for processes of regime formation. In the case of customs security, the 9/11 attacks were the shock that made the EU and US officials change their perceptions regarding the adequacy of the security controls in transatlantic supply chains. Therefore, a learning process took place where officials from both sides of the Atlantic gave an anti-terrorist role to customs functions; in particular, the US officials embraced the concept of smart borders as one of the solutions to the US security challenges, and in this sense the role of knowledge was prominent at the initial stages of regime formation.

Subsequently, the US moved first and their officials exercised all forms of leadership. In particular, intellectual leadership supported the other two forms of leadership. The US structural leadership (threatening the non-compliant states with sanctions) for the 24-hour rule and the US entrepreneurial leadership for CSI were backed with the idea of smart borders and the principle of risk management. When the US initiated the regime-formation process the issue of the identity of the participants emerged, which as previous regime research has shown is seldom neutral. While the US approached first the EU member states, the EU, which had competencies in the issue-area of customs, favoured an EU–US agreement. To change the US stance, the EU officials exercised structural leadership initiating legal proceedings against the member states that cooperated with the US thus raising the political costs for these states and for the US. Additionally, the EU officials exercised entrepreneurial leadership pointing out to the Americans the benefits in terms of both efficiency and security that an EU-wide agreement would confer.

The bilateralist approach of the US continued in the case of the mutual recognition decision where the EU could not change the US stance as easily as in the 2004 agreement. It was only when the EU AEO programme was implemented in all EU states that the US was convinced to negotiate at an EU level. This case highlights the importance of domestic developments for the regime-formation processes.

In a similar example of domestic political events and developments influencing regime formation, the emergence of a Democratic Congress in 2007 and the resulting 100 per cent scanning legislation created friction in transatlantic customs cooperation. Regime theorists have noted that there is nothing predetermined in the identity of participants in the regime-formation process and, indeed, in the 100 per cent scanning case the US Congress sought to influence this process. Interestingly, the stance of the Congress differed from the position of the US administration and an alliance was formed between the EU and the US administration against the US Congress. As a result, the EU officials focused their leadership efforts on two actors, the US Congress and the US administration; these efforts took the form of entrepreneurial campaigns in the US Congress and threats for legal action in the World Trade Organization (structural leadership).

Notes

1 This chapter is based on Anagnostakis, D. (2016) 'Securing the Transatlantic Maritime Supply Chains from Counterterrorism: EU–US Cooperation and the Emergence of a Transatlantic Customs Security Regime', *Studies in Conflict & Terrorism* 39 (5): 451–471. Reprinted by permission of Taylor & Francis LLC (www.tandfonline.com).
2 Smart containers are containers that have digital seals attached on them. These seals transmit information regarding the security of the container into a receiver device.

References

Advisory Committee on Commercial Operations to US CBP (2013), 13th Term Recommendations May–November 2013, 15 November 2013.
Aigner, S. (2010) 'Mutual recognition of Authorised Economic Operators and security measures', *World Customs Journal*, 4(1), pp. 47–54.
Allen, C. (2008) 'The International Supply Chain Security Regime and the Role of Competent International Organizations', in M.H. Nordquist, R. Wolfrum, J. Norton Moore and R. Long (eds) *Legal Challenges in Maritime Security*. Leiden: Brill, pp. 165–262.
Associated Press (2007a) 'EU, US businesses ask US lawmakers to scrap security rules that would scan all cargo', 12 April 2007.
Associated Press (2007b) 'EU says concerned that US cargo scanning would disrupt trade', 2 August 2007.
Associated Press Worldstream (2003) 'EU nations give Commission mandate for trans-Atlantic talks on port security', 18 March 2003.
Aviation Week's Homeland Security and Defense, 'Europeans objecting to US Container Security Initiative', 8 January 2003.
Booth, F. and Altenbrun, L. (2002) 'Maritime and Port Security, Piracy, and Stowaways: Renewed Concerns Over Old Problems', *University of San Francisco Maritime Law Journal*, 15(1), pp. 1–47.
Bowman, G. (2007) 'Thinking Outside the Border: Homeland Security and the Forward Deployment of the US Border', *Houston Law Review*, 44(2), pp. 189–251.
Caldwell, S. (2008) *Supply Chain Security: Challenges to Scanning 100 Percent of US-Bound Cargo Containers*. United States Government Accountability Office.
Council of the EU (1997) 'Act 98/C 24/01 of 18 December 1997 drawing up, on the basis of Article K3 of the Treaty on European Union, the Convention on mutual assistance and cooperation between customs administrations', OJ C 24, 23 January 1998.
Council of the EU (2003) 'Resolution of 2 October 2003 on a strategy for customs cooperation', OJ C 247, 15 December 2003.
Council of the EU (2004) 'Decision of 30 March concerning the conclusion of the Agreement between the European Community and the United States of America on intensifying and broadening the Agreement on customs cooperation and mutual assistance in customs matters to include cooperation on container security and related matters', OJ L 304, 30 September 2004.
Council of the EU (2005) 'EU–US Declaration on an "Initiative to Enhance Transatlantic Economic Integration and Growth" (20 June 2005) – Joint Work Programme', 15199/05, 1 December 2005.
EUobserver (2002) 'Member states attacked for signing US proposal', 27 December 2002.
EUobserver (2003a) 'Spain risks Commission wrath over US initiative', 10 January 2003.
EUobserver (2003b) 'Sweden joins rebels on US container security', 30 January 2003.

European Commission (2003a) 'Communication from the Commission to the Council, the European Parliament, the European Economic and Social Committee and the Committee of the Regions on Enhancing Maritime Transport Security', COM (2003) 229, 2 May 2003.
European Commission (2003b) 'Communication from the Commission to the Council, the European Parliament and the European Economic and Social Committee: a simple and paperless environment for Customs and Trade', COM (2003) 452, 24 July 2003.
European Commission (2010) 'Commission Staff Working Document – Secure Trade and 100 per cent Scanning of Containers', SEC (2010) 131, 11 February 2010.
European Commission (2016) 'United States', http://ec.europa.eu/trade/policy/countries-and-regions/countries/united-states/, accessed 19 June 2016.
European Report (2007) 'EU/US: 100 per cent Container Scanning Rule Arouses Commission IRE', 7 March 2007.
EU–US Joint Customs Cooperation Committee (2007) 'Terms of Reference EU–US JCCC Working Group on Mutual recognition', 22 January 2007.
EU–US Joint Customs Cooperation Committee (2009) 'Abridged External Partner Version of the US-EU Joint Customs Cooperation Committee Roadmap Towards Mutual recognition of Trade Partnership Programs', January 2009.
Frittelli, J. (2005) 'Port and Maritime Security: Background and Issues for Congress', Report for Congress RL31733, 27 May 2005. Congressional Research Service.
Grillot, S., Cruise, R. and D'Erman, V. (2010) *Protecting Our Ports: Domestic and International Politics of Containerized Freight Security*. Aldershot: Ashgate.
Haas, P. (1993) 'Epistemic Communities and the Dynamics of International Environmental Cooperation', in V. Rittberger (ed.) *Regime Theory and International Relations*. Oxford: Oxford University Press, pp. 168–201.
Inside US Trade (2007) 'US, EU Set To Unveil C-TPAT, AEO Mutual Recognition Road Map Today', 9 November 2007.
Interview EU (2012a), Interview with EU official, 9 February 2012.
Interview EU (2012b), Interview with EU official, 14 May 2012.
Interview EU (2012c), Interview with EU official, 16 May 2012.
Interview EU (2012d), Interview with EU official, 16 May 2012.
Interview EU (2012e), Interview with EU official, 21 June 2012.
Interview EU (2013), Interview with EU official, 14 May 2013.
Interview US (2012a), Interview with US official, 25 January 2012.
Interview US (2012b), Interview with US official, 25 January 2012.
Interview US (2012c), Interview with US official, 6 February 2012.
Interview US (2012d), Interview with US official, 7 February 2012.
Journal of Commerce (2002) 'Euro ports wary of US box security', 24 June 2002.
Journal of Commerce (2003) 'Brussels complains it's being left out; EC wants US Customs to negotiate a Europe-wide container security agreement', 3 February 2003.
Journal of Commerce (2007) 'Piece by piece on WCO framework; There's gradual progress on global model for security, trade', 12 February 2007.
New York Times (2002) 'US Port Security Plan Irks Europeans', 6 November 2002.
RAPID (2003) 'Frits Bolkenstein Member of the European Commission in charge of the Internal Market, Taxation and Customs EU Customs policy boosting security and modernising procedures Address at Freight Forwarders Day at Hotel Metropole Brussels', 1 December 2003.
Shipping Digest (2007) 'Customs close to C-TPAT deal with New Zealand', 29 January 2007.

Simon, S. and Knake, R. (eds) (2006) *The Forgotten Homeland-A Century Foundation Task Force Report*. New York: The Century Foundation Press.

The National Business Review (2002) 'US seeks to pre-screen container traffic to its ports', 16 August 2002.

The White House (2002) 'The National Security Strategy of the United States', 17 September 2002.

The White House Bulletin (2002) 'Bonner Announces Container Security Initiative', 17 January 2002.

US Coast Guard (2002) 'Maritime Strategy for Homeland Security', December 2002.

US Congress (2002) 'Maritime Transportation Security Act of (2002)', 107–795, 25 November 2002.

US Congress (2006) 'United States Security and Accountability for Every Port Act of (2006)', 109–347, 13 October 2006.

US Congress (2007) 'United States Implementing Recommendations of the 9/11 Commission Act of (2007)', 110–53, 3 August 2007.

US Customs Today (2001) September 2001.

US Customs Today (2002a) January 2002.

US Customs Today (2002b) February 2002.

US Customs Today (2002c) March 2002.

US Customs Today (2003) February 2003.

US Customs and Border Protection Today (2005) November 2005.

US Department of Homeland Security (2004) 'Securing Our Homeland: US Department of Homeland Security Strategic Plan', 2004.

US Federal Register (2002), Vol. 67 No. 211, 31 October 2002.

US Interagency Commission on Crime and Security in US Seaports (2000) 'Report of the Interagency Commission on Crime and Security in US Seaports', Fall 2000.

US National Commission on Terrorist Attacks Upon the United States (2004) 'The 9/11 Commission Report', 2004.

US Office of Homeland Security (2002) 'National Strategy for Homeland Security', July 2002.

US Senate (2003) 'Cargo Containers: The Next Terrorist Target?', Hearing 108–55, 20 March 2003.

US Senate (2008) 'Supply Chain Security: Secure Freight Initiative and the Implementation of 100 Percent Scanning', Hearing 110–1227, 12 June 2008.

Wilson, W. and Benson, D. (2009) *Container Flows in World Trade, US Waterborne Commerce and Rail Shipments in North American Markets*. Upper Great Plains Transportation Institute: North Dakota State University.

Young, O. (1994) *International Governance: Protecting the Environment in a Stateless Society*. Ithaca: Cornell University Press.

Young, O. (1998) *Creating Regimes: Arctic Accords and International Governance*. Ithaca: Cornell University Press.

3 Judicial cooperation between the European Union and the United States

The mutual legal assistance and extradition agreements

The agreements between the US and the EU on legal assistance and extradition were the EU's first international third-pillar agreements. These agreements granted implicit legal personality to the EU as an organisation and reflected the elevation of justice and home affairs to the forefront of the EU's political agenda and priorities. At the time of their conclusion, the EU–US deals were described as 'landmark', 'historic', and 'unprecedented' (Mitsilegas 2003: 533; International Enforcement Law Reporter 2008); these words, apart from reflecting the usual political rhetoric employed in such instances, also indicated a substantial development in EU–US judicial cooperation. The agreements provided for joint investigation teams between the US and EU member states, for the use of video-conferencing in the examination of witnesses, and for the ability of states to exchange information on bank accounts. In the words of Leslie Lebl, who served as Minister-Counselor for Political Affairs at the US Mission to the EU, 'a year earlier, even the video conferencing would have been an unprecedented step' (Lebl 2005).

The agreements were negotiated at a time when the relations between the US and certain member states and with the EU were strained due to its decision to invade Iraq. One would expect, therefore, that cooperation between the two actors would be limited at that time. Previously, similar tensions emerged with regard to the US transfer of Taliban and al-Qaeda militants to Guantanamo Bay, where special military tribunals were established. In reality, while these tensions fed into the two sides' talks on the extradition agreement, the judicial cooperation between the US and the EU continued uninhibited and expanded 'under the surface' of the above tensions (Interview EU 2012a; Interview US 2012a, 2012b, 2012c). The negotiations touched also upon the broader issues of data protection and human rights where the EU and the US approaches differed (Interview EU 2012c).

The aim of this chapter is to examine how the EU and the US cooperated on internal security matters, analysing the EU–US negotiations for the mutual legal assistance (MLA) and extradition agreements from a regime-theory perspective. These negotiations are conceptualised as a regime-formation process in which the EU and the US tried to establish a framework of rules that would guide the interactions between the US and the EU member states on legal assistance and extradition matters. These rules are part of the broader emerging internal security regime that the EU and the US started to build in the post-9/11 period.

This chapter shows that the EU–US relationship in the area of judicial cooperation can be characterised as a partnership based on common benefits. While the EU has often been portrayed as a passive actor in its relations with the US, in the case of the MLA and extradition agreements it was the EU that took the initiative and was the 'champion' for the start of the negotiations. A learning process occurred among the EU member states and the EU through which cooperation with the US emerged at the forefront of the political agenda after the 9/11 attacks as a new means in the fight against terrorism and organised crime. The US was persuaded to enter into talks with the EU after considering the information sharing advantages of a future legal assistance agreement. The US also took advantage of the political window of opportunity offered by the EU to include the topic of extradition to the EU–US negotiations on judicial matters. In other words, at the agenda-setting phase, in accordance with the interest-based approaches to regime formation (Young 1998: 10, 189), the political agenda was fluid with the EU and the US exercising equal influence to its shaping.

The negotiations were integrative in nature, characterised by the mutual adjustment of the two sides' positions and the use of side payments and quid-pro-quo arrangements for the establishment of rules acceptable to both parties. Additionally, the favourable strategic position of the EU in this issue-area enhanced its bargaining leverage. The US, as a result, could not translate its power into negotiating leverage as easily as in the negotiations for other agreements. This case confirmed, therefore, the argument of Young regarding the inability of powerful actors to exert influence under certain circumstances (Young 1994: 117–139).

Moreover, differences emerged between the EU and the US regarding the issues of data protection and human rights, in an example of Young's 'linked issues' problem where efforts of actors to establish a regime affect other regimes. To resolve these differences, the US was promoting the focal point and principle that the EU and the US data protection systems offered the same protections to individuals, and therefore the EU should not try to incorporate its data protection rules into the text of the agreements. This focal point clearly favoured the US position and supported the US interests, pointing towards the presence of interaction effects between ideational and interest factors.

The context

This section shows that before the 9/11 attacks the issue of transatlantic judicial cooperation against transnational threats such as organised crime, drug trafficking, and terrorism was mainly framed as a bilateral problem that the US had to address in its bilateral relations with the EU member states. The EU and the US did not give political priority to developing their mutual relations on third-pillar matters and this explains the absence of a regime at that period. While the US showed a strong interest in benefiting from the EU integration efforts in the area of justice and home affairs, the lack of progress of the EU in this field disappointed the Americans. The EU was preoccupied with deepening intra-EU judicial cooperation and it rebuffed the US advances, arguing that the Union should first put its own house in order. At the same time, the EU member states feared at that time that direct EU–US links on internal security issues could undermine their sovereignty in these issues. This section shows, therefore, that political priorities and broader socio-economic events affect whether an issue emerges high in the political agenda of actors and whether it is framed as a problem that the relevant actors need to address jointly (Young 1998: 24).

Before the 9/11 attacks, the relations between the EU and the US on judicial affairs had four main aspects. First, as with the area of police and law enforcement cooperation, which is examined in the next chapter, the US approach towards the EU on judicial issues was ambivalent. There was a fear among US officials and practitioners that stronger EU–US relations might compromise the already well-established and functioning bilateral relationships with European states (Cullen 1998: 96).

Second, prior to 9/11 the EU was not receptive to the US openings; the lack of substantial progress in intra-European cooperation in third-pillar matters meant that the EU prioritised enhancing cooperation among EU member states before focusing on developing the EU–US relationship. An additional factor that inhibited closer ties was the attitude of member states. France, in particular, was hostile to the idea of any formal or institutional EU–US cooperation in the judicial field (Gardner 1997: 57; Euro-East 2001).

Third, and related to the previous points, bilateralism with separate member states was the main pattern of US cooperation with Europe on judicial affairs. The network of relations with European states had its origins in the 1960s and 1970s when the US took a number of proactive and often extra-territorial measures to combat crimes that had increasingly a transnational character, such as drug trafficking, tax evasion, and terrorism (Nadelmann 1993; Den Boer 1998: 122; Snow 2002; Winer 2006). These measures included, among others, the conclusion of Mutual Legal Assistance Treaties (MLATS) and extradition treaties with European governments as well as the overseas posting of legal attachés from the Federal Bureau of Investigation (FBI).

Fourth, the cooperation between the EU and the US in the 1990s on judicial issues was limited and scattered and was developed more on an ad hoc basis. In 1995, the New Transatlantic Agenda and the accompanying Joint Action Plan were signed between the EU and the US, containing, among others, Justice and Home Affairs issues. However, no concrete results or actions were produced in this field.

From the above it can be seen that the issue of EU–US judicial cooperation and, in particular, the possibility of having EU–US framework agreements was not considered as a topic for discussion. Neither the US nor the EU considered at that time that having EU–US judicial cooperation agreements would significantly advance their interests, and there was lack of political prioritisation for such agreements on both sides of the Atlantic. Therefore, neither party made any effort in that period to exercise any form of leadership with the aim of influencing its counterpart.

Agenda formation after the 9/11 attacks

This section shows that the exogenous shock of the 9/11 attacks changed the political priorities of both the EU and the US. The EU became a champion (Young 1998: 7) of an EU–US agreement on judicial matters and its officials tried to popularise (Young 1991: 294) the importance of such an agreement during its exploratory talks with the US.

The judicial regime-formation process between the EU and the US started immediately after the terrorist attacks of 9/11. The initiative for the establishment of closer and formal judicial relations between the two sides came from the EU. This EU initiative appears surprising, especially if viewed in relation to two other instances of EU–US counter-terrorism cooperation that this book examines. In the cases of passengers' data transfers and customs security, it was the US which moved first – introducing new counter-terrorism rules and regulations. However, in the case of MLA and extradition agreements, and similarly with the Europol–US agreements, it was the EU which proposed and pressed for the start of negotiations.

The 9/11 events were crucial in creating the impetus for this EU initiative and in transforming the EU stance highlighting the importance of exogenous events for the emergence of international arrangements (Interview EU 2012a, 2012b). After 9/11 the cooperation with the US on counter-terrorism issues was elevated to the forefront of the political agenda both for member states and for the EU (Interview EU 2012a). In other words, a learning process occurred, stimulated by the new understandings regarding the post-9/11 security environment, through which the EU redefined the means it used in the fight against terrorism and organised crime.

In particular, in proposing the start of negotiations in the judicial field the main motive of the EU was the update of the existing mutual legal assistance treaties of the US with member states. Some of these treaties were considered outdated and therefore they were deemed to be ineffective counter-terrorism tools (Council of the EU 2011). For Europeans, special importance was given to the ability of judicial and law enforcement authorities to have access to financial and banking information as well as to the greater reliance on new telecommunication technologies (Interview EU 2012d). These innovative elements were already included in the EU's own mutual legal assistance convention, which was signed in 2000, and the aim of the EU was to transfer the same provisions into the transatlantic area (Interview EU 2013a; UK House of Lords 2003: 13).

This expansion of the EU's mutual legal assistance area to include the US also served two tactical purposes. First, according to the perspective of the EU officials interviewed, the EU 'showed its good will' at that time towards its 'most important ally' by making a concrete proposal that aimed to improve the practical cooperation between the two sides (Interview EU 2012d, 2013a). The

EU officials were expecting that through this practical initiative the credibility of the Union as an international counter-terrorism actor would be enhanced and trust would be built with the US (Interview EU 2013a).

Second, according to one of the EU interviewees, the start and the successful conclusion of the agreements would demonstrate the close relations between the two parties (Interview EU 2013a). Such a demonstration of a solid front was important if the preferences of the EU and the US, which were more converging than diverging, were to prevail globally at a time where international standards and responses for the fight against terrorism started to emerge (Interview EU 2013b).

The US officials were initially very reluctant to accept the EU proposals for the negotiation of mutual legal assistance and extradition treaties (Lebl 2005). Their biggest fear was that such treaties might compromise the bilateral treaties that the US already had with some member states and the already established and well-functioning bilateral ties with the judicial authorities of member states (ibid.). Apart from this fear of bypassing the member states, the US had also to be persuaded whether the agreements with the EU added any real value for them in the sense of specific advantages to be gained from cooperation at an EU level (Lebl 2005; Kerber 2007; Richard and Lebl 2009: 82). Additionally, and related to the above two factors, the US has been traditionally reluctant to enter into multilateral negotiations related to mutual legal assistance or extradition (Nadelmann 1993: 410). According to the American perspective, such negotiations usually worked under consensus rules and resulted in least common denominator solutions that were of little value; therefore, much more gains and concessions could be secured if the Americans approached key states separately (ibid.).

To change the US perceptions, the EU officials and negotiators presented the benefits that an EU framework agreement would bring to the US side: exercising in this way a form of entrepreneurial leadership. Similarly, they shaped the form in which the issue of EU–US judicial relations emerged for consideration by presenting the EU MLA Convention as the preferred model for the EU–US text (Interview EU 2013a). These entrepreneurial efforts were exercised in the context of the exploratory talks that officials from the Council, the Commission, and the member states had with their US counterparts during the first months after the 9/11 attacks. For example, the Belgian Presidency of the Council took the initiative to travel in Washington in October 2001 in order to present the EU arguments regarding an EU–US judicial deal.

The US side was finally persuaded to enter into formal negotiations for the judicial agreements. Regarding the substantial content of the talks, the US indeed shared the EU concerns regarding the update of the existing legal assistance treaties to make them more effective in the fight against terrorism; especially the provisions concerning the access to banking and financial information were perceived as extremely useful by the US officials (Interview US 2012c). Additionally, and from a practical point of view, an EU framework agreement covering all member states would be less costly in terms of resources and time than the US having to negotiate separate agreements with each member state (Interview US 2013).

Apart from the perceived benefits from an EU–US MLA agreement, the US saw the negotiations as a chance to bring a number of changes to the member states' extradition treaties with Washington. Indeed, the US was mainly focused on the extradition aspects of the EU–US talks, and during the EU–US exploratory discussions the US raised a number of issues related to extradition (Council of the EU 2002a). Therefore, during this stage of regime formation the agenda of the issues that would be subject to negotiation was fluid; despite the fact that the EU moved first, the US managed to expand the agenda of the negotiations from one focusing mainly on legal assistance to one that included both MLA and extradition issues.

Finally, key for the US acceptance of entering into negotiations with the EU was the fact that the EU reassured the US that any new MLA or extradition provisions would not compromise stronger or similar provisions in the existing bilateral treaties (Lebl 2005). This key 'principle of variable geometry' (Council of the EU 2011) was consistent with the US desire to secure the bilateral treaties and it was also shared by the EU member states themselves. In the draft negotiation mandate of the Council it was stressed that 'the future agreement [should in all cases safeguard the results achieved in the existing bilateral or multi-lateral agreements between the Member States and the USA]' (Council of the EU 2002a). The reassurances that the US received regarding bilateral treaties together with the innovative elements that the EU–US agreements would bring created the added value that the US sought from an EU–US deal.

From a theoretical perspective, the role of interest-based factors was prominent in the agenda-setting phase. The EU negotiators and officials exercised a form of entrepreneurial leadership towards the US, trying to make the case for a judicial agreement at the EU level and proposing a specific model for such an agreement based on the organisation's own MLA convention. After the US agreed to enter into negotiations and to work at an EU level, the two parties moved from the agenda-setting phase to the negotiations phase, envisioning a minimum of common interests to be gained from their cooperation.

Regarding the role of knowledge, the mutual legal assistance and extradition treaties were already well known and established anti-crime tools. The EU proposal for the negotiation of similar agreements with the US did not constitute any new anti-crime and counter-terrorism tool; rather, the innovation was that it was the first time that the US negotiated such treaties with an entity such as the EU and the first time that the EU negotiated an international third pillar-based agreement. It was only certain specific elements of the EU proposals, for example the use of videoconferencing, the establishment of joint investigative teams, and the rules on banking and finance information, that constituted innovative elements, and the EU's aim was to transfer these new ideas from the EU area where they were designed as anti-terror tools to the transatlantic area (Interview US 2013; Interview EU 2013a). Additionally, the 9/11 terrorist attacks triggered new understandings among Europeans concerning the post-9/11 security environment and the strategies and tools that fitted into this new environment.

Concerning power, structural factors did not play any role at the agenda-setting phase; rather than the US as a dominant law enforcement actor (in terms of material resources, budget, personnel, alliances, and control over ideas and technology) shaping the agenda unilaterally and monopolising the content of the items included for negotiation, both parties included the items that were of most interest to them (the discussion of the legal assistance provisions for the EU and the extradition issues for the US).

The negotiations for the agreements

The EU and the US entered the negotiations having a basis of common interests and the start of the two sides' talks resembled the interest-based patterns of regime formation. Both actors agreed on the need to update the extradition and legal assistance treaties and that an EU framework agreement was the most efficient way to proceed with this modernisation. At the same time, however, the EU had a number of additional aims related to its human rights and data protection regimes. The US was not part of these regimes and this created a potential source of conflict. Moreover, the US had to drop the aims of lifting the nationality bar to extradition and narrowing down the political offence exception given the negative reaction of the member states that maintained such provisions.

Regarding the extradition agreement, the US had three negotiating objectives. The first objective of the US was the elimination of obsolete provisions from the existing treaties of the US with the member states (US Department of Justice 2008: 2). For example, an outdated practice in the old treaties was to define the extraditable offences by a list of crimes for which extradition can be sought. Such an approach did not cover newly emerging forms of crime like cybercrime or antitrust crimes (US Department of Justice 2008: 3; US Senate 2008: 3). Additionally, providing a list of extraditable crimes would not allow the treaty to cover new types of offences that might emerge in the future, thus making a renegotiation necessary. For these reasons, the US proposed the 'penalty threshold' approach, according to which the extraditable offences were defined as those crimes that were punishable in both countries with a certain time of imprisonment (Council of the EU 2002a).

The second aim of the US was to safeguard the more advanced (from the US perspective) elements that were contained in certain bilateral treaties by ensuring that the provisions of the EU–US agreement did not undermine those elements (US Department of Justice 2008: 2). This objective reflected the concern of the US towards its bilateral ties with member states and it was a concern and negotiating objective that was shared by the EU member states and the Council (Council of the EU 2002a).

A third objective of the US was to come into agreement with the EU on adopting new provisions that were totally absent from the existing extradition treaties (US Department of Justice 2008: 3). Such provisions could include, for instance, the temporary surrender of persons who were already in custody in another country, the streamlining of the provisional arrest process, and the speeding up of extradition in cases where the fugitive agreed and consented to extradition. These issues would improve the efficiency and the speed of the extradition process, which, especially in older extradition treaties, was perceived as a cumbersome and time-consuming tool (US Senate 2006). For example, in the absence of a temporary surrender provision a person would be extradited only after he served his sentence in the requested country, a process that could take many years (US Department of Justice 2008: 4).

The US also raised in the negotiations the issue of the nationality bar to extradition and it proposed the narrowing down of the political offence exception in extradition (Council of the EU 2002a; Délégation de l'Assemblée Nationale pour l'Union européenne 2003: 27; Richard 2003: 278–281; Lebl 2005). These two bars to extradition have traditionally been a source of frustration for the US. In particular, the US criticised the legal tradition of many civil law countries to refuse the extradition of their own nationals (Richard 2003: 278), and during the last decades it has sought to limit the political offence bar to extradition so as not to cover, for example, terrorist acts (Garcia and Doyle 2010: 7–8; Doyle 2012: 30–31). Concerning the first issue, among the EU member states countries such as France, Greece, Germany, and Austria had provisions in their treaties with the US that forbade the extradition of their own nationals. The above two US aims were, however, dropped early in the talks given that the EU member states that maintained nationality and political offence bars and limitations to extradition were not willing to discuss any changes in the relevant provisions (Interview EU 2013a). In other words, the US could not monopolise the agenda of the negotiations due to the veto power that member states had in the Council of the EU. The latter situation enhanced the strategic position of the EU and weakened US bargaining leverage.

As far as the EU's negotiating aims for extradition were concerned, its stance was more reactive to the US aims than proactive, given that the main focus of the Europeans was on issues related to legal assistance. While the EU shared the US aim of reducing the delays related to extradition requests not all member states were willing to examine the two topics of political offence exceptions and extradition of one country's nationals (Council of the EU 2002a; Délégation de l'Assemblée Nationale pour l'Union européenne 2003: 27; Interview EU 2013a).

Additionally, the EU had as a general negotiating aim the protection and safeguarding of human rights and the incorporation into the agreement of the relevant guarantees (Council of the EU 2002a; European Report 2002; International Enforcement Law Reporter 2002). In particular, the issues of the death penalty, which was imposed in a number of US states, and of the special military tribunals created in the context of the war on terror were especially important from the EU perspective (Council of the EU 2002a; International Enforcement Law Reporter 2002; Stessens 2003: 266; UK House of Lords 2003: 11–12). Regarding the death penalty, the objective of the EU was to incorporate into the agreement a provision according to which the 'death sentence may not be imposed' or alternatively an article that would postulate that the 'death sentence may not be imposed or if imposed may not be carried out' (Council of the EU 2002a).

Concerning the special courts (military tribunals), the EU wanted to seek assurances from the US that the extradited persons would be brought and sentenced before 'ordinary US courts respecting fundamental rights and freedoms' (Council of the EU 2002a).

In the EU–US talks for the agreement for mutual legal assistance the EU was more proactive, making proposals that were directly influenced by the EU's own mutual legal convention (Interview EU 2013a; UK House of Lords 2003: 10). The objective of the EU was, first, to transfer its *acquis* in this field into the EU–US sphere and into the relations of member states with the US. In practice, the aim of Europeans was to include into the EU–US MLA agreements provisions that would improve mutual legal assistance and were related, among others, to the access to banking and financial information, the creation of joint investigative teams, and the use of videoconferences and other communication technologies (Stessens 2003: 264).

A second aim of the EU was to incorporate into the agreement guarantees and safeguards for the protection of human rights (Council of the EU 2002a). In this regard, the issue of data protection was particularly relevant given that the agreement would include the transfer of personal data from European authorities to US judicial and prosecutorial agencies. The negotiating objective of the EU, as described in the draft text of the EU mandate, was either to maintain the national data protection regimes or to include in the agreement strict provisions that were based however on 'solutions found in recent treaties, such as the Council of Europe Cybercrime Convention' (Council of the EU 2002a).

The US was willing to discuss the EU's proposals on mutual legal assistance and it had two main objectives. First, the US wanted to supplement the existing MLA treaties with new forms of legal cooperation (Interview US 2012c). An example of such a new form of cooperation was the provisions related to bank information, where the US responded positively to the EU suggestions. Second, the US wanted to make the legal cooperation more flexible, especially with regard to the use of the information that was shared in the context of the agreement. This US aim reflected the standard US position towards the use of information for law enforcement and judicial purposes according to which information should be shared freely among the relevant security agencies and with as few restrictions as possible (Richard 2003: 276–278; Richard and Lebl 2009: 85).

From the two sides' negotiating aims it can be seen that the EU and the US had a number of common objectives; both parties wanted to improve the efficacy of the extradition procedure and to include new provisions in the area of mutual legal assistance. However, there were three major areas where the EU and the US approaches differed; the protection of human rights, the data protection issue, and finally the relation of the European Arrest Warrant to the negotiated extradition agreement.

Interest-based factors and, to a lesser extent, knowledge and power factors played a role in the negotiation process for the MLA and extradition agreements. Negotiations were mainly integrative, and they were characterised by the mutual adjustment of the two actors' positions. A first interest-based feature of the talks between the two sides was that the US could not translate its power into bargaining leverage as easily as in other negotiations such as on passenger data. This US inability was related to the veto power that each member state had in the Council of the EU with regard to the EU–US negotiations. The negotiations were based on Articles 24 and 38 of the Treaty on European Union, which, combined, allowed the Council to negotiate agreements on third-pillar issues. According to the Treaty, the decision to conclude such agreements was taken by the Council acting unanimously, and this meant that each member state had the power to veto the conclusion of the EU–US deal. In terms of the EU–US judicial regime-formation process, this meant that during the negotiations the EU could extract concessions from the US by stressing that specific US demands could not be accepted by certain member states for constitutional or other reasons. Indeed, this institutional feature of the EU was an important factor in the negotiations and increased the strategic position and the bargaining leverage of the EU (Interview EU 2013a).

The difficulty of the US in enhancing its bargaining leverage was also connected to the fact that the US, compared with other issue-areas, such as in the case of PNRs, was less able to threaten the EU with defection from the negotiations and resort to bilateralism. In terms of a costs-benefits calculation, if the US wanted to update the existing legal assistance and extradition treaties with member states it would be costly both in time and in resources (Interview US 2013). At the same time, the resort to the previous status quo (no negotiations on MLA and extradition with either the EU or with member states separately) meant that the US would not benefit from improved extradition procedures and that the US would have difficulties in accessing bank and financing information. This was not considered an acceptable situation and a viable option given the perceived importance of these extradition and legal tools in the fight against terrorism (Richard 2003: 277; Kerber 2007). In the PNR case, the US would in any case have the data it needed, even in the absence of negotiations or a deal. In the case of a collapse of the MLA and extradition negotiations, however, the US could not identify, for example, the bank accounts and the financial information of a person suspected of criminal activities given that the existing bilateral MLA treaties of the US with member states did not provide for the sharing of such information (US Department of Justice 2008: 7–8; US Senate 2008: 4). This, in turn, weakened the overall strategic position of the US and its ability to threaten Europeans with defection during the negotiations in order to extract concessions from the EU.

Finally, the solution of the human rights and data protection issues became possible only through an agreement on the principle that the two sides' differences on such issues should not block cooperation (Council of the EU 2011: 33) and that despite these differences the EU and the US afforded the same level of protection to the rights of individuals. This principle was promoted by the US in order to support its interests and its position regarding data protection, pointing to an interaction effect between knowledge and interests. This ideational factor worked as a focal point that was influential in making the EU move away from maximalist positions (such as transferring the EU human rights and data protection *acquis* en bloc into the agreement) and to give concessions to the American side. The acceptance of the above principle by the EU reflected, however, a pragmatic analysis of what the Union was capable of achieving at the international level (Interview EU 2013a).

Human rights and data protection issues

One of the EU aims for the MLA and extradition agreements was the protection of human rights and fundamental freedoms. The EU and its member states were part of a comprehensive human rights regime based on documents such as the 'Charter of the Fundamental Rights of European Union' (CFR) (European Union 2000) and the Council of Europe's 'European Convention on Human Rights' (Council of Europe 1950) as well as on member states' specific constitutional provisions. This regime became relevant for the EU–US negotiations when the issues of the death penalty and US special courts emerged. On both issues, the obligation of a European state to extradite a person or to provide legal assistance could potentially clash with its obligations towards the human rights treaties. This section shows that the EU managed to get important concessions on the extradition agreement and the issue of the death penalty, for which most EU member states set a 'red line' (Interview EU 2013a). Regarding the issue of military tribunals, which was raised only by France, a salient solution was found in the form of an implicit provision that satisfied both parties.

The abolition and prohibition of the death penalty was part of the European human rights regime both at the national level (of states' constitutions)[1] and the international level (multilateral and EU treaties). The then 15 EU member states had undertaken an obligation to abolish the death penalty in peacetime under 'Protocol No. 6' of the ECHR. The ECHR was an international treaty focusing on the protection of human rights that was signed in 1950 by the members of the Council of Europe. Protocol No. 6 of the ECHR was opened for signature on 1983 and it stated that 'the death penalty shall be abolished. No-one shall be condemned to such penalty or executed' (Council of Europe 1983). Additionally, in 2002 the 'Protocol No. 13' of the ECHR, which prohibited the death penalty in all circumstances, including during wartime, was signed by all the then 15 EU member states. Moreover, on 7 December 2000, the European Charter of Fundamental Rights, which included into a single text the whole range of the rights of EU citizens (social, civil, political, and economic), was formally adopted in Nice by the EU organs.

Given the differences between European states and the US on the issue of the death penalty, the US was ready to accept that the Europeans could ask for assurances that the death penalty would not be imposed on extradited persons (Interview US 2012c). This American acknowledgement of the European position was indeed already incorporated into the existing bilateral agreements of the US with member states (US Senate 2008: 5); according to the relevant provisions of these agreements, the requested state *may refuse* [emphasis added] extradition unless the US provides assurances that the death penalty will not be imposed or if imposed not carried out (Stessens 2003: 266). Indeed, in the past, the US practice was to give and respect such assurances (Council of the EU 2011: 18; Interview US 2012c).

The aim of the EU was to elevate this death penalty protection from a case-by-case status to a general condition where the requested state *may grant* [emphasis added] extradition only after the receipt of the relevant US assurances (Stessens 2003: 267). This improved protection clause was incorporated into only two US treaties, with Austria and Lithuania, and the US argued in the negotiations that the improved provision was just an accidental coincidence; therefore, according to the US point of view, similar clauses could not be incorporated into the EU–US agreement (Interview EU 2013a).

In this issue, however, the EU's favourable strategic position stemming from member states' veto power in the Council and the weakened position of the US coming from its decreased ability to defect from the talks enhanced EU's bargaining leverage. For most member states the strengthened death penalty protection was a 'red line', and it was when the Union made clear that it would not agree to an agreement without these elevated assurances and only after several negotiation rounds that the Americans gave in (Interview EU 2013a).

A second example of the interaction between external regimes (in this case the European human rights regime) and the negotiation process for the MLA and extradition agreements was the two issues of special courts or military tribunals created by the US in the context of the war on terror and of Guantanamo Bay prisoners. Guantanamo Bay was a US military base in Cuba that was used as a detention centre for captured alleged Al-Qaeda members and Taliban fighters following the intervention in Afghanistan.

The position of the US administration was that these prisoners were 'unlawful combatants' (Agence France-Presse 2002) and therefore they could not be treated as prisoners of war and thus granted the rights that the Geneva Convention for prisoners of war postulated.[2] Additionally, the Bush administration claimed that Guantanamo Bay was not on US soil and that, therefore, the Constitution did not apply to the prisoners held there. This meant that the prisoners could not raise an appeal to the court for 'habeas corpus'.[3] Concerning the trial of the arrested Taliban and Al Qaeda fighters, President Bush authorised Military Order of November 13 2001 (US Federal Register 2001) for the establishment of military tribunals. From a legal perspective, the latter were not courts but rather military commissions where different standards were applied compared to ordinary civilian courts. A number of EU officials and member states such as Netherlands, France, and Sweden criticised both the existence of Guantanamo Bay as a legal no man's land and the establishment of special military courts (Agence France-Presse 2002).

The negotiations for the MLA and extradition agreements did not remain insulated from the above-mentioned differences between the EU and the US on the issue of military tribunals (Interview US 2012c; Interview EU 2012c;

European Report 2003a). In the negotiating mandate of the EU it was stressed that Europeans should 'seek assurances from USA that extradited persons from Member States will be subject of ordinary proceedings before ordinary US courts respecting fundamental rights and freedom' (Council of the EU 2002a). The reference to ordinary courts and ordinary proceedings contrasted with the US President's Military Order establishing the special courts; in this Order it was noted that the principles of law and the rules of evidence that were applied in the ordinary courts would not be applied in military commissions (US Federal Register 2001).

In practice however, among the EU member states, only France insisted on including safeguards in the agreement related to the military courts. This insistence was mainly due to pressure from domestic actors. In particular, when a first draft of the agreement emerged in the JHA Council on 8 May 2003 France refused to back it and the EU–US negotiations were suspended (European Report 2003b).[4] The main reason for France's veto was that the draft agreement did not make any reference to Article 6 of the Treaty on EU (TEU). The French Council of the State (Conseil d'État), which advised the government on, among others, constitutional issues, pressed the French negotiators to make the case for a provision that would explicitly mention Article 6 of the TEU and the respect towards fundamental rights (European Report 2003b).

Article 6 paragraph 2 of the TEU (Nice version) stated that 'the Union shall respect fundamental rights, as guaranteed by the European Convention for the Protection of Human Rights (ECHR) …' (European Union 2002). In other words, France wanted to include in the agreement a clause that would allow a state to refuse extradition if it suspected that the rights of the extradited, as postulated in the ECHR, would be violated. France's concern about the ECHR was mainly related to the article on the right to a fair trial given that France wanted to make sure that if it extradited persons to the US they would be subject to civilian courts and not military tribunals (Délégation de l'Assemblée Nationale pour l'Union européenne 2003: 40–41).

These French demands were not accepted by the US, which refused to consider any explicit reference in the legal text of the agreement to the European Convention of Human Rights (Stessens 2003: 270). Rather, they were more ready to accept implicit and non-legally binding references to rights such as, for example, the ones that were already incorporated into the preamble of the draft agreement (European Report 2003c). Instead of inserting general rules incorporated into the main text of the agreement, the US was also more in favour of providing ad-hoc and case-by-case, trust-based assurances when a situation emerged that demanded such assurances.

This conflict also revealed internal EU differences. In an example of internal dissensus (Young 1994: 91), the EU member states refused to support France, and the Greek Presidency of the Council of the EU ruled out publicly the possibility of reopening the negotiations (European Report 2003a). Tellingly, the Greek justice minister, who was keen to achieve a result in the EU–US negotiations before the end of the presidency period in June 2003 (Interview EU

2013a), emphasised that the 'French demands "do not need to be supported"' (EUobserver 2003).

The entrepreneurial solution to the deadlock emerged finally at the very last minute, in the form of an addition in one of the agreement's articles (UK House of Lords 2003: 11). In particular, a reference was made in Article 17 (paragraph 2) to pending 'final judicial decisions' and to constitutional principles that allowed a state to refuse extradition (European Report 2003c). This reference could cover, for example, a case where a person challenged her extradition in the European Court of Human Rights (ibid.). In such cases the agreement postulated that consultations would take place between the two states (Council of the EU 2011: 19).

Through this solution both parties' concerns were met. The US was satisfied with a reference that only implied the right to a fair trial and the European human rights charter instead of explicitly mentioning the latter. At the same time, France managed at least to have included in the agreement an implicit assurance that could alleviate the concerns of the Council of the State (European Report 2003b, 2003c).

The mutual legal assistance agreement concerned, among others, the transfer of personal data between law enforcement authorities and for this reason the issue of how personal data was protected was also relevant to the negotiations. The EU had a comprehensive data protection regime based on a number of regulations, rules, and international agreements and on central supervisory authorities (De Busser 2009: 225). This model of data protection is called a comprehensive legislative framework model (ibid.). The MLA agreement was a third-pillar issue where an overarching framework regarding the protection of data did not exist such as existed in the first pillar in the form of the Data Protection Directive; however, member states were bound by the Council of Europe's Data Protection Convention (Council of Europe 1981).

The US system was different and based on sector-specific laws, the self-regulation of the private sector, and technologies that enhanced privacy (De Busser 2009: 335; Interview EU 2012d). The EU positions and policies regarding the sharing of data were perceived by the US as extraterritorial efforts on behalf of the EU to export and impose its information processing and sharing standards globally and as a result they were traditionally met by US scepticism (Richard 2003: 276–278; Federal News Service 2006; Richard and Lebl 2009).

Concerning the negotiations for the MLA agreement, one of the explicit aims of the EU was to include data protection safeguards in the agreement (Council of the EU 2002a). However, the US viewed such safeguards as obstacles to effective judicial cooperation and favoured an approach based on flexibility and on 'much wider, quasi-automatic domestic sharing of critical information among interested agencies' (Richard and Lebl 2009: 85).

In practice, the particular data protection issue on which the two parties focused concerned the use of personal data and the limitations applied to this use. With regard to this issue, there were two interrelated rules specified in the European data protection regime: the speciality rule and the purpose limitation rule (De Busser 2009: 103, 353). According to these rules, the data that was requested and subsequently exchanged should only be used for the purpose for which the request was submitted. In the EU–USA MLA agreement, however, the permitted use of the exchanged data was broadened; the information that a state received could be used not only for the purpose for which a request was made but also in the course of 'its criminal investigations and proceedings' in general, as well as for non-criminal judicial or administrative proceedings related to criminal investigations and for 'preventing an immediate and serious threat to its public security' (European Union 2003).

Surprisingly, this broadening of the use of transmitted information was not only an American initiative as could be expected given the standard US views on this issue. It was the EU that took inspiration from its own MLA Convention and transferred the provisions related to the use of information from the EU area to the transatlantic space (Council of the EU 2011: 31; Interview EU 2013a). In the EU MLA Convention of 2000 there was an expansion too of the purposes for which data could be used after its transmission, based on three general categories similar to the ones in the EU–US agreement: criminal proceedings to which the EU's MLA Convention applied, judicial and administrative proceedings related to crime cases, and immediate threats to public security (Council of the EU 2000).

In addition to the above, the US managed to include in the agreement an even more aggressive provision, which prohibited the requested state from imposing 'generic restrictions' related to 'the legal standards of the requesting State for processing personal data' (European Union 2003). This provision, which was also included in the previously negotiated Europol–US agreement, reassured the US that in the future no member state could withhold information on the basis of the US having different data protection standards.

The US position on data protection was based on the principle that differences between the EU and the US on data protection should not block the two sides' judicial and law enforcement cooperation (Lebl 2005; US Cable 2009; Federal News Service 2011; Interview EU 2012d), and that the US and the EU data protection systems offered the same protections to individuals despite their differences (Interview EU 2012d). This principle was promoted by the US during the negotiations in the form of a focal point that could lead the two sides to reach a compromise. For example, the Deputy Assistant Attorney General, Mark Richard,[5] who was the lead US negotiator highlighted that:

> The European Union and the United States share fundamental values concerning the administration of justice.... That does not mean however that extradition and mutual legal assistance cannot be rendered unless the systems replicate each other in all respects.
> (Richard 2003: 276)

Regarding data protection, he noted in a similar vein that 'inflexible data protection regimes that in effect can only be satisfied in the international context by the adoption of identical methods for protecting data are an open invitation to the creation of safe havens for crime' (ibid.: 278).

This focal point became a normative vehicle for the US to neutralise the efforts of the EU to incorporate data protection principles into the text of the agreement in an example of the interaction between knowledge and interests during negotiations. The EU indeed accepted the above principle; in the Council's draft handbook for the implementation of the agreements it was explicitly mentioned that 'the Contracting Parties agreed that ... generic differences in the privacy protection legal frameworks of the United States and European Union should not be the cause for a denial of mutual legal assistance in a criminal case' (Council of the EU 2011: 33). The main reason for this acceptance was a pragmatic calculation on behalf of the EU, Council, and member states' officials that the EU could not transfer EU rules and regulations on data protection and human rights in their totality onto the US given the fact that such an imposition was politically unacceptable to the Americans (Interview EU 2013a). In other words, the Europeans realised that while the US could make partial concessions, such as on the issue of the death penalty in the extradition agreement, imposing the EU *acquis* on the US en bloc was an unrealistic aim.

Finally, the issue-area for which the above focal point was promoted shaped the reception of the principle by the EU officials (Interview EU 2013a). In judicial cooperation and legal assistance cases personal data was transmitted on a case-by-case basis for specific individuals. In the case of the PNR transfers, however, information was transferred and processed massively for every single passenger. It was therefore easier for the EU to make concessions on data protection in the MLA agreement, the negotiations for which were anyway an EU initiative. Additionally, prior beliefs influenced the reception of the US focal point by the EU and the member states' officials. The data protection principle of purpose limitation was already diluted in the Council of Europe's Committee of Ministers Recommendation R (87) 15 (Council of Europe 1987), the EU's own MLA Convention (Council of the EU 2000), and the Council of Europe's Convention on Cybercrime (Council of Europe 2001; Council of the EU 2002c: 8, 2011: 31–33; UK House of Lords 2003). In other words, Europeans conceded on broadening the purposes for which data was used in several other cases before the EU–US MLA negotiations and this set a precedent for them to accept a similar broadening in the EU–US agreement.

The European Arrest Warrant

Negotiations were suspended in May 2003 due to French concerns about the US military courts. An additional issue for which France blocked the draft agreement with the US was the presence of a paragraph that could compromise a potential future decision of the EU to grant priority to extradition demands coming under the framework of the European Arrest Warrant (EAW) (Statewatch 2003). As with the special courts issue, the negotiating block was overcome through a solution that was deemed fair and equitable by both sides.

The European Arrest Warrant had its origins in the Tampere European Council (European Council 1999) and the emphasis that the latter placed on the promotion of the mutual recognition of judicial decisions. The proposal from the Commission for a framework decision on the EAW came only days after the 9/11 attacks and it was adopted by the Council in June 2002 (Council of the EU 2002b). The EAW replaced the extradition system between member states, which was based in a number of agreements, treaties, and conventions, with a system where the request of a judicial authority for the surrender or arrest of a person was automatically recognised 'with a minimum of formalities' by the judicial authorities of the other member states (ibid.). Therefore, extradition in the formal sense of the term was no longer required among member states (the EAW came into implementation in January 2004).

One of the main aims of the US in the negotiations for the extradition agreement was to prevent the Europeans from granting priority to the European Arrest Warrant in relation to US extradition demands (US Department of Justice 2008: 5). As with the MLA negotiations, where the Europeans wanted to include the US into their own MLA convention and MLA area by transferring provisions from the latter to the EU–US agreement, the US wanted to be part of the EAW area and be treated as an EU member state as far as conflicting demands for extradition were concerned (Statewatch 2003). In the European framework decision for the EAW it was mentioned that in conflicting demands the requested state would take the final decision taking into account a number of criteria.[6] More importantly for the US, it was postulated in the EAW that in case of conflict between a third country's request and an EAW request the latter did not have priority but rather the requested state used the criteria.[7]

The US wanted to transfer the above-mentioned provisions, which did not grant priority to the EAW, into the EU–US agreement (EUobserver 2003). This was especially important for the US given that it was connected to the issue of the nationality-based ban on extradition that some European countries maintained (US Department of Justice 2008: 5). In particular, the US wanted to avoid a conflicting demands case where an EU country extradited semi-automatically an EU national, who was wanted by both the US and by one of the EU countries that did not extradite their own citizens, to his country of origin (Council of the EU 2011: 17). This scenario was averted in the EU–USA agreement, which did not grant priority to the EAW and copied the provisions related to conflicting demands from the EU's own EAW with some additional criteria included (Council of the EU 2011: 17).

Regarding the block in the negotiations brought by France, this was not related directly to the issue of whether the EAW would have priority. Rather, the particular provision about which France had concerns was the second paragraph of Article 10 of the draft agreement, according to which 'a request for arrest and surrender pursuant to the European Arrest Warrant received by a Member State shall be considered a request for extradition for the purpose of applying this Article' (Statewatch 2003). According to France, this paragraph could prevent a future EU decision to give priority to extradition demands coming in the context of the EAW and could inhibit the future creation of a common European judicial area (Délégation de l'Assemblée Nationale pour l'Union européenne 2003: 44–45).

The last-minute entrepreneurial solution that emerged was the removal of the controversial paragraph (European Report 2003c). Additionally, a 'verbal declaration' annexed to the main text of the agreement was made by the Council. In this declaration the Council noted that the EU states are in a process of developing an Area of Freedom, Security and Justice, 'which may have consequences that affect the agreements with the United States', especially as far as the article on conflicting extradition demands was concerned (Council of the EU 2003). As a result of the above middle-ground resolution, the US remained satisfied, given that its extradition demands would be treated as equal to the requests coming from EU member states. Moreover, the EU's verbal declaration was a non-legally binding text, a formula that was close to the US preference for informal and trust-based understandings. At the same time, the deletion of the paragraph that equated a request coming under the EAW context with an ordinary extradition request reassured France, which wanted to safeguard the option of granting priority to the EAW in the future.

Just as with the issue of military courts, France was alone in raising the issue of competing requests and for this reason its original demand, which was the deletion of the whole relevant article (rather than its second paragraph only), could not be satisfied (European Report 2003a). This French sensitivity reflected a French concern that the project of European integration could be compromised if very close and formal links were established between the EU and the US. After the 9/11 attacks the elevation of the fight against terrorism to the top of the Europeans' political agenda suppressed these concerns, but not completely – as the issue of the European Arrest Warrant revealed.

Conclusion

This chapter looked at how the EU and the US cooperated on internal security matters by examining the negotiations for the MLA and extradition agreements. The regime-formation process mostly confirmed the interest-based approaches in which mutual adjustment and integrative bargaining are the dominant characteristics. No evidence was found on the exercise of structural leadership on behalf of either the EU or the US.

As with the case of customs security, contextual factors were important for framing the issue of transatlantic judicial cooperation as a matter that deserved the attention of policymakers. Prior to the 9/11 attacks, the EU had an introvert stance and focused on expanding and consolidating the newly established third pillar, and therefore, relations with the US were not prioritised. Additionally, the member states viewed EU–US cooperation on internal security matters with suspicion at that time. The US, for its part, had an ambivalent stance concerning the added value that a linkage with the EU would provide. As a result of the above no cooperation emerged between the two sides in the pre-9/11 period.

The importance of contextual factors and external crises was highlighted by the fact that the 9/11 attacks triggered the EU initiative to propose to the US negotiations for judicial cooperation agreements. At this stage the EU officials exercised entrepreneurial leadership, becoming 'champions' of the agreements. The negotiations started subsequently with the two sides envisioning a number of benefits to be gained by the transatlantic agreements. In other words, the regime-formation process was one based on a minimum level of common interests. The main benefit of the agreements was the improvement of outdated provisions and the inclusion of innovative articles. As explained in Chapter 1 of this book, in an environment of uncertainty policymakers may seek to imitate or borrow ideas and solutions tried elsewhere. Indeed, in an example of the influence of the social factor of knowledge, the EU used its own MLA convention as a blueprint for the MLA agreement it negotiated with the US.

This case also highlighted the presence of linkages between various regimes. The EU was part of comprehensive data protection and human rights regimes in which the US did not participate, and therefore the transatlantic negotiations for the establishment of rules for an internal security regime affected the former regimes. Four main contentious issues emerged, which were solved through the mutual adjustment of the two sides' positions (mutual concessions). Power cannot not always be translated into bargaining leverage, and indeed in the case examined in this chapter the US made several concessions in the face of the strong strategic position of the EU. This strong strategic position was due to the presence of veto actors in the Council and the fact that the US could not have easy access to the judicial information it desired through other means. The EU, for its part, made a number of concessions due to the realisation that Europeans could not transfer the EU data protection and human rights *acquis* in its entirety into the US.

Regarding the role of knowledge at the stage of negotiations, ideas and knowledge in the form of focal points can facilitate the conclusion of a deal. Indeed, the US was promoting such a focal point for solving the EU–US differences on data protection issues. This focal point was used tactically by the US in order to support its interests, in an example of interaction effects between the social factors of knowledge and interests.

To sum up, this chapter has shown that the regime-formation process in the sub-case of judicial cooperation was based on joint gains expected to be derived as a result of the two sides' cooperation and on mutual adjustment, resembling thus the interest-based patterns of regime formation. The next chapter focuses on the relations between Europol and the US.

Notes

1 The constitutions of Austria, Germany, Netherlands, Italy, Portugal, Spain, and Sweden explicitly prohibited the imposition of the death penalty.
2 Later, however, (in February 2002) the US government decided to grant prisoner of war status to the members of the Taliban regime only.
3 Habeas corpus is a court order that compels the relevant authorities to justify the detention of a person. If the person under question successfully manages to argue that her detention is unlawful or unconstitutional then the court can order her release.

4 A second issue related to the French veto was that of the European Arrest Warrant and its relation with the EU–US extradition treaty. This issue is covered later in this chapter.
5 Mark Richard served from 1999 to 2007 as Justice Department representative to the EU and led the negotiations for the extradition and MLA agreements.
6 According to article 16 paragraph 1:

> [I]f two or more Member States have issued European arrest warrants for the same person, the decision on which of the European arrest warrants shall be executed shall be taken by the executing judicial authority with due consideration of all the circumstances and especially the relative seriousness and place of the offences, the respective dates of the European arrest warrants and whether the warrant has been issued for the purposes of prosecution or for execution of a custodial sentence or detention order.

7 According to article 16 paragraph 3,

> [I]n the event of a conflict between a European arrest warrant and a request for extradition presented by a third country, the decision on whether the European arrest warrant or the extradition request takes precedence shall be taken by the competent authority of the executing Member State with due consideration of all the circumstances, in particular those referred to in paragraph 1 and those mentioned in the applicable convention.

References

Agence France-Presse (2002) 'Rumsfeld denies any mistreatment of Guantanamo detainees', 22 January 2002.
Council of Europe (1950) 'Convention for the Protection of Human Rights and Fundamental Freedoms', 4 November 1950.
Council of Europe (1981) 'Convention for the Protection of Individuals with regard to Automatic Processing of Personal Data', 28 January 1981.
Council of Europe (1983) 'Protocol No. 6 to the Convention for the Protection of Human Rights and Fundamental Freedoms Concerning the Abolition of Death Penalty', 28 April 1983.
Council of Europe (1987) 'Committee of Ministers Recommendation No. R (87) 15 Regulating the Use of Personal Data in the Police Sector', 17 September 1985.
Council of Europe (2001) 'Convention on Cybercrime', 23 November 2001.
Council of the EU (2000) 'Act of 29 May 2000 establishing in accordance with Article 34 of the Treaty on European Union the Convention on Mutual Assistance in Criminal Matters between the Member States of the European Union', OJ C 197/1, 12 July 2000.
Council of the EU (2002a) 'Request for a negotiation mandate for the Presidency on judicial cooperation in criminal matters on the basis of Articles 38 and 24 TEU', 6438/2/02, 5 April 2002.
Council of the EU (2002b) 'Framework Decision of 13 June 2002 on the European arrest warrant and the surrender procedures between Member States', 2002/584/JHA, 13 June 2002.
Council of the EU (2002c) 'Informal explanatory note: Europol–US Supplementary Agreement', 13696/02, 4 November 2002.
Council of the EU (2003) 'Note Verbale', 25 June 2003.

Council of the EU (2011) 'Handbook on the practical application of the EU–US Mutual Legal Assistance and Extradition Agreements', 8024/11, 25 March 2011.
Cullen, D. (1998) 'Transatlantic Relations in the Fields of Justice and Home Affairs-can the EU Really Deliver?', in J. Monar (ed.) *The New Transatlantic Agenda and the Future of EU–US Relations*. London: Kluwer Law International, pp. 79–108.
De Busser, E. (2009) *Data Protection in EU and US Criminal Cooperation*. Antwerp: Maklu.
Délégation de l'Assemblée Nationale pour l'Union européenne (2003) 'Rapport d'information sur la coopération judiciaire entre l'Union européenne et les Etats Unis d'Amérique', No. 716, 19 March 2003.
Den Boer, M. (1998) 'Defying a Global Challenge: Reflections About a Joint EU–US Venture Against Transnational Organised Crime', in J. Monar (ed.) *The New Transatlantic Agenda and the Future of EU–US Relations*. London: Kluwer Law International, pp. 109–126.
EUobserver (2003) 'EU–US extradition agreement on hold', 9 May 2003.
Euro-East (2001) 'EU Enlargement: Candidates' Justice and Home Affairs Ministers Meet in Brussels', 27 March 2001.
European Council (1999) 'Tampere European Council 15 and 16 October 1999-Presidency Conclusions', 15–16 October 1999.
European Report (2002) 'Justice and Home Affairs Council: Deal on Freezing of Assets Initiative Hangs in Balance', 27 February 2002.
European Report (2003a) 'EU/US: Extradition Agreement Suspended Over French Concerns', 1 March 2003.
European Report (2003b) 'EU/US: France Blocks Extradition Agreement', 10 May 2003.
European Report (2003c) 'EU/US: Extradition and Legal Assistance Accords Can Be Signed', 7 June 2003.
European Union (2000) 'Charter of Fundamental Rights of the European Union', OJ C 364/1, 18 December 2000.
European Union (2002) 'Consolidated Version of the Treaty on European Union', OJ C 325/5, 24 December 2002.
European Union (2003) 'Agreement on mutual legal assistance between the European Union and the United States of America', OJ L 181/34, 19 July 2003.
Federal News Service (2006) 'Remarks by Homeland Security Secretary Michael Chertoff at the Federalist Society for Law and Public Policy's Annual National Lawyers Convention', 17 November 2006.
Federal News Service (2011) 'Prepared Remarks of Attorney General Eric Holder to the European Parliament's Committee On Civil Liberties, Justice, And Home Affairs Location: Brussels, Belgium', 20 September 2011.
Gardner, A.L. (1997) *A New Era in US–EU Relations? The Clinton Administration and the New Transatlantic Agenda*. Aldershot: Ashgate.
Garcia, M., and Doyle, C. (2010) 'Extradition To and From the United States: Overview of the Law and Recent Treaties', Report for Congress 98–958, 17 March 2010. Congressional Research Service.
International Enforcement Law Reporter (2002) 'International Cooperation against Transnational Terrorism Continues', January 2002.
International Enforcement Law Reporter (2008) 'US Senate Committee Holds Hearing on Extradition and Mutual Legal Assistance Treaties', July 2008.
Interview EU (2012a) Interview with EU official, 9 February 2012.

Interview EU (2012b) Interview with EU official, 16 May 2012.
Interview EU (2012c) Interview with EU official, 16 May 2012.
Interview EU (2012d) Interview with EU official, 7 December 2012.
Interview EU (2013a) Interview with EU official, 28 January 2013.
Interview EU (2013b) Interview with EU official, 14 May 2013.
Interview US (2012a) Interview with US official, 25 January 2012.
Interview US (2012b) Interview with US official, 25 January 2012.
Interview US (2012c) Interview with US official, 8 February 2012.
Interview US (2013) Interview with US official, 28 February 2013.
Kerber, F. (2007) 'US-EU Cooperation on Counter Terrorism', *American Diplomacy*, June 2007, www-test.unc.edu/depts/diplomat/item/2007/0406/kerb/kerber_useu.html, accessed 10 June 2016.
Lebl, L. (2005) 'Security Beyond Borders', *Policy Review*, No. 130, April–May 2005.
Mitsilegas, V. (2003) 'The New EU–USA Cooperation on Extradition, Mutual Legal Assistance and the Exchange of Police Data', *European Foreign Affairs Review*, 8(4), pp. 515–536.
Nadelmann, E. (1993) *Cops Across Borders: The Internationalization of US Criminal Law Enforcement*. University Park, PA: Pennsylvania State University Press.
Richard, M. (2003) 'Some Observations Concerning International Law Enforcement Co-operation and the European Union', in G. de Kerchove and A. Weyembergh (eds) *Sécurité et justice: enjeu de la politique extérieure de l'Union européenne*. Bruxelles: Editions de l'Université de Bruxelles.
Richard, M. and Lebl, L. (2009) 'Security and Data Sharing', *Policy Review*, No. 154, April–May 2009.
Snow, T. (2002) 'The Investigation and Prosecution of White-Collar Crime: International Challenges and the Legal Tools Available to Address Them', *William & Mary Bill of Rights Journal*, 11(1), pp. 209–244.
Statewatch (2003) 'EU–USA agreements – the drafts on the table', 1 April 2003.
Stessens, G. (2003) 'The EU–US Agreements on Extradition and on Mutual Legal Assistance: how to Bridge Different Approaches', In G. de Kerchove and A. Weyembergh (eds) *Sécurité et justice: enjeu de la politique extérieure de l'Union européenne*. Bruxelles: Editions de l'Université de Bruxelles, pp. 263–273.
UK House of Lords (2003) 'EU/US Agreements on Extradition and Mutual Legal Assistance', 38th Report, HL Paper 153.
US Cable (2009) 'US–EU Justice and Home Affairs Ministerial Meeting in Prague', Cable #09USEUBRUSSELS681, 13 May 2009, http://wikileaks.cabledrum.org/cable/2009/05/09USEUBRUSSELS681.html, accessed 12 May 2016.
US Department of Justice (2008) 'Statement of Bruce C. Swartz Deputy Assistant Attorney General Criminal Division Department of Justice Before the Committee on Foreign Relations United States Senate Entitled "Treaties"', 20 May 2008.
US Federal Register (2001) Vol. 67 No. 222, 16 November 2001.
US Senate (2006) 'Extradition Agreement with the European Union', Treaty Document 109–14, 28 September 2006.
US Senate (2008) 'Extradition Treaties with the European Union', Executive Report 110–12, 11 September 2008.
Winer, J. (2006) 'Cops across borders: The evolution of transatlantic law enforcement and judicial cooperation', in A. Dalgaard-Nielsen and D. Hamilton (eds) *Transatlantic Homeland Security: protecting society in the age of catastrophic terrorism*. Abingdon: Routledge, pp. 106–125.

Young, O. (1991) 'Political Leadership and Regime Formation: On the Development of Institutions in International Society', *International Organization*, 45(3), pp. 281–308.

Young, O. (1994) *International Governance: Protecting the Environment in a Stateless Society*. Ithaca: Cornell University Press.

Young, O. (1998) *Creating Regimes: Arctic Accords and International Governance*. Ithaca: Cornell University Press.

4 Transatlantic law enforcement cooperation

The agreements between Europol and the United States

Europol was the first body of the EU that concluded an agreement with the United States that involved the transfer of personal data for law enforcement and counter-terrorism purposes (De Busser 2010: 99). The protection of personal data was central to Europol's mission and to the organisation's founding texts (Storbeck 1999: 9; Dubois 2002: 331; De Busser 2009: 142). The US did not have a similar system of data protection. Therefore, the case that this chapter examines posed for the first time a number of questions related to the transatlantic protection and transfer of personal data in the fight against terrorism and organised crime.

The Europol–US agreements and the posting of US liaison officers to the organisation's headquarters constituted the first formal connection between Washington and an EU body related to Justice and Home Affairs (Dubois 2002: 329). While there were instances of *ad hoc* and informal cooperation between Europol and the US prior to the conclusion of the agreements (Federal News Service 1997b), this relationship was streamlined into a more permanent form of formal law enforcement cooperation and exchange of strategic and operational intelligence with the 2001 and 2002 agreements.

The negotiations for an agreement that covered the exchange of strategic information between Europol and the US started in 2000 through a Europol initiative. The negotiations for this agreement did not pose significant problems and they were concluded in December 2001. At the same time, negotiations started for an agreement that covered the exchange of personal data. These negotiations presented more difficulties given that they touched upon the issue of data protection, and a deal was finally reached in December 2002.

This chapter addresses this book's main research question of how the two sides cooperated on internal security matters employing a regime-theory perspective. The interactions between Europol and the US are conceptualised as a regime-formation process in which power, interests, and knowledge can play a role. Through this process, Europol and the US tried to establish a framework of rules that would guide law enforcement cooperation and data sharing between the US and Europol and the member states. These rules were part of the broader internal security regime that the EU and the US started to build in the post-9/11 period.

This chapter shows that before the 9/11 attacks Europol and the US did not conclude any agreements, highlighting the significance of broader socio-political events and political priorities in affecting whether an issue emerged high on the political agenda of actors (Young 1998: 24). While there was a convergence between Europol and the US on the importance of international police cooperation in general, the establishment of close and formal relations between the two sides was not seen as an important political priority on either side of the Atlantic. The US wanted to benefit from the integration efforts of Europeans in the area of justice and home affairs (Interview US 2012c). At the same time, however, the Americans were disappointed with the slow EU progress in this field (for example, it took three years for the Europol Convention to be ratified by member states). Additionally, the US feared that if they enhanced the relations with Europol, long-established and well-functioning bilateral relationships with European states could be undermined.

The lack of political prioritisation for Europol–US relations was evident in Europe too in the pre-9/11 period, undermining any progress in the regime-formation process. The EU member states prioritised relations with the Central and East European candidate countries and with the non-EU Schengen countries (for example, Iceland and Norway). Moreover, before the 9/11 attacks, France was sceptical of any attempt to formally link the EU and the US on justice and home affairs issues, fearing that such a link might undermine the process of EU integration.

At the same time, Europol officials were at that period much more in favour of negotiating agreements with third countries. For Europol, the establishment of relations with third states would facilitate the organisation's ability to fulfil its mission. When, finally, Europol was given the green light to negotiate international agreements in 2000, Europol officials initiated the regime-formation process inviting the US, among other states, to an international seminar. In this seminar, but also in various international forums and in international media, Europol officials drew attention to and 'popularised' (Young 1991: 294) the work of Europol and highlighted the importance of the Europol agreements with third states. These entrepreneurial (ibid.) efforts were backed with the broader normative principle that international policing and law enforcement was absolutely necessary, pointing to a synergistic effect of knowledge-based and interest-based factors. Additionally, the Europol initiatives indicate that the organisation was much more proactive than normally assumed in the literature on transatlantic relations.

This chapter also shows that the 9/11 attacks worked as an external crisis (Haas 1993: 188) that initiated a learning process (Goldstein and Keohane 1993: 13–17) among both Europeans and Americans. Through this external shock, Europeans and the US redefined their political priorities and an agreement between Europol and the US was framed as essential. In the context of the new post-9/11 security environment the US changed its initially ambivalent position. Among others, the US calculated that Europol could provide all-sources strategic intelligence and it could also function as a one-stop point for US law enforcement information enquiries. Europol and the EU member states, for their part, calculated that the ability of the organisation to fulfil its mission could be significantly enhanced if Europol established formal links with the US. In other words, this chapter shows that the relationship between Europol and the US could be characterised as a partnership based on the perceived benefits to be gained from cooperation.

While the negotiations for the strategic agreement did not pose any difficulties and were concluded very quickly, the negotiations for the personal data agreement touched upon the issue of data protection on which Europol and the US had different positions. These negotiations were mainly integrative (Young 1994: 100) in nature, characterised by the mutual adjustment of the two sides' positions and the establishment of rules that were perceived as fair by both parties. At the same time, Europol's bargaining leverage was reduced by the fact that a collapse of the negotiations would hurt Europol much more than it would hurt the US. In such a scenario the US could resort to bilateralism while Europol would neither have access to US information nor could it include data protection safeguards into the data transfers between member states and the US. Europol therefore made several concessions on the issue of data protection, realising that the organisation could not transfer Europol's data protection regime in its totality into the text of the agreement. Moreover, the US negotiators and officials promoted the principle that the US and European data protection systems offered the same protections to individuals despite the differences between these systems. This focal point (Goldstein and Keohane 1993: 18) supported the US interests by neutralising Europol's efforts to include data protection provisions into the text of the agreement, thus revealing the existence of interaction effects between knowledge and interests (Young 1994: 97).

The context

This section presents the historical context of the relations between Europol and the US and it shows that both sides placed emphasis on the importance of international law enforcement cooperation. This convergence did not lead, however, to any form of formal cooperation given the slow ratification of Europol's Convention and the fact that the Council authorised the organisation to negotiate international treaties only in 2000. The slow development of Europol was related to the internal disagreements among EU member states regarding the form and the functions of the nascent organisation, pointing to the importance of political context for regime formation.

Europol was a European criminal intelligence and law enforcement agency that emerged under the framework of European Union in 1992 when the Treaty on European Union (Maastricht Treaty) was signed (Rijken 2001: 581; Deflem 2006: 341). It was governed by a management board, which reported directly to the Council of the EU, and was assisted and supervised by a Joint Supervisory Board (JSB). Europol became an EU agency in 2009 with the entry into force of the Lisbon Treaty. Europol did not have operational powers and it relied on member states for information as well as on its international partners with which it concluded cooperation agreements. Its mission was to facilitate intra-EU law enforcement cooperation by providing expertise and critical strategic intelligence[1] to the member states' law enforcement and criminal intelligence agencies (Rijken 2001: 581; Deflem 2006: 342).

Europol had its origins in the informal intergovernmental TREVI group, which was created in 1976 by the then 12 members of the European Community (EC) (Bunyan 1993: 1). TREVI consisted of the EC interior ministers and its mission was the coordination of the EC governments in the fight against terrorism and the exchange of best practices and techniques in the area of policing. In the context of TREVI, a working group (working group 'Trevi 3') was created in 1985 that was responsible for international organised crime with a special focus on drug trafficking (ibid.: 3). It was from this working group that the Europol Drugs Unit (the predecessor of Europol) emerged in January 1994.

Europol emerged out of the 'Europol Drugs Unit', with a remit covering the fight against drugs and drug trafficking. The Europol Convention, which described the functions of the organisation in detail, was signed a year later (1995) coming finally into operation in 1998. Europol's mandate expanded gradually to cover, apart from drug trafficking, other serious forms of transnational crime like money-laundering, child pornography, cybercrime, terrorism, trafficking of vehicles and human beings, and money forgery (Occhipinti 2003: 60; Andreas and Nadelmann 2006: 186–187).

Internationalisation of law enforcement in the 1990s: the role of Europol and the US

This section shows that both Europol and the US placed emphasis during the 1990s on the internationalisation of law enforcement. Europol officials were urging the EU member states to be swifter in giving powers to Europol and in ratifying the organisation's Convention. At the same time, Europol emphasised that agreements between Europol and third states were crucial tools in the fight against organised crime. The US, for its part, agreed on the importance of international law enforcement cooperation and established globally a network of contacts with governments and national law enforcement agencies.

Europol saw the institutionalisation and formalisation of its global contacts as part of the solution to the growing problem of transnational crime in the post-Cold War security environment. Jürgen Storbeck, who was co-ordinator of the 'Europol Drugs Unit' from 1994 and Director of Europol between 1999 and 2004, played an important role at that time in promoting the idea of international police cooperation and in trying to change the perceptions that the relevant stakeholders (both EU member states and third states) had about policing. In this way, Storbeck exercised a form of intellectual leadership (Young 1991: 298). In particular, in a 1996 speech, he emphasised that there was an 'urgent need for Europol cooperation with third states and international organisations' (Fortress Europe Circular Letter 1996). Storbeck believed that the transnational features of organised crime made the internationalisation of law enforcement necessary; however, according to him, this idea of international police cooperation clashed 'headlong into the concept of national sovereignty', and 'the difficulties encountered in international police cooperation [stemmed] from this attachment to sovereignty in law enforcement' (Storbeck 1999: 5). Similarly, in a policing conference in Ireland in 2000, Storbeck noted that providing internal security was a complex task that no state could fulfil on its own, and, as a result, such a task 'requires intensive international cooperation among police, customs, border guards and judicial authorities' (EUobserver 2000).

Concerning institutional developments, the exchange of information between Europol and third countries was at the centre of Europol's agenda from the start. The Dublin European Council of December 1996 created a High Level Group with the aim of examining the issue of organised crime and drawing an Action Plan against this threat (European Council 1996). The Action Plan was adopted by the Council of the EU in 1997 (Council of the EU 1997); among the Plan's recommendations was the enhancement of Europol's ability to liaise with third countries and international organisations with the creation of suitable legal instruments.

In December 1997 the Justice and Home Affairs Council adopted three reports related to the exchange of police and criminal intelligence between Europol and third countries (Statewatch Bulletin 1997). These reports dealt with issues like the posting of liaison officers and the transmission of personal data from Europol to a third country. In 1998 Europol prepared a 'Draft Model agreement on cooperation with Third States' for the international exchange of information related to Europol's remit (Statewatch Bulletin 1998; Rijken 2001: 593; UK House of Commons 1999). According to Europol's plans, the agreements with third parties would be supplemented by a number of memorandums ('Memorandum of Understandings') signed between Europol and the national criminal intelligence agencies of third countries; these memorandums would cover, among others, the issues of 'contacts between representatives', 'technical arrangements', and 'secure communications' (Statewatch Bulletin 1998). Finally, in 2000, the Council of the EU authorised Europol's Director to start negotiations with non-EU states and with international bodies and organisations (Council of the EU 2000a; International Enforcement Law Reporter 2000).[2]

While Europol was growing in stature during the 1990s, US law enforcement agencies strengthened their overseas presence in the fight against drug trafficking and organised crime (Winer 2006: 100; Andreas and Nadelmann 2006: 169). The FBI was pushed outward with the creation of liaison offices abroad and the posting of law enforcement agents in the US embassies and consulates (Nadelmann 1993: 135; Winer 2006: 100). A number of other US agencies too, such as the US Customs Service, the Immigration and Naturalization Service, the Secret Service, the Treasury Bureau of Alcohol, Tobacco, and Firearms, and the Drug Enforcement Administration followed the FBI's example establishing liaison offices overseas (Zagaris 1998: 1412; Winer 2006: 100). As a result of this pattern of external projection, the number of US law enforcement agents stationed abroad in 1994 was estimated to be around 2,000 (Winer 2006: 100).

The internationalisation of the US law enforcement agencies reflected a similar belief to Europol in that the fight against transnational organised crime and drug trafficking demanded an international approach to crime fighting. There was a convergence of the US law enforcement professional community around the idea that part of the solution to the problem of transnational crime lay in the development of stronger ties with third countries and the enhancement of the US presence overseas. In a 1996 speech in the US Congress, the FBI Director, Louis Freeh, stressed the fact that the internationalisation of organised crime was one of the biggest challenges that the US faced, and he proposed that the FBI should have an active role and presence abroad. In his words,

> we [the US] are at a unique position in modern history where we can help contribute to the development of professional law enforcement agencies in foreign countries, promote the rule of law in the newly independent states, and build the cop-to-cop relationships between American [sic] and our overseas counterparts.
> (Federal News Service 1996)

In the same spirit, he added in 1997 that 'we [the US] need agents in other countries to protect Americans, to have a perimeter of defence for Americans and let us do our investigations, not for other countries, but for the United States' (Federal News Service 1997a). Similarly, Jamie Gorelick, US Deputy Attorney General, noted to the US Congress in 1995 that 'international cooperation is crucial to combatting international crime' (Federal News Service 1995c). Additionally, a year later, he explained that 'all we are doing is following cases here in the United States to their origins abroad' and that 'we're performing a very traditional law enforcement function', which, however, took place in foreign countries (Gorelick 1996, cited in Andreas and Nadelmann 2006: 169). What the above quotations show is that during the 1990s the internationalisation of the US crime-fighting functions was a central topic in the agenda of the US law enforcement community.

This section showed that the US and Europol officials shared the belief that international law enforcement cooperation was crucial for the fight against transnational organised crime. The next section shows that even if the two sides agreed on the particular form that this cooperation would take (for example, Europol favoured the negotiation of international treaties with the US and with other states) Europol was 'paralysed' from a lack of authorisation to conclude deals with international partners.

Relations between Europol and the United States before 2000

This section shows that the convergence of ideas between Europol and the US did not lead to regime formation or to any form of formal institutional cooperation between the two sides despite the US interest. To the frustration of the US (Federal News Service 1998), the Europeans were very slow in giving powers to and enhancing Europol; it was only in 2000 that the Council authorised the Director of Europol to start negotiations with third parties (International Enforcement Law Reporter 2000). This lack of progress was due to the fact that the establishment and the granting of more powers to Europol and the deepening of integration in the third pillar in general were highly contested issues among the EU member states at that period of time (*Guardian* 1994; European Report 1995b; European Report 1999). This, in turn, highlights the centrality of broader political and contextual factors for the emergence of international regimes. As a result, during the 1990s, the Europol–US relationship was one of *ad hoc*, informal, and scattered cooperation (Intelligence Newsletter 1998; The Associated Press 2000; Rijken 2001: 590).

The international fight against organised crime and drug trafficking was at the centre of the US security agenda in the 1990s. The US was eager to see the EU stepping up its efforts in the area of the third pillar and improving intra-EU cooperation on organised crime, terrorism, and drugs issues (Federal News Service 1995a, 1998; Interview US 2012c). Additionally, the US had a keen interest in seeing Europol come into operation and in establishing relations with this European criminal intelligence agency (European Report 1995a; Federal News Service 1995b, 1997b; Interview US 2012c).

Starting from the New Transatlantic Agenda signed in December 1995, the EU and the US pledged their support in establishing 'active, practical cooperation between the US and the future European Police Office, EUROPOL' (EU–US 1995). Europol–US relations were the subject of discussions during the following years in the context of the EU–US summits held twice per year (Federal News Service 1997b). In the May 1998 EU–US summit, the EU and the US issued a joint statement regarding counter-terrorism where it was stressed that 'information is also shared on significant developments on either side of the Atlantic, e.g. the creation of Europol, which will include terrorism within its remit soon after its launch' (EU–US 1998). Informal talks and discussions were also taking place when Europol officials were meeting their US counterparts in international fora and venues, conferences and meetings (Intelligence Newsletter 1998; The Associated Press 2000).

Europol and the US could not, however, at this stage establish formal means of communication. The Europol Convention came into force only in 1998 and international agreements could be negotiated and concluded only after the Council gave its consent in 2000. This delay caused frustration in both Europol and the US, and, in this respect, the words of a senior US official were telling:

> The institutional arrangements simply don't exist. Europol, for example, there's still no convention. I have met with the Europol people, they're anxious to cooperate but they don't even have a convention which allows them to deal yet with third countries.
>
> (Federal News Service 1995a)

In a similar tone, when the New Transatlantic Agenda was signed, US officials conceded in private that 'the fact that the EU's police organization, EUROPOL, was still in a fledgling state made the new agenda's policing aims harder to achieve', and, therefore, the US would continue to work bilaterally with member states on issues like terrorism, drugs, and organised crime (United Press International 1995). Similarly, Undersecretary of State Stuart Eizenstat noted in a 1998 conference that the US has waited 'anxiously' and 'impatiently' for the Europol Convention to enter into force and for the organisation to be fully functional (Federal News Service 1998).

In conclusion, this section has shown that the US saw the gradual European communitarisation of policing and law enforcement, part of which was the creation of Europol, in a positive light and wanted to benefit from the developments in this field. While Europol was eager to establish relations with third states, including the US, the organisation did not have the authority to negotiate agreements until 2000. The next two sections focus on the period of time when Europol was fully operational.

Negotiations in the years 2000–2001

The process of Europol–US regime formation started in the years 2000–2001 under the initiative of Europol with the launch of negotiations between the two sides for a strategic agreement. As this section shows, however, there were no talks for a personal data agreement and, at the same time, the negotiations for a strategic agreement did not lead to the conclusion of a deal. On the one hand, the instructions of the Council to Europol prioritised the relations with the East European EU candidate countries and the non-EU Schengen countries (Council of the EU 2000a); therefore, Europol did not focus on the US at that time and there were only isolated and scattered instances of entrepreneurial leadership on behalf of the Europol officials (European Report 2000; *Washington Post* 2000). Moreover, France was highly sceptical of giving the green light to EU institutions and agencies to establish formal and closer relations with the US on justice and home affairs matters (Gardner 1997: 57; Euro-East 2001). On the other hand, while the US was interested in establishing relations with Europol, this interest was not as strong and urgent as to justify a more assertive approach by Washington, and the US did not make any significant efforts at this phase to influence the regime-formation process.

In other words, this section shows that the issue of Europol–US relations was given low political prioritisation by both the US and the EU member states, and it was not framed as an issue that demanded immediate action. Apart from the importance of contextual factors for the process of regime formation, this section also shows that Europol had a proactive approach regarding the cooperation with third states. This approach contrasts with what is normally assumed in the literature, where the European side is often portrayed as reacting passively to prior US initiatives.

In March 2000, the Council of the EU authorised the Director of Europol to start negotiations with third countries for the conclusion of operational and strategic agreements (Council of the EU 2000a; International Enforcement Law

Reporter 2000). Consequently, the Director of Europol organised a seminar on 26 and 27 April 2000 to which 23 non-EU countries (including the US) and three international bodies were invited (International Enforcement Law Reporter 2000). While the US was not at the top of the Council's priority list, Europol sought a strategic and technical agreement with Washington. At that time, Europol was preoccupied with strengthening its abilities to fight forgery and counterfeiting of the Euro in preparations for the launch of the new European currency (in January 2002) (Associated Press International 1998; *The Times* 2001; *Guardian* 2001). Europol wanted, therefore, to establish closer relations with the US Secret Service, which dealt with currency forgery issues; a strategic and technical agreement with the US would serve this role and would allow Europol to benefit from the US expertise and technical advice (Rijken 2001: 590).

At this stage of the Europol–US regime-formation process the entrepreneurial leadership (Young 1991: 294) of Jürgen Storbeck, who was Director of Europol, played an important role. First, the fact that he convened the international seminar after the Council's green light reflected Storbeck's personal interest in expanding Europol's connections globally. Second, through the international seminar held under the aegis of Europol, Storbeck acted as a 'populariser' (Young 1991: 294) of the issue of transnational organised crime. Third, he shaped the form in which this issue was presented for consideration and set the agenda of talks by presenting to the seminar participants the Convention of Europol, the data protection rules of the organisation, the different scenarios and levels of cooperation between Europol and third states, and, more importantly, Europol's draft 'Model Cooperation Agreement' (European Report 2000; International Enforcement Law Reporter 2000;). The latter contained provisions ranging from the transmission and exchange of personal data to the stationing of liaison officers and the confidentiality of information (UK House of Commons 1999). It was prepared by Europol in order to use it as the basis for negotiations with third parties (Rijken 2001: 593–594), and, in this sense, it could allow the organisation to put its 'stamp in the process of regime formation as clearly as possible' (Young 1998: 10).

The entrepreneurial factors mentioned above (that is the 'populariser' and 'agenda setter' roles) could also be seen in the context of a conference organised by Europol and the EU in Washington in December 2000 with the aim of introducing 'Europol to the American security establishment' (*Washington Post* 2000). The Director of Europol addressed a number of high-ranking US officials from the US Customs, FBI, State Department, DEA, and other federal bodies and agencies, and he presented a global threat assessment regarding terrorism and drugs (*Washington Post* 2000). In this way Storbeck sought to present to Americans the benefits of working closely with Europol and the utility of Europol in the fight against organised crime, drug trafficking and terrorism.

The above efforts of Europol were only partially successful. While talks for a strategic agreement commenced, it was only after the 9/11 attacks that the negotiations for this agreement were concluded. Additionally, there were no discussions in the pre-9/11 period about a personal data agreement. The US had an ambivalent stance, doubting whether an agreement with Europol would provide added value. The EU member states, for their part, gave priority to the Central and East European candidate countries. Moreover, France was hostile to the idea of formalising the links between Europol and the US. In other words, in the pre-9/11 period there was no strong political will (Young 1994: 173) in the US or in Europe for the negotiation and conclusion of Europol–US agreements and therefore the regime-formation process stalled.

The absence of political will in Europe for the negotiation of agreements between Europol and the US could be seen in the Council document authorising Europol to initiate discussions with third countries in which the US was not at the top of its priority list for negotiations (Council of the EU 2000a). The Council's view concerning Europol's external relations was that the priority areas for the organisation were the EU candidate countries and the non-EU Schengen countries, rather than the US. In 2000, in a report from COREPER (Committee of Permanent Representatives of member states to the EU) to the Council about the EU foreign policy priorities in the area of justice and home affairs, COREPER noted that 'the EU must prioritize bilateral or multilateral cooperation, especially in the context of the enlargement of the EU' and that when the EU selects partners it should 'prioritize states that have "structured relations" with the EU, such as Norway and Iceland' (International Enforcement Law Reporter September 2000). Similar emphasis on the relationship between Europol and the EU and the EU candidate countries was evident in the JHA Council meetings and actions and texts in general during both this phase (2000–01) (European Report 2001; Euro-East 2001) and the previous one (1995–2000) (European Report 1998; International Enforcement Law Reporter 1999). The above emphasis reflected an EU concern about the problems of organised crime and drug trafficking in the Central and East European candidate countries.

Apart from this prioritisation of the Council, certain member states disagreed politically with the establishment of closer links between Europol and the US, which they saw as a premature move. This was the view especially of France, which argued at that time that an enhanced EU–US dialogue on justice and home affairs could only take place when there was a clear EU position on this matter. According to the then deputy police attaché at the French Embassy in Washington, discussions with the US for a personal data agreement 'would not happen immediately, because political support will have to be found' (*Washington Post* 2000).

The lack of political will among Europeans was accompanied by an American scepticism with regard to the benefits that the establishment of formal Europol–US relations would confer to the American side. Despite the general interest of the US in having access to Europol's information pool, the Americans proceeded cautiously (Lebl 2005). According to Leslie Lebl, who was a Foreign Service officer who served in the US mission to the EU, '[before September 11] the lack of support from EU national police forces brought into question Europol's effectiveness: Just how much information would Europol be able to provide US authorities in return?' (ibid.). As long as Europeans were slow in giving powers to and sharing information with Europol, the Americans were reluctant to spend time and resources in establishing closer ties with this European organisation.

In conclusion, it was between 2000 and 2001 that the US–Europol regime-formation process started under the initiative of Europol. No agreement was concluded during that period; the focus of the European side was rather on the EU candidate countries and the non-EU Schengen countries, and indeed Europol signed two agreements for the exchange of information with Iceland and Norway in June 2001 (European Report 2001a). At the same time, the establishment of formal relations with Europol was not a highly prioritised issue for the US and, as a result, the US did not make any energetic effort in the second phase to press Europol with regard to the two sides' negotiations. The lack of political prioritisation on both sides of the Atlantic meant that no significant instances of leadership on behalf of Europol and US officials were evident at that period and this affected negatively the progress of the Europol–US regime-formation process.

Negotiations after the 9/11 attacks

The terrorist attacks of 9/11 constituted a crucial point in the Europol–US regime-formation process, precipitating the conclusion of the strategic agreement and the start of negotiations for a personal data exchange deal. The 9/11 attacks were an exogenous shock (Young and Osherenko 1993: 15) that triggered a sense of urgency among Europeans and Americans and worked as a catalyst for the regime-formation process. This section shows that the shock from the 9/11 attacks was important in moving the topic of the Europol–US agreements to the top of the regime participants' political agenda and in framing this topic as an issue that demanded immediate action. In other words, this external crisis changed the political and security environment and prompted a learning process in Europe and in the US.

This section focuses only on the agreement for the exchange of personal data given that the strategic agreement was routinely negotiated and concluded without any blocks emerging (Interview US 2012b). In the context of the changed security environment, Europol and the US sought to realise joint benefits through the conclusion of a personal data agreement. Europol's ability to fulfil its mission would be enhanced from the intelligence that it would receive from the US. The latter would benefit from Europol's function as a one-stop point for US information enquiries and from Europol's all-sources intelligence that member states alone could not provide. Difficulties emerged, however, with regard to four distributive issues related to data protection, where the positions of the two sides diverged. While these differences were overcome mainly through integrative bargaining and mutual adjustment, Europol's bargaining leverage was reduced. Europol had more need of a formal agreement with the US than the latter had, pointing to the existence of unequal opportunity costs of change. Finally, in an example of interaction effects between knowledge and interest factors, the US demands were backed with the argument and focal point that the US and European data protection arrangements provided the same level of protection to individuals despite their respective differences. The receptivity of Europeans to the US demands and to the above focal point was influenced by an already established belief among Europeans that the purpose limitation data protection principle should be broadened.

Agenda formation and the conclusion of the strategic agreement

As with the strategic information agreement, the initiative for the negotiation of a supplemental personal data agreement between Europol and the US was taken by the European side. In the extraordinary Justice and Home Affairs Council meeting of 20 September 2001, the Director of Europol was invited to 'take all the measures necessary ... [in order] to establish informal cooperation with the United States, pending the conclusion of a formal agreement' (Council of the EU 2001). The Council called for Europol's Director to finalise the strategic agreement with the US by November and to open negotiations for a formal personal data agreement (ibid.).

The informal cooperation of Europol with the US started immediately, and the first initiative of the Americans was to take advantage of an emergency provision in the rules that governed the transmission of data from Europol to third countries (Sénat 2002). This provision allowed the director of Europol to authorise, in exceptional circumstances, the transfer of personal data to third countries without the existence of an agreement in place, in order to 'safeguard the interests of the Member States' and 'in the interests of preventing imminent danger associated with crime' (Council of the EU 1999). After the 9/11 attacks, the US sought to benefit from this emergency procedure in order to establish an informal and urgent line of communication with Europol regarding the transfer of personal data (Sénat 2002).

In that period, the perception among the US security officials who dealt with European matters was that the US could not afford to spend time on formal negotiations with Europol and the European Union, which were perceived as cumbersome and slow moving organisations, especially at a time when US law enforcement officials were busy investigating the 9/11 attacks (Lebl 2005; Interview US 2012a). In addition, there was the fear among the US officials that a formal connection with Europol could compromise or undermine the bilateral relations of US with the police agencies of member states. In the words of a US official:

> The last thing an American investigator pursuing an al Qaeda link wanted to hear was that his German counterpart, who had been communicating directly with him, had just been told everything now must go through Brussels – and that no one could say how long that would take.
>
> (Lebl 2005)

In other words, immediately after the 9/11 attacks the US stance towards Europol continued to be ambivalent.

This initial negative stance of the Americans towards a formal legal-based relationship with Europol and towards Europol's data protection framework was the first problem that Europeans faced. The Director of Europol authorised the exceptional transfer of personal data to the US in order to assist the US investigation into the 9/11 attacks. According to Willy Bruggeman, who was Deputy Director of Europol, 'all [the exchange of information] that's linked to Sept. 11 is no problem' (Associated Press Online 2002). The Joint Supervisory Body of Europol, however, stressed at that time that this exceptional authorisation 'may not replace on a permanent basis the standard rule for the transmission of personal data' (Joint Supervisory Body of Europol 2002). Put differently, the exceptional transfer of data could not continue indefinitely, and a more permanent and formal arrangement was needed.

The Americans finally realised the importance of legal certainty and the need for a formal deal for data to continue to flow from Europol to the US (Sénat 2002). Additionally, the response of the EU to the 9/11 attacks was seen as a positive development by the Americans who recalculated the benefits of working more closely with Europol (Interview US 2012c). The European willingness to strengthen EU's third pillar, as demonstrated by the measures that were taken by the EU in the first weeks after the 9/11 attacks, addressed the concerns voiced by the Americans previously regarding the slow pace of integration in the Justice and Home Affairs area (European Report 2001b). Such measures included the European Arrest Warrant, a common definition of terrorism and a common list of terrorist organisations, an Action Plan against terrorism, and a decision on the freezing of terrorist assets. More importantly for US–Europol relations, the EU called on the member states to share more information with Europol and it strengthened the latter by creating an anti-terrorism unit inside the organisation (Task Force for the Fight against Terrorism) (International Enforcement Law Reporter 2001). These developments in Europol and, generally, in the field of EU internal security in the first weeks after the 9/11 attacks, together with the new security environment, changed US perceptions and, as a result, the US agreed to the start of negotiations for a formal personal data exchange agreement (Interview US 2012b).

The two sides perceived, therefore, that there was a minimum of common interests to be derived from the proposed agreement, and these common interests formed the basis on which the US–Europol negotiations and regime construction were developed. According to the US ambassador to the EU, Rockwell Schnabel,[3] an agreement with Europol would benefit the US especially in the long term; it was expected that Europol would gradually evolve into 'a major organizational law enforcement institution both within the EU as well as in international law enforcement fora' (US Cable 2004). The conclusion of agreements with Europol would allow the US 'to develop a deepening cooperative relationship with Europol as it grows in stature within the EU' enhancing in this way the US fight against terrorism and organised crime (US Cable 2003). For the US, the added value of Europol was that the organisation analysed and processed information coming from more than one member state and, therefore, its analyses and intelligence work contained a critical and strategic element that Washington's bilateral national contacts could not provide (US Cable 2003, 2004). According to Schnabel, however, it would take time before the US could truly benefit from Europol's intelligence work:

> At least in the short run, it is anticipated that US agencies will be providing more data to Europol than it will provide us ... [and] it is expected that the initial flow of information will largely be from the USG [United States Government] to Europol....
>
> (US Cable 2003)

Similarly, according to another US official, the real value of the Europol–US agreements 'might become clear only at a future date' (Lebl 2005).

Regarding Europol and the member states, the 9/11 terrorist attacks moved cooperation with the US to the top of Europeans' political agenda. The external shock of the 9/11 attacks prompted a learning process through which the pre-9/11 European political priorities were reevaluated, and France reconsidered its objections concerning transatlantic cooperation. This changed political and security environment made the EU member states more receptive to Europol's position that agreements with third states and especially with the US were crucial in the organisation's fight against organised crime and terrorism.

In particular, according to an EU official speaking two days after 9/11, '... so far the US has been way down on its [Europol's] list. After this week's horrific events the need for stronger Europol–FBI links is clear' (Deutsche Presse-Agentur 2001). Europol wanted to enhance its relationship with the US, from which the organisation could receive information relevant to its mandate. In the words of Willy Bruggeman, the 9/11 attacks presented 'a young organisation with a huge responsibility' and 'there never has been such a need to have such close co-operation between ourselves and the US' (EUobserver 2001). Similarly, after the 9/11 attacks the Director of Europol, Jürgen Storbeck, lamented that Europol received 'very scant information' from the US and he called for stronger transatlantic cooperation in the area of counter-terrorism (BBC Monitoring Europe 2001).

At the same time that Europol and the US agreed to start negotiations for a personal data agreement they concluded the talks over a strategic and technical agreement (Agence France-Presse 2001). The negotiations were concluded at the end of November 2001, and the agreement was finally signed in December 2001. During these talks no significant problems emerged given the non-controversial nature of the issues discussed and the urgency of the time (Interview US 2012b; Interview US 2012c). Among the discussion subjects were the practicalities of how Europol and the US could communicate and exchange strategic information with each other and how both parties could benefit from each other's experiences.

This progress was, however, dismissed as insufficient from the US Secretary of State, Colin Powell, who attended the signing ceremony. Powell noted during the ceremony that 'it is hard to see how [Europol and the US] can work together in criminal investigations without sharing (personal) data on suspects' (Associated Press Worldstream 2001), pointing to the lack of a personal data agreement. The discussions for the latter started immediately after the signing of the strategic agreement, and, given the fact that the negotiations touched upon the 'legal and logistical minefield' (European Report 2001c) of data protection, they were much more difficult to conclude.

This sub-section presented the stage of agenda formation for the Europol–US agreements and highlighted the role of external shocks and broader political events for processes of regime formation. It also showed that Europol and the US entered negotiations expecting to derive common interests and benefits from their cooperation. The next sub-section focuses on the subsequent negotiations for a personal data agreement.

The negotiations for a personal data agreement

This section shows that the Europol–US negotiations were characterised by mutual adjustment and by the establishment of solutions that were deemed acceptable by both parties. At the same time, however, Europol had more need of an agreement with the US than the latter had, which reduced Europol's bargaining leverage. The US supported its demands in the negotiations with the promotion of the principle that the US and Europol offered the same level of protection to individuals' personal data, and therefore, there was no need for data protection safeguards to be included in the agreement. Europol accepted this principle for reasons related to the structural inability of the organisation to transfer the European data protection regime in its entirety into the text of the agreement. Finally, regarding the US demands about the purpose limitation principle, the previous beliefs and experiences of Europeans on this issue partially influenced Europol's position; Europol was therefore more receptive to the US arguments over this principle.

The main point of friction in the Europol–US negotiations for a personal data exchange agreement concerned the issue of data protection (US Cable 2003; Lebl 2005). The protection of personal data had a central place in Europol's mode of operation, as reflected in the organisation's convention. In general, the way personal data was protected among European countries was different from the system that was in place in the US. The EU had a detailed data protection regime (the comprehensive legislative framework model) (De Busser 2009: 225) based on a number of international agreements, rules and regulations, and on data protection supervisory authorities. The US system was based on sector-specific laws, the self-regulation of the private sector, and technologies that enhanced personal privacy (ibid.: 335).[4]

Practically, the Europol data protection framework had a number of consequences for the US–Europol negotiations on a personal data agreement. On the one hand, Europol's aim was to incorporate into the agreement as much data protection safeguards as possible (Sénat 2002). On the other hand, the aim of the Americans was to ensure that data flowed unhindered by data protection rules and that the data protection safeguards were as flexible as possible (European Report 2001b). According to the US ambassador to the EU,

> The handling and sharing of data, including personal data, is one of the more difficult issues.... The challenge for the US is to craft a relationship that lets us join forces with EU members in combating crime and terrorism through expansive exchanges and sharing all forms of data, including personal data.
>
> (US Cable 2004)

In other words, the topic of data protection in the Europol–US negotiations was a distributive issue in that losses for one party were translated into gains for the other party. In particular, four data protection issues were central in the negotiations: the assessment of whether the US data protection system was 'adequate', the purpose limitation principle, the issue of data accuracy and correction, and the issue of data retention (Joint Supervisory Body of Europol 2001).

Starting from the power-based factors, the strategic position of Europol was not favourable and this reduced the organisation's bargaining leverage. Europol had more need of an agreement than the US had; the US could always resort to the well-tried path of bilateralism and continue working only with the EU member states (Sénat 2002). As the dominant international law enforcement actor, the US made use of a global network of relationships with governments and law enforcement agencies. Additionally, the US perceived that in the short term Europol did not have much to contribute (US Cable 2003; Lebl 2005). Europol did not possess the vast resources that the US had at its disposal with regard to law enforcement, and the intelligence that the US could provide was deemed important and crucial by Europol officials for the fulfilment of Europol's mission (BBC Monitoring Europe 2001). Moreover, in the absence of an agreement, Europol would not be able to regulate the personal data transfers between the US and member states with data protection provisions (Sénat 2002).

The above factors created an asymmetrical situation (Interview EU 2012) where Europol's range of options and, consequently, bargaining leverage were reduced. For example, according to the President of the Joint Supervisory Body of Europol, there was a real possibility that if the US was heavily pressured with regard to data protection then Americans would defect from the negotiations (Sénat 2002). The Europeans realised that they could not incorporate en bloc Europol's data protection regime into the text of the agreement. The least bad option for them was, therefore, to tie the US in the negotiation process and to try to safeguard as many data protection principles as they could (ibid.).

The above structural framework and asymmetry played a role first in the primary stage of the negotiations. According to Europol's rules, before the start of negotiations the data protection system of the US should have been assessed according to the European standards (Joint Supervisory Body of Europol 2001). In practice, this never happened; when the director of Europol asked before the start of the negotiations the opinion of the JSB about the US law and practice in the area of data protection, they replied that 'since Europol did not provide a report on the data protection law and practice in the United States, the JSB is not able at this point to express an opinion on the adequacy of the US data protection level' (ibid.). Despite that, the JSB noted that the negotiations could start and it highlighted a number of points related to data protection that should be raised by the European negotiators in their talks with the US (ibid.). It can be seen, therefore, that one of the requirements stemming from the data protection regime that Europol was part of was not adhered to.

The reasons that the JSB gave for this stance were the prevalent sense of urgency at that time and the realisation that if the JSB insisted then the US would defect and would continue with the other two alternative routes: the bilateral contacts with member states and the exceptional transfer of data (Sénat 2002). In other words, Europeans adapted to the US preferences under the pressure of political costs that would occur otherwise and the political exigencies of the time (UK House of Lords 2003: 17). According to Alex Türk, who was president of the JSB of Europol between 2000 and 2002, if the negotiations collapsed, the relations between Europol, the member states, and the United States would continue in the framework of a system deprived of any control (Sénat 2002).

An additional data protection issue was the formulation of Article 5 of the agreement, which was the most difficult to negotiate (Council of the EU 2002a: 8). This article concerned one of the main principles of data protection, the principle of 'purpose limitation'. According to this principle, the data that was requested and subsequently transferred should only be used for the purpose for which the request was submitted.

In the Europol–US agreement, however, the allowed use of the shared data was broadened; while the beginning of Article 5 stated that the transmission of information 'shall be for the purposes set forth in the request', the article continued presupposing that these purposes 'shall be deemed to include the prevention, detection, suppression, investigation and prosecution of any specific criminal offences, and any specific analytical purposes, to which such information relates' (Europol–US 2002). In other words, the shared information could be used not only for the purpose for which a request was made but also for broader non-criminal proceedings and intelligence-related purposes (Council of the EU 2002b: 3; De Busser 2009: 326). Moreover, and on the insistence of the US (Council of the EU 2002a: 11), the two parties included in the exchange of letters document that accompanied the agreement a statement that 'imposition of generic restrictions with respect to the sharing of personal data' was not permitted (Council of the EU 2002b: 3). In this way, the US removed the possibility that a party might raise objections in the future with regard to data protection. This broadening of the purpose limitation principle was in line with the US position that transatlantic information flows and exchanges should be unhindered by data protection provisions and that the grounds for refusal of sharing information should be as limited as possible (US Cable 2004.)

The negotiations focused on two additional data protection issues: data retention and data accuracy. Regarding the first, the Europol Convention stated that the organisation could not store data for more than three years (UK House of Lords Paper 2003: 18), and Europol's Supervisory Body highlighted that this time limit should be applicable to the data transferred to the US too (Joint Supervisory Body of Europol 2001). However, the final text of the Europol–US agreement did not include any time-limitation to the storage of data, in accordance with the US preferences on this topic (US Cable 2004).

Concerning the accuracy of data, the European data protection regime specified that incorrect data should be either corrected or deleted (Joint Supervisory Body of Europol 2001). The US practice however was different; both the correct and the incorrect pieces of data were retained in order 'to have a complete overview of what happened with the information' (Council of the EU 2002a: 14). Finally, Europol conceded to the demands of the US; the latter set at the start of the negotiations the 'red line' that the provisions of the deal should not force the US to change its laws (ibid.: 2). The inclusion in the agreement of a rule that would oblige the parties to delete incorrect data would indeed force the US to change its laws and, therefore, such a rule was not accepted by the US negotiators (ibid.: 14).

During the negotiations for the above data protection issues the US backed their position with the promotion of the principle and focal point that despite the differences between the US and the European systems for data protection both systems afforded the same protection to individuals (Council of the EU 2002a: 17; European Report 2002). According to this principle, rather than emulating each other's data protection frameworks the two sides should proceed by trusting each other's system for the protection of personal data (European Report 2001c). Through this focal point the US negotiators sought to influence their European counterparts and to neutralise any efforts of the latter to press for data protection provisions in the agreement. Thus this example reveals the existence of interaction effects between intellectual and entrepreneurial leadership.

The above principle and focal point was indeed accepted by Europol. Europol mentioned explicitly in its explanatory report to the Council that the agreement 'reflects the idea that the US legal system, though different in many aspects, is recognised as offering a comparable level of assurances as to the appropriate usage of information, and adequate remedies for individuals' (Council of the EU 2002a: 17). Similarly, the President of the Supervisory Board noted that despite the philosophical differences between the US and Europe on data protection 'no one could doubt the fact that the US has a legislation which genuinely protects the rights of the individuals' (Sénat 2002).

Regarding the purpose limitation principle in particular, the previous experiences of Europeans influenced the receptivity of Europol's negotiators to the US demands and the above focal point. Europeans themselves accepted the broadening of the purpose limitation principle in the Council of Europe's Committee of

Ministers Recommendation R (87) 15 (Council of Europe 1987), the EU's own MLA Convention (Council of the EU 2000b), and the Council of Europe's Convention on Cybercrime (Council of Europe 2001) (Council of the EU 2002a: 8, 2011: 31–33). This dilution by Europeans of the purpose limitation principle in several other cases set a precedent for Europol to accept a similar dilution in the case of the Europol–US agreement (Council of the EU 2002a: 8).

The intellectual and entrepreneurial leadership of the US officials who promoted the above focal point did not take place in a vacuum; in this sense, the acceptance by Europol of the US principle cannot be separated from the structural framework under which negotiations took place. Europol's acceptance of the US focal point was predominantly related to the political costs that would occur to Europeans in the case of non-compliance and a US defection from the negotiations (Sénat 2002; UK House of Lords 2003: 17). In other words, the US interests were supported through an interaction of power-based and knowledge-based factors.

Indeed, the President of the Joint Supervisory Board invoked the exceptional character of the relations with the US and the status of the US as a dominant power to justify the concessions made by Europol and to argue that these concessions did not create any precedent for future agreements of Europol with third states (Sénat 2002). For example, at the later negotiations of the EU with Russia and Australia the JSB insisted on the adequacy requirement and on a stricter application of the Europol's data protection framework; in other words, the focal point promoted by Americans was not used in other cases, something that would hint towards a genuine intellectual conversion of Europol and European officials to this principle.

Despite the above deviations from the European data protection principles, the Europol–US agreement was perceived as fair and equitable by Europol and EU officials given that the US side made several concessions too (Council of the EU 2002a: 17). For example, the US accepted for the first time the inclusion in the agreement of a provision on the sharing of sensitive personal data (related, for example, to race or political and religious beliefs), and the inclusion in the final deal of the purpose limitation principle, even in its diluted form, was also seen by Europol as a positive element (Associated Press Worldstream 2002; Council of the EU 2002a: 12).

The conclusion of a mutually acceptable agreement was facilitated by the formula of the 'exchange of letters'. The 'exchange of letters' was a document that was attached to the agreement and was almost one third as long as the agreement itself (Statewatch Analysis 2002). When differences emerged between the two sides about the wording or the meaning of certain provisions then the two parties explained and clarified their position in this document. Europol noted that the document was explicitly devised as an agreement-facilitating formula and salient solution that was 'used in the process of coming to a final approval of the text both on the Europol and the US side' (Council of the EU 2002a: 3). For example, the two parties' clarifications regarding the highly contested article on the purpose limitation principle covered almost one page in the exchange of letters document (Council of the EU 2002b: 3).

Conclusion

This chapter addressed the question of how the EU and the US cooperated on internal security matters looking at the negotiations between Europol and the US from a regime-theory perspective. Both interest-based and power-based factors influenced the regime-formation process between the two parties while knowledge was only used tactically in the form of a focal point promoted by the US in order to neutralise the EU demands.

Before the 9/11 attacks, cooperation between Europol and the US was not considered a high priority issue in either the EU or the US. Additionally, it was only in 1998 that the Europol Convention came into power and only in 2000 that Europol was authorised to negotiate agreements with third countries. Even then, Europeans prioritised relations with the Central and Eastern European Countries rather than with the US. The US, for its part, had an ambivalent stance fearing that cooperation with Europol could undermine bilateral relations with member states. At the same time, the US was disappointed with the slow progress that the European organisation made. The broader political and security environment and in particular the lack of an emergency situation or crisis that would highlight the importance of transatlantic cooperation influenced the regime-formation process, resulting in a lack of progress on the Europol–US relations.

The start of the regime-formation process came with an initiative of Europol; after the organisation was authorised to conclude agreements with third countries, the Director of Europol initiated an entrepreneurial campaign in which he sought to emphasise to third countries the benefits from concluding deals with Europol, to draw attention to the issue of transnational organised crime, and to present a draft model agreement and Europol's data protection framework. An agreement with the US was not concluded at that period given the previously mentioned political context. In other words, the influence of the political environment was crucial for determining whether the issue of the Europol–US cooperation would be framed as an issue for consideration.

The external shock of the 9/11 attacks changed the political environment and worked as a catalyst for Europol–US relations. In the post-9/11 period the Europol–US agreements were framed as absolutely necessary by officials from both sides. This, in turn, confirms the interest-based approaches that emphasise the existence of common interests. Indeed, Europol and the US perceived that by formalising their cooperation they would achieve joint gains. Europol would have access to US intelligence while the US would have access to Europol's all-source strategic intelligence, which member states could not provide on their own.

Despite the existence of a minimum level of common interests, the negotiations of the two parties touched upon Europol's data protection regime, and differences and friction emerged. Data protection was ultimately a distributive issue in which gains for one side amounted to losses for the other side. Research on regime theory has shown that disagreements over distributive issues leads to distributional bargaining and the use of threats or coercion. Indeed, in the case that this chapter examined, the US used the threat of defecting from the negotiations in order to extract concessions from Europol. Such a defection would hurt Europol more than it would hurt the US; in other words, the opportunity costs of change were bigger for Europol, which as a result conceded to the US demands. Additionally, the US officials, exercising intellectual leadership, used a focal point to neutralise the Europol demands and to justify their positions regarding data protection.

Despite the above, the Europol–US rules constituted ultimately a negotiated regime and not an imposed regime. The US made several concessions too, accepting for the first time the inclusion of data protection provisions in its international agreements, even if the provisions were diluted. In other words, the interest-based argument that international regime-formation processes are successful when the deals are perceived as equitable by both parties is confirmed.

To sum up, this chapter addressed the question of how the EU and the US cooperated on internal security issues by showing that the Europol–US agreements were based on a minimum level of common interests. In terms of regime formation, the interest-based and power-based approaches had stronger explanatory value, with the latter being especially pertinent for the issue of data protection. The next chapter looks at the PNR agreements.

Notes

1 Strategic intelligence in this context is intelligence that is produced from the analysis of raw information and material coming from more than one member state.
2 The Council mentioned that negotiations can start with the following countries: the EU candidate countries, Canada, Iceland, Norway, the Russian Federation, Switzerland, Turkey, the United States, Bolivia, Colombia, Morocco, and Peru. Attached to the decision of the Council was an annex noting that the EU candidate countries, Norway, Iceland, Switzerland, and Interpol had priority with regard to the start of negotiations.
3 Ambassador Schnabel served in this position from 2001 to 2005.
4 According to De Busser, there are four models for data protection worldwide: general laws, sectoral laws, self-regulation by companies, and privacy-enhancing technologies. While the EU followed the first model (general laws) the US used a combination of the other three models (De Busser 2009: 335).

References

Agence France-Presse (2001) 'EU police agency to tighten links with US on terrorism, crime', 4 December 2001.
Andreas, P., and Nadelmann, E. (2006) *Policing the globe: criminalization and crime control in international relations.* Oxford: Oxford University Press.
Associated Press (2000) 'Conference explores ways to fight international cybercrime', 15 May 2000.
Associated Press International (1998), 'Europol wants major role in fight against counterfeit euros', 1 November 1998.
Associated Press Online (2002) 'Sept. 11 Sways Europe Terror Stance', 17 August 2002.
Associated Press Worldstream (2001) 'With US-Attacks EU, US sign deal on closer anti-terrorist cooperation', 6 December 2001.

Associated Press Worldstream (2002) 'EU nations agree data exchange with US crime-fighters', 19 December 2002.
BBC Monitoring Europe (2001) 'Europol chief views problems in establishing "European FBI"', 3 December 2001.
Bunyan, T. (1993) 'Trevi, Europol and the European state', in T. Bunyan (ed.) *Statewatching the New Europe*. London: Statewatch.
Council of Europe (1987) 'Committee of Ministers Recommendation No. R (87) 15 Regulating the Use of Personal Data in the Police Sector', 17 September 1985.
Council of Europe (2001) 'Convention on Cybercrime', 23 November 2001.
Council of the EU (1997) 'Action plan to combat organized crime', OJ C 251/1, 15 August 1997.
Council of the EU (1999) 'Act of 12 March adopting the rules governing the transmission of personal data by Europol to third States and third bodies', OJ C 88, 30 March 1999.
Council of the EU (2000a) 'Decision of 27 March authorising the Director of Europol to enter into negotiations on agreements with third States and non-EU related bodies', OJ C 106, 13 April 2000.
Council of the EU (2000b) 'Act of 29 May 2000 establishing in accordance with Article 34 of the Treaty on European Union the Convention on Mutual Assistance in Criminal Matters between the Member States of the European Union', OJ C 197/1, 12 July 2000.
Council of the EU (2001) 'Extraordinary Council Meeting–Justice, Home Affairs and Civil Protection', 12019/01, 20 September 2001.
Council of the EU (2002a) 'Informal explanatory note: Europol–US Supplementary Agreement', 13696/02, 4 November 2002.
Council of the EU (2002b) 'Exchange of letters related to the Supplemental Agreement between the United States of America and Europol on the exchange of personal data and related information', 13996/02, 11 November 2002.
Council of the EU (2011) 'Handbook on the practical application of the EU–US Mutual Legal Assistance and Extradition Agreements', 8024/11, 25 March 2011.
De Busser, E. (2009) *Data Protection in EU and US Criminal Cooperation*. Antwerp: Maklu.
De Busser, E. (2010) 'EU data protection in transatlantic cooperation in criminal matters: Will the EU be serving its citizens an American meal?', *Utrecht Law Review*, 6(1), pp. 86–100.
Deflem, M. (2006) 'Europol and the Policing of International Terrorism: Counter-Terrorism in a Global Perspective', *Justice Quarterly*, 23(3), pp. 336–359.
Deutsche Presse-Agentur (2001) 'Europol and FBI must sign cooperation pact, EU urges', 13 September 2001.
Dubois, D. (2002) 'The Attacks of 11 September: EU–US Cooperation Against Terrorism in the Field of Justice and Home Affairs', *European Foreign Affairs Review*, 7, pp. 317–335.
EUobserver (2000) 'Organised crime biggest security threat to EU', 28 September 2000.
EUobserver (2001) 'New role for Europol', 19 November 2001.
Euro-East (2001) 'EU Enlargement: Candidates' Justice and Home Affairs Ministers Meet in Brussels', 27 March 2001.
European Council (1996) 'Dublin European Council 13 and 14 December 1996 –Presidency Conclusions', 13–14 December 1996.
European Report (1995a) 'Justice/Home Affairs Council: Agreement Expected on Requests for Asylum from EU Citizens', 7 March 1995.

European Report (1995b) 'Law and Order: UK throws Europol into a state of paralyses, 25 November 1995.
European Report (1998) 'Justice/Home Affairs Council: Little Headway but Willingness to Boost Cooperation', 21 March 1998.
European Report (1999) 'Justice and Home Affairs Council: Starting Signal for Scoreboard on Area of Freedom, Security and Justice', 4 November 1999.
European Report (2000) 'Europol Seminar Prepares Fight against International Organised Crime', 29 April 2000.
European Report (2001a) 'Justice and Home Affairs: Move to Boost Europol Role in Transfer of Personal Data', 9 June 2001.
European Report (2001b) 'EU/US: US Favours More Justice and Home Affairs Co-Operation', 7 November 2001.
European Report (2001c) 'EU/US: Tough Talks Ahead With Europol on Transfer of Personal Data', 19 December 2001.
European Report (2002) 'EU/US: Agreement on Transfer of Personal Data with Europol Imminent', 16 November 2002.
EU–US (1995) 'The New Transatlantic Agenda and the Joint EU–US Action Plan', 3 December 1995.
EU–US (1998) 'European Union/United States Joint Statement on Shared Objectives and Close Cooperation on Counter-Terrorism', 18 May 1998.
Europol–US (2002) 'Supplemental agreement between the Europol Police Office and the United States of America on the exchange of personal data and related information', 20 December 2002.
Federal News Service (1995a) 'USIA Foreign Press Center Background Briefing Subject: US-European Union Summit', 14 June 1995.
Federal News Service (1995b) 'USIA Foreign Press Center Briefing Topic: Upcoming US-European Union Summit in Madrid with President Clinton', 29 November 1995.
Federal News Service (1995c) 'Prepared Statement of Jamie Gorelick Deputy Attorney General Before the House Committee on International Relations', 7 December 1995.
Federal News Service (1996) 'Prepared Statement of Louis J. Freeh Director Federal Bureau of Investigation before the House Appropriations Committee', 1 May 1996.
Federal News Service (1997a) 'Prepared Statement of Louis Freeh Director, Federal Bureau of Investigation Before the Senate Appropriations Committee', 10 April 1997.
Federal News Service (1997b) 'White House Press Briefing by Deputy National Security Advisor James Steinberg and Assistant to the President for International Economic Affairs at the National Economic Council Dan Tarullo and Press Secretary Mile McCurry The Carlton Hotel', 28 May 1997.
Federal News Service (1998) 'Stuart Einzenstat, Undersecretary of State for Economic Affairs', 4 May 1998.
Fortress Europe Circular Letter (1996) 'Europol Chief Storbeck on the State and the Prospects of His Agency', November 1996.
Gardner, A.L. (1997) *A New Era in US-EU Relations? The Clinton Administration and the New Transatlantic Agenda.* Aldershot: Ashgate.
Goldstein, J., and Keohane, R. (1993) 'Ideas and Foreign Policy: An Analytical Framework', in J. Goldstein and R. Keohane (eds) *Ideas and Foreign Policy: Beliefs, Institutions, and Political Change.* Ithaca: Cornell University Press, pp. 3–30.
Guardian (1994) 'Kohl Plan for Europol gets thumbs down – Bonn's EU presidency totters as France and Britain dig in against powerful cross-border police agency', 27 October 1994.

Guardian (2001) 'Europol comes of age as it gets ready for battle with euro-forgers: Briton in the hot seat for the January launch of the new currency', 8 June 2001.

Haas, P. (1993) 'Epistemic Communities and the Dynamics of International Environmental Co-Operation', in V. Rittberger (ed.) *Regime Theory and International Relations*. Oxford: Oxford University Press, pp. 168–201.

Intelligence Newsletter (1998) 'Closed-Door Conclave on Terrorism', 1 October 1998.

International Enforcement Law Reporter (1999) 'European Union Holds Justice and Home Affairs Council Meeting', January 1999.

International Enforcement Law Reporter (2000) 'Europol Begins Cooperation with Non-EU States and Bodies to Combat Transnational Organized Crime', July 2000.

International Enforcement Law Reporter (2001) 'EU Initiates New Counter-terrorism Cooperation', November 2001.

Interview EU (2012) Interview with EU official, 7 December 2012.

Interview US (2012a) Interview with US official, 25 January 2012.

Interview US (2012b) Interview with US official, 6 February 2012.

Interview US (2012c) Interview with US official, 8 February 2012.

Joint Supervisory Body of Europol (2001) 'Opinion 01/38 of the JSB in respect to the data protection level in the United States of America', Opinion 01/38, 26 November 2001.

Joint Supervisory Body of Europol (2002) 'Opinion 02/08 of the JSB in respect to the decision of the Director of Europol on transmission of personal data to law enforcement authorities in the United States of America', Opinion 02/08, 6 March 2002.

Lebl, L. (2005) 'Security Beyond Borders', *Policy Review*, No. 130, April–May 2005.

Nadelmann, E. (1993) *Cops Across Borders: The Internationalization of US Criminal Law Enforcement*. University Park, PA: Pennsylvania State University Press.

Occhipinti, J. (2003) *The Politics of EU Police Cooperation: Toward a European FBI?* London: Lynne Rienner.

Rijken, C. (2001) 'Legal and technical Aspects of Co-operation Between Europol, Third States, and Interpol', in V. Kronenberger (ed.) *The European Union and the International Legal Order: Discord or Harmony?* The Hague: T.M.C. Asser Press, pp. 577–603.

Sénat (2002) 'Projet d'accord entre les États-Unis et Europol relatif à l'échange de données à caractère personnel', Texte E 2141, 10 December 2002.

Statewatch Bulletin (1997) Vol. 7 No. 6, 1997.

Statewatch Bulletin (1998) Vol. 8 No, 5, 1998.

Statewatch Analysis (2002) 'Proposals to amend the Europol Convention', No. 15/2002, October 2002.

Storbeck, J. (1999) 'Organised Crime in the European Union-The Role of Europol in International Law-Enforcement Co-operation', *The 1999 Police Foundation Lecture*. London: The Police Foundation.

The Times (2001) 'Europol prepares to enter a wider arena', 19 January 2001.

UK House of Commons (1999) 'European Scrutiny – Twenty-Eighth Report, 9 November 1999.

UK House of Lords (2003) 'Europol's Role in Fighting Crime', Fifth Report, HL Paper 43, 6 February 2003

United Press International (1995) 'Clinton to sign transatlantic initiative', 2 December 1995.

US Cable (2003) 'EUROPOL – US Cooperation', Cable #03BRUSSELS2375, 6 May 2003, http://wikileaks.cabledrum.org/cable/2003/05/03BRUSSELS2375.html, accessed 5 July 2016.

US Cable (2004) 'EUROPOL – Feeling its way Forward', Cable #04BRUSSELS4536, 21 October 2004, http://wikileaks.cabledrum.org/cable/2004/10/04BRUSSELS4536.html, accessed 5 July 2016.

Washington Post (2000) 'Member of Party He Ousted May Represent Fox in Washington', 13 December 2000.

Winer, J. (2006) 'Cops across borders: The evolution of transatlantic law enforcement and judicial cooperation', in A. Dalgaard-Nielsen and D. Hamilton (eds) *Transatlantic Homeland Security: protecting society in the age of catastrophic terrorism*. Abingdon: Routledge, pp. 106–125.

Young, O. (1991) 'Political Leadership and Regime Formation: On the Development of Institutions in International Society', *International Organization*, 45(3), pp. 281–308.

Young, O. (1994). *International Governance: Protecting the Environment in a Stateless Society*. Ithaca: Cornell University Press.

Young, O. (1998) *Creating Regimes: Arctic Accords and International Governance*. Ithaca: Cornell University Press.

Young, O. and Osherenko, G. (1993) 'Testing Theories of Regime Formation: Findings from a Large Collaborative Research Project', in V. Rittberger (ed.) *Regime Theory and International Relations*. Oxford: Oxford University Press, pp. 223–250.

Zagaris, B. (1998) 'US International Cooperation Against Transnational Organized Crime', *Wayne Law Review*, 44(Fall), pp. 1401–1464.

5 The passenger name record agreements between the European Union and the United States

The negotiations of the passenger name record agreements had at their core a number of issues related to data protection and for this reason they were the most difficult to conclude compared with the other cases that this book examines. The EU–US talks on PNRs concerned the transfer of personal data of European travellers contained in the airlines' reservation systems to the US Customs for law enforcement purposes. The way personal data was protected in the US and in the European Union differed (De Busser 2009: 370) and this divergence of the two systems created friction during the negotiations and stood as a block to the successful conclusion of an agreement.

The PNR case touched on other vital aspects of the EU–US relationship. First, with regard to the economic aspect, the US PNR regulations specified that the airlines that failed to comply with the US rules would face fines or have their landing rights revoked (EUobserver 2003). The transfer of travellers' data to the US authorities also meant that the airlines had to make changes to their computerised reservation systems, which created costs for the companies (*Washington Post* 2003). Second, the issue of PNR transfers touched upon the EU–US security relationship. The US enacted the PNR legislation in order to enhance its security, but this legislation was extra-territorial since it created a number of obligations for the European airlines.

The negotiations for the PNR agreements covered a period of more than 10 years. After the enactment of the relevant US legislation in 2001 (US Congress 2001) and 2002 (US Congress 2002), the first understanding between the EU and the US was the February 2003 'Joint Statement' on PNR transmission (European Commission–US 2003). After intense negotiations this was followed by the conclusion of a first agreement between the EU and the United States on 28 May 2004 (European Community–US 2004). The European Parliament, however, challenged the legality of this agreement at the European Court of Justice and asked the latter to comment on the content of the agreement (UK House of Lords 2007: 21). On 30 May 2006, the Court announced that the EU–US agreement was not based on an appropriate legal basis but, to the disappointment of the European Parliament, it did not make any comment on the content of the text (Agence France-Presse 2006a). According to the European Court of Justice, the European travellers' PNR data was transferred to the US authorities for public security and law enforcement purposes, and therefore the correct legal base for a PNR transfers agreement was not the first pillar of the EU (on which the first agreement was based) but rather the third pillar (European Court of Justice 2006).

The Court decision for the annulment of the EU–US deal was followed by an interim agreement in October 2006, which allowed the continued flow of PNR data (EU–US 2006). A more permanent deal was concluded by the two sides in July 2007 (EU–US 2007). In December 2009 the Lisbon Treaty entered into force, which gave increased powers to the European Parliament in the area covered by the former third pillar of the EU. At that time, however, the EU–US 2007 PNR agreement was not ratified by all the EU member states, and the European Parliament demanded that a new EU–US PNR agreement was negotiated and concluded with the consent of the Parliament. This third agreement on PNR was signed in December 2011 and it was finally approved by the European Parliament in April 2012 (Council of the EU 2011).

The agreements regulated the transfer of European PNR information to the US security agencies and the usage of this information by the latter for law enforcement and counter-terrorism purposes. In particular, PNR information could be used for stopping known terrorists from entering the US. Additionally, the same information could be cross-checked with intelligence from other sources for the identification of previously unknown terrorists or crime offenders. The agreements came with a reciprocity clause, which meant that the US would provide Europeans with any piece of data that concerned Europe's interests and security.

This chapter addresses this book's research question of how the EU and the US managed their cooperation on internal security issues by analysing the EU–US PNR negotiations through the regime-theory model presented in the first chapter. The explicit rules of the PNR agreements are conceptualised as being part of an emerging EU–US internal security regime. This chapter therefore examines the role of power, interests, and knowledge in the agenda-setting phase and in the negotiations of the three EU–US PNR agreements.

This chapter shows that, in the agenda-formation stage, power interacted with knowledge in the form of the unilateral US measures, which were backed with the threat of penalties and which were based on the concept of 'smart borders'. Negotiations were dominated by the issue of data protection, which was a distributive issue; and, therefore, the bargaining was predominantly distributive in nature. The bargaining leverage of the EU was weakened by the exogenous fact that the PNR data was predominantly held in US computer databases and by the member states' readiness to negotiate bilateral deals with Washington. In the negotiations, the US promoted the principle that the EU and the US data protection systems offered the same protection to individuals despite their differences. This ideational 'focal point' served mainly the US agenda and interests, revealing interaction effects between knowledge and power and interests. While the EU position on data protection differed from the US position, the EU was convinced about the utility of using PNR information for law enforcement and counter-terrorism purposes. In other words, a learning process took place through which the EU changed its perceptions on the basis of new knowledge. To sum up, on the one hand the dominance in the negotiations of the distributive issue of data protection gave to the negotiations a conflictual character, and distributive bargaining based on threats and coercion was prominent. On the other hand, the agreements were based on common interests (highlighted by equitable provisions and the presence of side payments) and on consensual knowledge in the form of a shared EU–US belief that the sharing of information (including PNR data) was essential in the fight against terrorism and organised crime. Therefore, the relationship between the EU and the US on the issue of PNR transfers has been more akin to a partnership defined by common interests.

The context of the problem and agenda formation

It is argued in this section that before 9/11 the use of PNR for law enforcement purposes was not considered an option by either the EU or the US. The shock of the 9/11 attacks changed this situation and the US policymakers and officials converged around the idea of 'smart borders', part of which was the exchange of PNR transfers. In practice, the concept of smart borders and its specific PNR element was enforced globally through a series of unilateral US measures and this is how the agenda was set for the EU–US negotiations.

The 9/11 attacks constituted in other words an external shock or crisis which changed the way the US perceived its goals and its means to achieve these goals. Uncertainty regarding the security environment was prevalent, and the concept of smart borders promised to dispel this uncertainty by offering a partial solution to the problems of border controls and counter-terrorism intelligence. This learning process was most prominent in the US which was the victim of the 9/11 attacks. A similar learning process took place however in Europe too prompted by the new security environment together with the US example in the area of border controls.

The impact of the 9/11 attacks

In the immediate aftermath of the 9/11 attacks the concept of smart borders and the utility of PNRs for security purposes acquired dominant status only in the US. In other words, at this initial stage there was no consensual knowledge about what could be an effective solution to the problems of border controls and counter-terrorism. While the US had previous experience with employing computer-based risk-management approaches and with using PNRs, the EU was not as experienced as the US was in this field (Interview US 2012a, 2012b).

Before 9/11 the border and transport security approach was one of physical screening, access control in the airport facilities, and border and immigration controls at the points of arrival. While there were measures related to the advance provision of passenger information (such as the use of passenger name records for law enforcement and counter-terrorism purposes and the US

Customs' Advance Passenger Information System – APIS) these measures were not compulsory or they only concerned domestic flights. The idea of passenger screening based on risk assessment and of relying on information given in advance (before a plane landed on US soil) had already started to form in the period prior to 9/11. However, the political and security environment was not mature enough for the policymakers to accept the new security paradigm in its entirety (Interview US 2012a, 2012b).

APIS was first initiated by the US Customs Service and the US Immigration and Naturalisation Service in the late 1980s and early 1990s, in cooperation with the air industry, following the increase of passenger traffic to the US (US Department of Homeland Security 2005: 1). It was a voluntary programme according to which biographical information contained in the passports of passengers – including name, gender, data of birth, nationality, country of residence, travel document type, and travel document number – could be collected by the airlines prior to the aircraft's departure from the foreign airport in order to be sent to the US authorities. In this way, controls at the US airports' immigration and border points would be expedited since the US authorities would make the immigration and visa-related checks before the plane landed. The APIS system contained both a security and a travel facilitation element.

Concerning the use of PNRs for security purposes, the idea emerged in 1996 when the Federal Aviation Reauthorization Act allowed the development of the Computer-Assisted Aviation Pre-screening System (CAPS).[1] In 1998 the US Federal Aviation Authority proposed a rule about the screening of passengers through the PNR data held in the airlines' reservation systems (Krouse and Elias 2009: 13). The software and the selection algorithms for CAPS would be provided from the government to the airlines, which would have an obligation to apply the selection system to the PNR data of passengers who were travelling with luggage. The passengers who would be selected and flagged according to the CAPS system would have their luggage checked and inspected for explosives and other dangerous materials. The CAPS system concerned domestic flights in the US operated by US airline companies.

With regard to the EU and its member states in the period prior to 9/11, measures such as the use and advance transmission of PNRs and of the information contained in passengers' passports for border and transport security purposes were not on the agenda. The focus at that time was rather on checking passengers' luggage with X-rays or through physical inspection and on the more traditional immigration and border control checks at airports.

In 1995 the Schengen Convention removed the internal borders among the EU countries, with the exception of Ireland and United Kingdom, and created the so-called 'Schengen Area' (Den Boer 1997a, 1997b). The external borders of the Schengen Area were governed by common principles, but the implementation of the checks at the EU's external borders was left to member states. The use of passenger information was not among these principles since the focus of the European governments at the time was on increasing intra-EU cooperation on organised crime and drug trafficking as well as on the traditional threat of domestic terrorism in countries like Spain, Italy, Greece, Germany, and the UK (Mitsilegas et al. 2003: 37). There was not any perceived need to target passengers in advance, before they arrived at EU airports; rather the focus was on the internal EU borders and on coordination and information exchange between the member states' relevant law enforcement authorities (Bruggeman 1997a, 1997b; De Kerchove 1997: 109).

The 9/11 terrorist attacks changed the US threat perceptions regarding aviation and border security and led the US to search for and try to plug any vulnerabilities in the border and transportation security system. The official documents that appeared after 9/11 pronounced, in particular, a number of threats: (1) attacks against land-based targets using aircraft, including the possibility of delivering chemical, biological, radiological, and nuclear weapons or conventional explosives; (2) hijacking of commercial aircraft; (3) on-board attacks against aircraft using explosive devices or conventional and non-conventional weapons; (4) attacks against aircraft using stand-off weapons like man-portable air-defence missiles (MANPADs); (5) cyber-attacks or physical attacks against the air traffic control and navigation systems; (6) the smuggling of weapons, operatives, explosives, and nuclear weapons by terrorists; (7) attacks against and exploitation of air cargo aircraft (US Department of Homeland Security 2006; Elias 2010: 103).

Additionally, the 9/11 Commission report highlighted a number of shortcomings in the US border security system. Prior to 9/11, officials from the Immigration and Naturalisation Service (INS) had instructions not to focus on terrorists, and, with the exception of the FBI, only a very small part of the US law enforcement community dealt with counter-terrorism (US National Commission on Terrorist Attacks Upon the United States 2004: 81–82). The Federal Aviation Administration (FAA), for its part, focused on explosives and on the threat of aircraft bombings rather than on hijackings and air-piracy. While there was a layered defence system based on intelligence, passenger pre-screening, checkpoint screening, and on-board security, 'each layer ... was seriously flawed' (US National Commission on Terrorist Attacks Upon the United States 2004: 83). For example, the FAA's list of the names of people who should not be allowed to travel – the 'no fly' list – contained only 12 names, despite the fact that the similar lists of the FBI and the Central Intelligence Agency (CIA) contained thousands of names. In addition, according to the CAPPS pre-screening system, only passengers with checked luggage could be selected for additional security checks, the fear being that of hidden explosives. Summarising the pre-9/11 situation, the Commission noted succinctly that: 'border security ... was not seen as a national security matter' and that 'in national security circles ... only smuggling of weapons of mass destruction carried weight, not the entry of terrorists who might use such weapons or the presence of associated foreign-born terrorists' (US National Commission on Terrorist Attacks Upon the United States 2004: 384).

The shock of the 9/11 attacks prompted a change in the way the US conceptualised and framed border security (States News Service 2007; Interview US

2012c). At a time of uncertainty and in an atmosphere of crisis, US policymakers and security officials converged around the concept of smart borders and the idea of projecting the US border functions abroad, which promised to offer a solution to the perceived US security vulnerabilities (US Office of Homeland Security 2002: 22; Flynn 2003; *US Customs Today* 2003). The post-9/11 security environment and the new threat perceptions initiated a learning process where the US redefined the means through which they pursued the goals of border and transport security.

The US border security epistemic community had a central role in this learning process and in disseminating and advocating the concept of smart borders (Interview US 2012a, 2012b, 2012c). An epistemic community is a group of professionals and experts who have 'an authoritative claim to policy-relevant knowledge within their domain of expertise' (Haas 1992: 3). In border security the relevant epistemic community consisted of security experts and officials coming from the US Customs and Border Protection unit, the Department of Homeland Security, and from other federal agencies with a border security-related mandate and who had a common 'policy enterprise' (Haas 1993: 180). In particular, this US epistemic community had a professional belief that the idea of smart borders could significantly reduce the risks related to international terrorism.

The concept of smart borders was based on the idea of screening people and goods abroad before they arrived at US territory. In this way, low-risk and high-risk traffic would be identified and the US security assets and resources would focus on high-risk traffic, facilitating the swift clearance and transit of low-risk traffic (Federal News Service 2004).[2] A layered approach to border defences was envisioned, with the first security layers being abroad (Federal News Service 2010a).

In terms of official strategic documents, this new approach of layered homeland defence was reflected in the first National Strategy for Homeland Security, where the creation of smart borders was highlighted as one of the US objectives in the field of border and transportation security and where the new 'border of the future' was described in detail (US Office of Homeland Security 2002: 22). Visa checks in the US consular offices abroad, biometric identifiers in passports, the screening of people through risk-based analysis systems before 'they can reach our shores', and the inspection and control of people when they finally arrived at the US entry points were all part of the US border and transportation security system that was envisioned for the future (US Office of Homeland Security 2002: 22; States News Service 2011a).

Concerning the EU, while in the immediate aftermath of the 9/11 attacks there was an increased mobilisation of efforts and resources in the area of counter-terrorism, no border security initiatives similar to the ones launched by the US were taken by the EU. At that time, the responsibility for the monitoring and surveillance of the EU external borders was predominantly held by the EU member states. As far as the Schengen Area and external borders control were concerned, the focus of member states and the EU was mainly on illegal immigration and on organised crime, especially the smuggling of drugs and weapons, through land and sea borders, rather than on the threats emanating from the aviation transportation system.

One of the first steps that was taken after the 9/11 attacks at an EU level was the re-emergence and start of discussions in October 2001 for the creation of an EU external border guard unit. In Laeken in December 2001 the European Council asked the Council and the Commission 'to examine the conditions in which a mechanism or common services to control external borders could be created', with the purpose of helping the fight against terrorism, illegal immigration, and human trafficking (European Council 2001: 12). Additionally, during the next year, there was both a Communication from the Commission and a plan from the Council, which focused on the management of the Union's external borders, the creation of an EU border guard unit, and the coordination of member states' efforts in the area of border controls under 'the framework of an integrated strategy which takes progressively into account the multiplicity of aspects to the management of the external borders', with the intention of arriving 'at a coherent framework for common action in the medium to long term' (European Commission 2002; Council of the EU 2002).

While the attacks of 9/11 worked as a catalyst for the emergence of new European policies and plans in the area of border security, these initiatives did not initially include the use of advance passenger information or PNRs for law enforcement and counter-terrorism purposes. It was only when the US started implementing its plan for the establishment of smart borders that the EU sought to benefit from the American example in this field (Interview EU 2012a, 2012b, 2012c). In other words, in the immediate aftermath of the 9/11 attacks, the idea of relying on PNRs was dominant only in the US. New knowledge and ideas in the form of the smart borders concept played a prominent role at this stage shaping the US response to the threat of terrorism.

The agenda-formation stage

This part of the chapter shows how the issue of PNR transfers entered the arena of EU–US relations and became the subject of EU–US negotiations. In this agenda-formation stage, power and knowledge interacted with each other stimulating the regime-formation process; the US officials exercised intellectual leadership by propagating the idea of smart borders and PNR transfers, and, at the same time, exercised structural leadership by making the PNR exchanges compulsory for other countries and legislating fines and penalties for the non-compliant airlines. This pattern was similar to the US behaviour in the area of customs security, as shown in Chapter 2. Both cases resembled Haas' 'modified follow-the-leader' regime pattern in which regime formation starts with the initiative of a powerful actor that has, however, been influenced by the beliefs of an epistemic community (Haas 1993: 187–188).

The realisation of the US plan for the creation of smart borders started with the November 2001 Aviation and Transportation Security Act. With this legislation, the provision of advance passenger information (API) from the airlines to US authorities became mandatory. Additionally, the air carriers had an obligation to make the PNRs they collected 'available to the Customs Service upon request' (US Congress 2001: 623). The US intentions were presented in a joint meeting between US representatives and officials from the EU's Strategic Committee on Immigration, Frontiers and Asylum (Council of the EU 2001). In this meeting the US expressed its willingness to exchange various types of data on a reciprocal basis (for example, passenger lists and customs information) (Council of the EU 2001: 2). The US authorities would use the information from PNRs and API first to identify potential threats to US security and second to prevent the entrance of known terrorists or unwanted persons to the US. In other words, the PNR data was used both as a border control tool and as an intelligence tool.

As far as EU–US relations were concerned, the problem with the US demands and the PNR legislation was that it clashed with the EU data protection legislation. The information that the US demanded contained passengers' personal data that was collected within the EU by airline companies; according to the Data Protection Working Party of the EU, the handling of such data was regulated by the provisions of the EU Data Protection Directive (European Union 1995), which set a number of rules concerning the protection of personal data and which was legally binding for the EU airline companies (Article 29 Data Protection Working Party Opinion 2002: 4). The Directive specified the principles that were related to the processing, storage, and transfer of data of personal character (De Busser 2009: 72–77). More specifically, with regard to the transfer of data from the EU to a third country, it was stipulated that the latter should have an adequate level of data protection (De Busser 2009: 361).

The crux of the problem was that the airline companies faced a situation where they had to comply at the same time with two different sets of rules. If European airlines complied with the US requirements then they would violate the EU data protection rules, and the national data protection authorities of member states could bring these companies to national courts and impose fines on them. Yet if European airlines conformed to the EU data protection rules and decided to disregard the US laws then they would face fines from the US and their landing rights to the US would be revoked. In other words, the extraterritorial rules of the US clashed with the data protection regime of the EU. This situation of linked issues and regimes (Young 1994: 24–25) made the negotiation of an agreement necessary in order to relieve legal uncertainty and find a compromise with regard to the conflicting rules.

The negotiations for the PNR agreements

This section shows that there was a minimum of common interests that the EU and the US envisioned achieving from a PNR agreement. Both parties wanted to ensure that there was legal certainty for airlines and, therefore, they sought to fix the problem of clashing requirements. Apart from this technical or legal aspect of the agreement, at the core of the EU–US PNR deal was a real security issue (Interview EU 2012b, 2012c). Officials from the Commission, the Council, and from member states were convinced that the sharing of PNR data was indeed a useful measure in the fight against terrorism and crime (Interview EU 2012a, 2012b, 2012c; US Cable 2010). In other words, a learning process occurred through which the EU and the member states changed their perceptions. The new post-9/11 security environment and the example of the Americans, who acted as historical first-movers, constituted a new body of knowledge for Europeans and they were the two factors that prompted this learning process (Interview EU 2012b, 2012c, 2012d).

The mutual perception of joint gains to be achieved through an agreement did not lead automatically to the conclusion of a deal given the two sides' differences on the issue of data protection. The latter was a distributive issue in that losses for one party were translated into gains for the other party. In particular, the aim of the EU was to incorporate into the agreement a number of safeguards related to data protection. The aim of the US was to ensure that PNR data flowed as unhindered as possible by data protection regulations. This distributive conflict gave rise to distributive bargaining based on threats and coercive tactics as expected by the realist regime-formation patterns. At the same time, however, the EU and the US were motivated by a concern about the equitability of the final deal. The role of knowledge in the stage of negotiations was not as prominent as it was in the agenda-setting phase. Knowledge, in the form of a focal point, was used tactically by the US in order to advance its interests in the conflict with the EU on the topic of data protection.

Starting from the power-based regime-formation perspective, it can be seen that the power asymmetry between the EU and the US created a structural framework that constrained the EU's range of options and reduced its bargaining leverage. Four factors in particular weakened the EU's strategic position. First, the US accompanied the PNR rules with a number of threats against the airlines that failed to comply. These threats ranged from fines amounting to several thousand dollars to the refusal of landing rights on US soil (US Congress 2002: 17; EUobserver 2004). The US threats raised the costs of non-compliance for the EU; if the EU maintained a hard stance towards the US then there was the possibility that the EU companies would be hurt and that there would be serious economic consequences. Transatlantic travel would be disrupted, the companies would face economic losses from the US fines, EU travellers to the US would face increased waiting times and huge queues due to the additional security checks that the US authorities would impose, and the EU airlines would be perceived as less safe than the airlines that conformed to the US anti-terrorist measures (Statewatch 2003a). In the extreme case that landing rights were completely revoked for the EU airlines, then transatlantic trade, business, and economy would be severely affected (*International Herald Tribune* 2007).

Second, and related to the above, as it became clear in 2006, the airlines were much more inclined to comply with the US requirements than to the EU data protection regulations (US Fed News 2006a; Interview EU 2012c). This meant that, in the absence of an EU–US deal, the airlines, being more willing to take the risk of penalties from national data protection authorities than to risk the US fines, would in any case give the PNR data to the US (*Independent* 2006). In this way, the behaviour of the airlines weakened the EU position.

Third, from a technical point of view, the PNR data of airlines was not located in one centralised computer database; rather, the PNRs were stored in four main computer reservation systems (CRS), three of which were physically located in the US (Sabre, Galileo, and Worldspan) (Hasbrouck 2010). Concerning the fourth one, Amadeus, while it was EU-based it had offices in the US (Hasbrouck 2010). Practically, this situation meant that the US could demand from the US-based CRSs or from the US offices of the EU-based Amadeus system the disclosure of their stored PNR data, even in the absence of an agreement with the EU. US courts, for instance, could issue subpoenas demanding that the US-based CRSs disclose the PNR information they stored in their databases (*New York Times* 2004). This could not happen if, for example, all the CRSs were located in Europe, as the case of SWIFT – regarding the transatlantic transfer of bank data – demonstrated at a later time (Interview EU 2012c). In other words, this technical feature of passenger name records meant that Europeans did not have control of the airlines' data and this weakened their bargaining power (Interview EU 2012c).

Fourth, the US had the option of working separately with member states and concluding bilateral PNR deals. While in terms of efficiency it made sense for the US to conclude an EU wide agreement, the US was ready to defect from the negotiations with the EU and to start working at a bilateral, member state level if the EU's data protection demands crossed Washington's red lines (European Report 2007a; Interview EU 2012c). The 'bilateral card' of the US was reinforced by the fact that after the 2004 EU enlargement the new East European member states were also exploring the option of bypassing the EU and working directly with the US on issues like PNR and the visa waiver programme (EUobserver 2008a, 2008b). While the Commission insisted that the negotiation of agreements related to the exchange of PNR data with third countries was a competency of the EU as a whole, member states such as Estonia, the Czech Republic, and Hungary were ready to sign bilateral PNR deals with the US in exchange for being admitted to the visa waiver programme (European Report 2008). This bilateral option of the US together with the EU's own internal differences with regard to EU–US relations reduced the EU's negotiation power and its ability to extract concessions from the US.

The above four factors constituted a permanent feature of the EU–US PNR talks and a structural frame that constrained the EU and weakened its strategic position in negotiations. In practice, these structural constraints meant that the EU had more need of an agreement than the US had, and the latter was in a better position to extract concessions from the EU. Under such pressure, the Europeans were aware that it was impossible to demand the transfer of the EU's data protection regime in its totality to the text of the agreement; the least bad option was for them to keep the Americans on the track of negotiations and to try to safeguard some of the EU's data protection principles (Interview EU 2012c).

The first PNR agreement

The influence of the structural framework on the choices of the Europeans can be seen at the start of the regime-formation process when the US began implementing the PNR regulations. The Europeans had two options at that time. The first option would be to reject the US legislation as unacceptable and contrary to the EU's data protection regulations and to urge the national data protection authorities to penalise the airlines that would conform to the US rules. The second option would be to accept as a starting point the legitimacy of the US demands and then try to engage in talks to achieve a compromise solution.

As the EU Commissioners Patten and Bolkenstein admitted (Statewatch 2003a), the first option was not feasible. Their explanation about why the EU accepted the US measures and started talks with Washington on the issue of PNR transfers pointed to the structural factors mentioned previously:

> Airlines operating flights across the Atlantic risked being caught between two sets of incompatible measures and suffering severe losses as a result of penalties the United States threatened to impose, including fines and even the withdrawal of landing rights.
>
> (Patten, cited in Statewatch 2003a)

> In the absence of discussions with the United States, the airlines – as Commissioner Patten has already explained – would have been left in an impossible situation. They would have faced a whole range of penalties, starting with the practice of secondary inspections of arriving passengers. That indeed had already started.
>
> (Bolkenstein, cited in ibid.)

In other words, the consideration of political and economic costs shaped the EU response, in a pattern similar to the typical realist cases where actors adapt their behaviour to avoid the penalties that a powerful actor has threatened to impose.

Additionally, the two Commissioners stressed that if there were not talks with the Americans, the US would in any case have access to airlines' PNRs, especially given the fact that a number of the airlines' reservation systems were based on US soil:

> although there is no agreement as yet, the effect is nonetheless that data is being accessed where it was not accessed before. That is true. It is clear that in the absence of discussions the airlines would have provided the data anyway. The airlines know that the US airlines and US-based reservations systems are already doing this....
>
> (Bolkenstein, cited in ibid.)

The fact that the PNR data of airlines was mostly stored in computer databases in the US was a factor exogenous to the negotiations that nevertheless reduced the EU's range of options significantly. Concerning the airlines' intentions, the airline companies were not willing to stop their flights to the US just because there was an unsafe legal situation (Interview EU 2012c).

The Europeans, pressured by the factors mentioned previously, decided as a result to engage in talks with the US, trying through these discussions first to convince the Americans about the need for an EU–US agreement and second to incorporate in the text of the agreement as many data protection safeguards as possible in an effort to export the EU's own rules (Interview EU 2012c).

The acceptance of the US regulations was not related only to structural reasons. In addition to the power factors, a learning process also took place among Europeans – which points to the simultaneous work of knowledge factors. In particular, the Europeans were convinced that the exchange and use of PNR information was a useful measure in the fight against terrorism and organised crime (Bolkenstein 2003a; US Fed News 2006a; UK House of Lords 2007; Interview EU 2012b, 2012c). In other words, a learning process took place in which European perceptions about what constituted an effective solution to the problem of transnational terrorism changed under the influence of new knowledge; in the PNR case, the new knowledge was the US PNR rules and regulations, which were instrumentally imitated, and the post-9/11 security environment.

According to one of the EU interviewees, the fact that the EU was insisting on the US sharing with the EU member states any pieces of PNR-derived information that was important for Europeans indicated that the EU was deeming that such PNR-related measures could be useful and effective (Interview EU 2012c). It was acknowledged that there was a real security need for the US as well as for the EU (Agence France-Presse 2007), and an exceptional transfer of data to the US (an EU–US PNR agreement would constitute such an exceptional transfer) would never be authorised and approved without this realisation and acknowledgement (Interview EU 2012c).

The fact that in the last months of 2003 EU officials started (European Commission 2003; European Report 2003b) to think about creating an EU PNR system is further evidence of this learning process. The EU, having seen the value in the US program of PNR exchanges, initiated the necessary debates and procedures in the direction of building an EU PNR policy and system (Agence France-Presse 2007; Interview EU 2012a, 2012b). Commissioner Frattini noted, in particular, that the use of PNR information has been an important law enforcement tool and emphasised that the 'Union is at least as much a potential target of a terrorist attack as the United States' (Agence France-Presse 2007; EUobserver 2007). An EU PNR system would also serve as a safeguard in case the US decided in the future to withhold PNR-derived intelligence related to Europe, and it would enable Europeans to have a better oversight of the data protection provisions that were contained in the PNR agreements (*Europolitics* 2010c; Interview EU 2012b, 2012d).

The need for an EU PNR system was similarly advocated by several EU member states, indicating a similar acceptance on behalf of European states of the utility of PNR sharing (UK House of Lords 2008: 40; Interview EU 2012a, 2012b). In January 2003, Spain suggested to the Commission and to member states the initiation of legislation that would require airlines to transfer PNRs to the EU member states (Council of the EU 2003). National legislation regarding the collection of PNR was enacted in the UK, France, and Denmark (UK House of Lords Paper 2008: 7). Germany, Estonia, Poland, and Italy also supported the idea of establishing a European PNR collection system (UK House of Lords Paper 2008: 20; EUobserver 2011a).

The regime-formation process started, therefore, in the context of the two factors mentioned previously: that is, the structural constraints the EU faced, and the learning process of the EU accepting new knowledge and changing its perceptions. The US agenda was not merely imposed; instead there was a process of instrumental imitation taking place on behalf of the EU officials as well as on behalf of the member states. There was, in other words, a basis of consensual knowledge between the two sides. At the same time, the US accepted entering into negotiations with the EU to avoid a situation of legal uncertainty that could compromise US anti-terrorist measures (US Cable 2004; States News Service 2011a).

The negotiations for the first EU–US PNR agreement started in 2003 and ended in 2004. From the three PNR agreements that the two sides concluded, the 2004 text contained the most safeguards. A puzzle thus emerges regarding the reasons for which the data protection safeguards in the 2004 agreement were stronger than the ones in the later treaties, especially given the fact that the structural constraints of the EU (fines, location of data in the US soil, US bilateralism, and airlines' conformity to US rules) did not change over that time period.

The answer lies in the fact that structural power could not always be translated into bargaining leverage. In the case of the 2004 agreement, there were two main factors that inhibited the successful conversion of structural power into negotiation leverage on the part of US; these factors were the domestic differences inside the US, as well as the EU invocation of a situation of legal chaos should the negotiations collapse.

First, the EU managed to gain a number of concessions from the US by arguing that legal uncertainty must be avoided otherwise the results would be catastrophic for both sides. The EU warned during its talks with the US that in the absence of a deal a chaotic situation would ensue. The national data protection authorities would bring the airlines to court, and the airlines would stop the transfer of data to the US, undermining a counter-terrorism programme perceived as extremely useful in the US. This scenario was implied in the letter sent by Commissioner Bolkenstein to DHS Secretary Tom Ridge: 'if current efforts fail, we risk a highly charged trans-Atlantic confrontation with no obvious way out. Such confrontations are best avoided' (Bolkenstein 2003b). Similarly, in a US–EU meeting in July 2003, Commission officials insisted that the February 2003 joint statement was legally frail and that 'agreement on PNR must be reached by end of July to avoid negative adequacy findings in September' (US Cable 2003).

The tactic of the EU to wave the threat of negative adequacy findings during the negotiations with the Americans, which would lead to 'complete disarray' (EUobserver 2004), was supported by a favourable EU strategic position. The first PNR agreement was negotiated under the first pillar of the EU; this meant that the national data protection authorities had the power to bring airlines to court for violation of member states' and EU's data protection regulations (in the absence of an adequacy agreement); and, at the same time, the European Parliament had to be consulted on any EU–US agreement (European Report 2003a; Associated Press International 2003). In practice, while these actors did not have veto powers on any of the Commission's movements, the Commission used their pressure for the support of its argument concerning the negative situation that would emerge if the talks did not lead to a deal acceptable by both parties. EU officials explicitly warned that if there was no agreement between the EU and the US then 'the EU would have to instruct national data agencies to stop sharing data with Washington and fine carriers that do so' (Associated Press International 2003). Similarly, in the EU–US meeting in July 2003, Commission officials noted to their US counterparts that the temporary February 2003 EU–US statement 'was severely attacked by the European Parliament and Data Privacy Authorities (Article 29 Committee members)' and they remarked that 'the US must do more' (US Cable 2003).

The EU tactic described previously appears to have been successful: according to Stewart Baker, who was Assistant Secretary for Policy in the Department of Homeland Security (DHS) (2005–2009) and who negotiated the later PNR agreements, in the negotiations for the 2004 deal, 'the risk of chaos in the skies over the Atlantic had been used' by the 'European prophets of doom ... to bludgeon DHS into a quick settlement' (Baker 2010: 114–115). Similarly, in a US State Department diplomatic cable on the EU–US PNR negotiations it is noted that at that time 'there was a perceived risk that, absent such agreement, any carrier complying with US law would be at risk of fines or other penalties under the Data Protection Directive or implementing Member State law' (US Cable 2007).

The Commission benefited in its negotiations with the US from the dissent that the national data protection authorities and the European Parliament raised regarding the EU–US PNR negotiations. At the same time, however, the Commission did not want the objections that these actors expressed to impede in any way the discussions with the US. For the Commission officials, having a hard-line approach towards the Americans, as the European Parliament suggested, would be a counterproductive approach. The hard-line approach of the European Parliament could have a detrimental effect on the Union's credibility and trust-building campaign towards the US and, consequently, on the EU's efforts to protect and export some of its data protection standards (Interview EU 2012c).

Second, according to DHS Assistant Secretary for Policy, Stewart Baker, another factor that weakened the US position was the challenge that Congress raised in 2003 against the domestic aspects of PNR collection. While Congress allowed the collection of passengers' data only for overseas flights, it was discovered that the government, with the cooperation of several airlines, was testing a domestic PNR collection programme (Hasbrouck 2004). This programme raised concerns among privacy organisations and in the Congress, and in late 2003 the DHS finally imposed restrictions on the usage of domestic travellers' data.

According to Baker this internal fight, and domestic lack of consensus regarding PNR use, influenced negatively the ability of the US to resist the EU demands:

> DHS was embroiled in claims that JetBlue and other airlines had violated privacy standards when testing the domestic program. Bolkenstein welcomed the flap.... Under siege on the Hill and facing hard lobbying from a financially strapped air industry, DHS had no stomach for a fight with Brussels. It buckled, agreeing to European demands and setting limits on how it would handle travel reservation data.
>
> (Baker 2010: 99)

These two factors, namely the domestic lack of consensus inside the US and the successful tactic of the EU to use the threat of legal uncertainty in case negotiations collapsed, resulted in the first PNR agreement being closer to the EU standards than the later agreements (Interview US 2012c). For instance, the PNR information that was sent to US Customs could only be transmitted to other agencies under very strict conditions, the retention periods were limited, and the use of sensitive data was totally prohibited. For these reasons, the new leadership in 2005 in the DHS had a negative view of the agreement, and the general perception was that it was a bad agreement that significantly limited the ability of the US to conduct counter-terrorism investigations (Baker 2010: 100–101; Interview US 2012c).

To sum up, in the initial stage of the negotiations for the first agreement the role of power was evident in the US threat of penalties, which restricted the EU's options. At the same time, however, the new post-9/11 security environment together with the US PNR initiatives convinced the EU about the utility of using air passengers' data for counter-terrorism and law enforcement purposes. Moreover, the domestic disagreements in the US regarding PNRs and the contextual factor that the EU was negotiating under the framework of the first pillar enhanced EU's strategic position.

The second PNR agreement

The collapse of the first PNR agreement and the start of negotiations for a second PNR agreement confirmed Young's remarks that the identity of participants in regime formation is often fluid and that factors and events exogenous to the negotiations influence the establishment of regimes (Young 1994: 123, 1998: 24). The European Parliament, which felt excluded from the EU–US negotiations, sought to assert its power and challenged the 2004 PNR agreement in the European Court of Justice (Agence France-Presse 2004). This section shows that in the negotiations for the second PNR agreement the EU had an unfavourable strategic position; both the member states and the airlines had parallel talks with the US, which undermined the EU's negotiating position in an example of how internal dissent can influence bargaining leverage. The context of the negotiations also changed in that the EU negotiated the second PNR agreement under the framework of the third pillar. On the one hand, this meant that the EU could not draw as easily on the threat of legal chaos given that in the third pillar there was not any overarching data protection regulation similar to the first pillar's Data Protection Directive (O'Neill 2010). On the other hand, the negotiation arithmetic (Young 1994: 123–124) changed with the inclusion in the negotiations of the Justice, Freedom and Security Directorate General of the Commission. Through this change, the issue of PNR transfers could more easily be framed during the negotiations as a security issue rather than as an issue of data protection as the US argued from the beginning (US Cable 2003; Statewatch 2003b).

Soon after the conclusion of the first PNR agreement, US officials started voicing concerns about how the data protection provisions of this agreement impeded the work of the DHS (Interview US 2012c). The halt that the agreement was putting on the ability of the US agencies to share PNR information with each other was considered especially negative since this intelligence 'wall' was specifically identified as one of the main shortcomings behind the 9/11 attacks (Baker 2010: 91). The 9/11 Commission Report stressed that prior to 9/11 'information was not shared, sometimes inadvertently or because of legal misunderstandings' and that 'analysis was not pooled' (US National Commission on Terrorist Attacks Upon the United States 2004: 353). Therefore, the committee suggested that all sources of information should be integrated so as to enable the relevant agencies 'to see the enemy as a whole' (US National Commission on Terrorist Attacks Upon the United States 2004: 401). This suggestion was put into practice with the Intelligence Reform and Terrorism Prevention Act (US Congress 2004). Under these circumstances, DHS officials were 'appalled at the idea that foreign governments would re-impose such a catastrophic policy [the impediments to the sharing of PNR information with other law enforcement agencies] on the United States within a few years of 9/11' and desired a new agreement (UK House of Lords 2007: 43; Baker 2010: 100).

Ironically, this opportunity was given to the US by the European Parliament, which challenged the legality of the agreement at the European Court of Justice. The European Court of Justice issued its verdict in May 2006, challenging the legal base on which the EU–US agreement was based (the first-pillar framework and the functioning of the internal market) and declaring that a new agreement should be concluded under the framework of the third pillar (European Court of Justice 2006; Agence France-Presse 2006a). To the disappointment of the European Parliament, the Court did not comment on the content of the text, and the third-pillar framework that was suggested by the Court as the right basis for an EU–US PNR agreement provided less scope for the Parliament to play a role and make its voice heard than the first pillar did (*Aviation Daily* 2006a). The nullification of the agreement by the Court influenced the regime-formation process, giving the US the window of opportunity that it sought to change the rules of the deal with the EU. Jonathan Faull, the EU negotiator and Director-General for Justice, Freedom and Security, expressed his dismay about the behaviour of the Parliament, noting that a 'perfectly good agreement' had to be reopened (*International Herald Tribune* 2006b).

At the same time, the cancelling of the agreement changed the overall strategic position of the EU and consequently its negotiation power. First, the Court stressed that law enforcement was the essence of the agreement and therefore the text should have been negotiated under a third-pillar framework (European Court of Justice 2006). This meant that while the previous agreement was framed by Europeans as an internal market and data protection issue (the Data Protection Directive was applicable only to first-pillar issues) (Bolkenstein 2003b), the new agreement would be negotiated under the third pillar, which at that time did not have any overarching data protection framework. This favoured the US, which from the beginning sought to include the opinion and input of people coming from a law enforcement perspective into the negotiations and stressed that PNR sharing concerned not only data protection but also, and mainly, counter-terrorism and security. For example, in an EU–US meeting in 2003, the US officials remarked tellingly that 'a glaring omission in the discussion of PNR ... is the law enforcement perspective (Justice and Home Affairs – JHA). For the US, PNR is a question of security and we would welcome the JHA point of view' (US Cable 2003). The Commission officials replied that while they were aware of the value of the JHA perspective this should not 'be used to circumvent data protection issues' (US Cable 2003). Second, and related to the above, the Court decision changed the negotiation arithmetic, bringing the JHA Commissioner into the discussions and removing the Commissioners Patten and Bolkenstein. The participation in the negotiations of EU officials who had a security background meant that in the subsequent negotiations for the second and third PNR agreements there was a stronger framework of consensual knowledge, and the issue of PNR would be framed as mainly an issue of security. These conditions could potentially enhance the receptivity of EU negotiators to the arguments (intellectual leadership) of US officials about the utility of as much unhindered data sharing and transfers as possible (Baker 2010: 134).

Finally, the negotiation under a third-pillar framework meant, in practice, that the EU could not invoke with the same credibility the threat of legal chaos and uncertainty in case the talks collapsed given that under this context the national and EU data protection authorities had less powers than previously (UK House of Lords 2005: 19–23). As a result, the bargaining power of the EU was reduced in the negotiations.

After the Court ruling, the aim of the EU was to keep the status quo of the previous agreement and just replace the legal base on which the agreement was based before the 30 September expiration date set by the Court (UK House of Lords 2007: 43). If the two sides wanted to change the content of the agreement substantially then this could happen in later negotiations in 2007 and certainly after an interim agreement based on the previous deal was in place. In several instances Commission officials and representatives emphasised and stressed that the content of the agreement should remain the same, given that the Court did not comment on the content, and that only the mere formality of changing the legal base should be addressed (*Aviation Daily* 2006a; Associated Press International 2006a; European Report 2006a). They warned that the replacement of the old text with a new one based on the third pillar should happen by 30 September to avoid putting the airlines in a difficult position of having to comply with two different and conflicting regulations (US Fed News 2006a).

On the part of the Americans, the aim of the DHS leadership was to convince Europeans about the need to rework the content of the 2004 agreement immediately and not later in 2007 (US Fed News 2006b; Associated Press International 2006b). The US negotiators and officials exercised for this purpose all types of leadership (structural, entrepreneurial, and intellectual). The position of the DHS became clear immediately after the Court ruling, when the DHS Secretary and other DHS officials highlighted the need for greater sharing of the PNR data among US agencies and for an expansion of the PNR data collected. As one DHS official stressed, 'as we negotiate with our European allies for a replacement agreement, we will not forget the key lessons of 9/11 – the necessity of sharing information so dots can be connected before attacks materialize' (Federal News Service 2006). Similarly, the DHS Secretary made the DHS position clear in an article he wrote for the *Washington Post*, exercising in this way a combination of entrepreneurial and intellectual leadership (*Washington Post* 2006). In this article he noted emphatically that the US remains 'handcuffed' by the provisions of the 2004 agreement and that more data categories and more flexibility in the sharing of information was needed if the DHS was to accomplish its mission. The mandate that was given to Stewart Baker for the September 2006 talks was to convince the Europeans to rework and change the 2004 agreement by 30 September (Baker 2010: 122).

A power and distributive contest ensued between the two parties' conflicting positions; the EU insisted on keeping the old agreement in place while the DHS pressed for an immediate change (*Aviation Daily* 2006b). At this contest two tactics were used by the EU. First, and similar to the negotiations for the first agreement, the EU invoked the risks of leaving the agreement to expire: 'just a threat of data protection litigation could cause chaos if no agreement had been reached, he [the EU negotiator] said. Airlines might withhold data from the DHS. They might refuse to fly across the Atlantic at all' (*The International Herald Tribune* 2006a; Baker 2010: 125). The second tactic used by the Commission negotiators was a tactical issue-linkage between the EU–US PNR case and Canada–US PNR sharing. The EU argued that if the agreement was left to expire on 30 September then the US would no longer be deemed adequate under EU data protection law and this would prevent Canada from sharing PNR with the US (Baker 2010: 125–126). In other words, the EU threatened that the US would lose not only the EU PNR but also the Canadian PNR data.

These EU tactics did not work, however, for reasons related to the weak EU strategic position mentioned previously and the EU's own internal inconsistency. In particular, two factors played a role in this power contest. First, the US played the bilateral card and approached the member states individually in an effort to ascertain the EU governments' position in case the talks collapsed (US Cable 2006a, 2006b, 2006e). The US found that several European governments were taking measures to avoid the possibility of lawsuits or the stop of transatlantic flights in case the talks ended without any agreement (US Cable 2006a, 2006b, 2006e; Baker 2010; 120). In meetings with officials from France (US Cable 2006c), Germany (US Cable 2006d), Italy (US Cable 2006e), and the Czech Republic (US Cable 2006b) the US was reassured that the airlines in their flights from these countries to the US would continue the transfer of PNR data even in the absence of an EU–US agreement. Apart from ascertaining the intentions of the European governments, the US even considered having bilateral agreements with member states if the EU–US talks collapsed (Agence France-Presse 2006c). The Czech Republic, for instance, was prepared for such an option if there was no EU–US PNR deal (US Cable 2006b).

Second, and related to the above, the airlines themselves were ready to continue the flow of data to the US even if this meant that they could possibly face the risk of litigations in member states. As early as May 2006, British Airways, for example, noted that it had been liaising with the UK government and understood 'that the UK data protection legislation does not prevent British Airways from providing passenger data to the US authorities' (*Independent* 2006). Similarly, Air France representatives met with US officials from the US Embassy in Paris reassuring them that with or without an agreement the airline would continue transferring PNR information after the expiration date of 1 October (US Cable 2006c).

The above two factors, namely the stance of the airlines and of member states, reduced the credibility of the EU position and as a result weakened the EU's negotiation power. If both the airlines and the member states admitted privately in their conversations with US officials that the data would continue flowing after 1 October even if there was no agreement in place, then the EU's main negotiation chip was rendered void. According to some of the EU officials interviewed, the consistency between the collective EU position and the behaviour of member states was a crucial element that could enhance the Union's credibility with the US (Interview EU 2012d, 2013). The EU officials were aware of the pragmatic approach of the US, which sought in general to maintain a position as flexible as possible regarding the fora in which they pursued their interests (Interview EU 2012d). Therefore, what the EU could do was to make sure that member states carried the same message as the EU in their talks with the US (Interview EU 2012d, 2013). In the case of the PNR negotiations this did not work, however, because the member states were not willing to risk economic losses for their airlines by enforcing a stop to PNR transfers (Interview EU 2012c). As a result, the EU threats were not credible.

The internal inconsistency and dissent within the EU was coupled with a clear message by the US negotiator Stewart Baker that the US was not afraid to let the agreement expire. The result was that the EU negotiator was forced to accept that at least some elements of the 2004 agreement should change before the full renegotiation of the deal in the next year.

Given the above situation, the EU negotiator agreed to accept the US changes, some of which he found reasonable in any case (UK House of Lords Paper 2007: 42–43; Baker 2010: 126). The problem was that the only mandate that was given to the EU negotiator was to renew the agreement; he was not authorised to make any changes (UK House of Lords 2007: 43). A solution was needed that, on one hand, would nominally keep the previous agreement intact and, on the other, would deliver the changes that the DHS desired. The salient formula that could overcome this impediment was finally proposed by the EU negotiator, Jonathan Faull, who exercised a form of entrepreneurial leadership. Faull proposed that instead of the 2004 agreement being changed it could just be reinterpreted in order to accommodate the US demands (Baker 2010: 126–127). This could take place through a provision of the 2004 agreement that allowed the DHS to change the agreement's US undertakings if this was necessary due to a change in US law (UK House of Lords Paper 2007: 43).

Such a law was the 2004 Intelligence Reform and Terrorism Prevention Act (US Congress 2004), which encouraged the US agencies to share intelligence with each other with the aim of creating a federal 'information sharing environment' (Agence France-Presse 2006c; UK House of Lords 2007: 43; Baker 2010: 127). The interpretation formula was based and justified on the changes in US law that had occurred since 2004; in the words of Baker, 'the 2004 agreement could be rolled over, in accordance with the commission's instructions, but with a sweeping set of changes based on the new US law' (Baker 2010: 127).

However, when the US prepared the interpretation letter the EU realised that some of the changes moved beyond mere interpretation and constituted a substantial change in the agreement. As a result, the EU negotiators left the talks, since they did not have a mandate to accept changes in the text, and negotiations collapsed on Friday 29 September (Agence France-Presse 2006b). The expiration of the agreement was crucial for the EU's strategic position since it nullified its main tactic, which was to invoke the threat of legal chaos, cancelled flights, and no data flows. On the contrary, there were no flights cancellations, and the airlines continued to provide data to the US (European Report 2006b). Under this unfavourable strategic position, the EU had more need of an agreement than the US had and this in turn forced the EU to concede to an interim agreement a week later (on 6 October 2006) (Agence France-Presse 2006c). The latter was accompanied by the US letter of interpretations, which was negotiated with the EU. In parallel with the EU concessions, a number of concessions were also made by the US towards Europeans, ensuring in this way that the arrangements were perceived as acceptable and fair by both parties. The DHS would grant access to its PNR files to other agencies only under certain conditions, and the retention period remained at the low level of three and a half years, at least until the negotiation for a permanent agreement in the next year (Baker 2010: 138).

The negotiations for an interim agreement were followed by negotiations in 2007 for a new, more permanent deal. In these negotiations further concessions were made by the EU on the scope of the agreement, the sharing of data to other agencies, and the data retention period (Associated Press International 2007; European Report 2007c). As with the previous negotiations, the weak strategic position of the EU meant that it could not bring any substantial bargaining leverage to the negotiations. More importantly, the EU's main negotiation chip – the consequences of not having any agreement in place – was rendered an empty threat after the 2004 agreement expired without any consequences for transatlantic flights, travel, and the economy. Baker summarised the EU's position succinctly, noting that in the 2007 negotiations 'because DHS was willing to live without an agreement, the EU had to make further concessions just to hang on to an agreement of some sort' (Baker 2010: 140). Similarly, an EU interviewee highlighted that there were several moments during the negotiations in which the Americans made clear that certain topics were considered as hard core security issues, refused to discuss anything about these issues, and were ready to leave the talks (Interview EU 2012c). In these negotiations, which resembled the realist and distributive patterns of regime formation, the EU was in need of an agreement more than the US was and this reduced the power of the EU to resist the US demands; if an EU–US agreement was not concluded, the US would simply negotiate separate deals with EU member states (European Report 2007a), while the EU would lose any chance it had to incorporate data protection safeguards into the text of the deal (Agence France-Presse 2006c).

On the negotiations for the 2007 agreements three issues were noteworthy. Young's remark (1998: 26) that the design and the format of international arrangements are highly political issues rather than a mere technical exercise was confirmed. Additionally, interaction effects were revealed between knowledge and power and interests in the form of a focal point promoted by the US. Finally, a salient solution was proposed for the issue of data retention that was at the core of the EU–US negotiations.

First, the US sought to change the format of the new agreement from one detailed and heavy in content text into a more flexible kind of deal, which specified general principles and rules and which was based on trust rather than on strictly legal rules. The US had concerns with the 'detailed, "code of conduct" mentality' (US Cable 2006f; Agence France-Presse 2006d) and the 'detailed and prescriptive security and procedural rules' (Baker 2010: 142) that underlay the 2004 agreement. The aim was therefore to have

> a different kind of PNR agreement, based on general principles, not a list of detailed 'dos and don'ts', and more modelled on mutual legal assistance treaties, which envision the sharing of data between law enforcement agencies, and less on the data privacy rules the EU applies to the commercial sector.
> (US Cable 2006f)

The US preference for an agreement framed and modelled on law enforcement treaties was strengthened by the European Court's decision that a new treaty should be negotiated under a third-pillar context.

Practically, the move towards a more flexible set of rules based on trust rather than legal requirements could be seen in the format of the 2007 agreement; the latter was very brief and it was accompanied by a DHS letter to the EU where the way the DHS would handle the PNR information was described. In other words, the essential parts of the deal were incorporated not into the treaty itself but into a non-legally binding text. This US preference towards trust-based arrangements ultimately served the US interests given that in this way the EU's detailed data protection rules were diluted.

Second, the US started promoting in the issue-area of PNR the idea that the EU and the US data protection systems, despite their differences, offered the same protections to individuals (Federal News Service 2007a, 2007b; Interview EU 2012d). This idea served as a focal point that allowed the swift conclusion of the EU–US agreement; instead of the US copying the EU data protection provisions in total, the two sides would rather agree that both the EU and the US systems afforded the same level of protection and that they would commit themselves to a number of trust-based undertakings. This principle could be seen in the preamble of the 2007 agreement, which highlighted that 'US and European privacy law and policy share a common basis and that any differences in the implementation of these principles should not present an obstacle to cooperation between the US and the European Union' (EU–US 2007).

The EU's tacit acceptance of this principle cannot be separated from the reality of US structural power and from the structural context under which the agreement was conducted. For the US, the invocation of this principle was used as the ideational and normative means to argue against the need to adopt data protection principles identical with European ones. For Europeans, the same principle, which, apart from the PNR case, could be found also in the MLA and extradition agreements and in the Europol–US agreements, reflected the reality that the EU could not impose its data protection regulations on the US in their entirety (en bloc).

Third, the main data protection issue in the negotiations was the data retention period for the PNRs; the three-and-a-half-year limit that was contained in the 2004 agreement was considered to be very strict for the US and thus harmful for law enforcement and counter-terrorism investigations (European Report 2006d; Baker 2010: 139). This view was also shared by the key Commission officials involved in the EU–US negotiations (European Report 2006c; UK House of Lords Paper 2007: 44–46; Baker 2010: 134, 139), confirming the previous US insistence on including in the talks the 'law enforcement and judicial side of the Commission' (US Cable 2004). The compromise that was finally found with the EU was that data would be held for 15 years. In order for this to be accepted by the EU, however, it was agreed that during these 15 years, data would be accessible for the first seven years, and then held in a 'dormant' database, with limited access, for the following eight years.

The third PNR agreement

The EU member states were slow in ratifying the second PNR agreement. When the Lisbon Treaty entered into force in December 2009, the 2007 PNR agreement had not yet been ratified by all member states. This fact, together with the new powers that the Lisbon Treaty gave to the European Parliament, had a number of consequences for the EU–US regime-formation process. The European Parliament could contest the legality of the agreement, given that it did not give its assent as the new Lisbon Treaty postulated. The Commission and the Council therefore agreed in December 2010 to reopen the negotiations for a third agreement with the US, taking into account the views of the Parliament, which would have the right to accept or reject the third deal. The US, which was initially reluctant to enter into another round of PNR negotiations, agreed in the end to launch a fresh round of negotiations with the EU, but on condition 'that the new text would not degrade the operational effectiveness of the 2007 Agreement' and that "additional security enhancements" would be incorporated into the agreement where necessary' (States News Service 2011a).

This section shows that contextual factors can change the negotiation arithmetic and the dynamic of the regime-formation process. After the Lisbon Treaty entered into force, the European Parliament became a veto player and sought to play an active role in the EU–US PNR talks and negotiations. The US adapted its tactics, and US representatives started an entrepreneurial and intellectual campaign among members of the European Parliament in order to convince and persuade them about the utility of PNR transfers and about the US positions. Similar to the previous negotiations, the US threat of defection from the talks significantly constrained the EU options and reduced its bargaining leverage (Interview EU 2012a). Additionally, and in accordance with the realist patterns of regime formation, the US tactically connected the issue of PNR sharing with the issue of granting visa waiver status to European governments. To defend and justify its positions regarding data protection, the US was promoting the same focal point as in the negotiations for the second agreement. Finally, a number of concessions were made by the US, ensuring that the final text was deemed fair and acceptable by all parties.

Starting from the new negotiation arithmetic, the veto power that the European Parliament gained changed the dynamics of the EU–US relationship and the EU strategic position. According to both the EU and the US officials interviewed, the new powers of the Parliament changed the power balance between the EU and the US and resulted in the latter making a number of concessions in order to gain the Parliament's approval (Interview US 2012d; Interview EU 2012a, 2012c). An additional factor that played a role was the precedent of the rejection (in February 2010) by the European Parliament of a previous EU–US agreement concerning the transfer of financial data, which had been a shock to the Americans (*Europolitics* 2010b; Interview EU 2012c). This previous demonstration of power by the European body added to the credibility of the threat that there was a real possibility that the European Parliament might reject the EU–US PNR agreement. This in turn made the US adapt its tactics by organising a lobbying campaign with speeches and individual contacts and meetings with members of the European Parliament (Agence France-Presse 2010; EUobserver 2010a; States News Service 2011a). The US lobbying campaign was made easier by the fact that in the European Parliament elections of 2009 the Conservative and right-wing parties, which traditionally were less critical of US policies, increased their power compared to the previous 2004 elections (*Europolitics* 2010a; Federal News Service 2011a; EUobserver 2011b). For example, Timothy Kirkhope, who was the European Conservatives and Reformists justice and home affairs spokesman in the European Parliament, wrote an editorial in the *Guardian* where he stressed the importance of PNR transfers and the EU–US PNR agreements (*Guardian* 2011).

At the same time, however, the Commission negotiators were afraid that the involvement of the Parliament might affect the Union's credibility and as a result weaken its position (*Europolitics* 2009). The fear was that the involvement of the Parliament and the resulting institutional complexity might frustrate the US, which might decide to work with EU member states and defect from the EU–US negotiations (Interview EU 2012c).

The US had a bargaining chip too, which came from its ability to offer side payments to European member states as a means of gaining support. In particular, since late 2007 and early 2008 the US, bypassing the EU, linked the issue of PNR transfers with the issue of removing the visa requirement for travellers coming from certain European countries (European Report 2007b; EUobserver 2008a). The US offered side payments to the governments that were more forthcoming with regard to data transfers in general (including PNR data).[3] This US tactic was based on the Implementing Recommendations of the 9/11 Commission Act of 2007 (US Congress 2007), which mandated, among others, the modernisation of the Visa Waiver Program and that the granting of visa-free travel privileges to the nationals of a country was linked to each country's cooperation 'with the Government of the United States on counterterrorism initiatives, information sharing, and preventing terrorist travel' (US Congress 2007: 340). Within this context, the members of the European Parliament feared that if they did not vote in favour of the EU–US PNR agreement then the visa-waiver status of EU member states would be revoked (*Europolitics* 2010b, 2011).

In addition to the above, the US made a clear warning to the EU (both to the Commission and to members of the Parliament) that if the Parliament rejected the agreement then there would be no renegotiation (EUobserver 2010b). This scenario, where the US would defect from the negotiations, meant that no data protection at all would be available for the PNR data transferred to the US. In other words, and similar to the negotiations for the 2007 agreement, if the US defected from the negotiations then this would harm the EU more than it would harm the US. The bargaining leverage of the EU was therefore reduced.

Additionally, the demands of the US were similarly supported with the focal point that the data protection systems of the two sides offered the same level of protections to individuals and that therefore there was no need to include data protection provisions in the agreement (Federal News Service 2010b, 2011b).

The agreement that the two sides finally signed differed from the previous text; the US making a number of concessions to accommodate the demands of the Parliament. On the main data protection issue of data retention, where the US desired to keep the data as long as possible, the solution that was found was that after a certain period of time the data would be 'masked' and 'depersonalised' (Agence France-Presse 2011). This salient solution, which facilitated the conclusion of the negotiations, was perceived as fair by both the European Parliament and the US. Additionally, the scope of the agreement was defined more clearly: PNR data would be used only for transnational crimes that were punishable in the US by three years of imprisonment or more (States News Service 2011b). Finally, the agreement provided for the adoption of the 'push' system for access to the PNR data. This meant that the US would not pull data from the airlines' reservation systems; rather, the airlines would transfer the PNR data to the US authorities (European Commission 2011). In this sense, while certain members of the European Parliament dismissed the new agreement (EUobserver 2011b), the EU acknowledged that the US made a lot of concessions and it could not give more (Interview EU 2012a, 2012c).

Conclusion

This chapter addressed the research question of how the EU–US cooperation on internal security emerged by looking at the negotiations for the PNR agreements through a regime-theory perspective. Power and knowledge factors were prominent in the regime-formation process of this case. At the same time, the agreements reflected and served the interests of both parties.

The initial factor that triggered the regime-formation process was the 9/11 attacks, which prompted a change in the way the US officials thought and conceptualised border and transport security. As shown in Chapter 1 of this book, external shocks create an uncertain environment for policymakers, who seek to address this uncertainty by looking for solutions in the professional or scientific (epistemic) communities. Indeed, the US policymakers converged around the idea of smart borders, which was promoted in the US by security officials as a way of addressing the security gaps identified in the post-9/11 period. In this sense, the role of knowledge was prominent at this agenda-setting stage of regime formation, confirming previous research that showed that knowledge had a more prominent role at the initial stages of regime formation (before the start of negotiations). The concept of smart borders framed the issue of border and transport controls as an issue to be dealt with outside US borders through, among others, the collection of PNR data.

The regime-formation process started with US legislation that made the sharing of PNR data by foreign airlines compulsory. In other words, US officials initiated the regime-formation process through the exercise of structural leadership, threatening non-compliant actors with costs. This form of structural leadership was based on the smart borders concept and in this way intellectual leadership worked synergistically with structural leadership.

In an example of regime linkages, the US initiatives clashed with the EU data protection regime. The EU, rather than challenging the US demands, complied with the US legislation under the pressure of political and other costs; in other words, the US structural leadership was successful. At the same time, the EU officials were convinced about the utility of PNR collection, influenced by the post-9/11 security environment and by the US example. As with the US learning processes, the EU officials too framed the issue of enhanced border and transport controls as absolutely necessary after the 9/11 attacks. Therefore, both types of the US leadership (intellectual and structural) influenced the positions of the EU.

Additionally, the PNR case highlighted the importance of an actor's strategic position and the broader context for the bargaining leverage of the two sides. The EU's strategic position was weakened by the fact that the PNR data was mainly located in US computer servers and by the stance of the airlines and member states, which were not willing to confront and challenge the US in case the negotiations collapsed. In other words, the EU's internal lack of consensus weakened its strategic position. Another contextual factor that had a similar influence was the move of the negotiations from the first to the third pillar. The challenge and interference of the European Parliament in the regime-formation process confirmed that the identity of participants and the negotiation arithmetic are not always fixed issues and that they can be fluid. The only instance in which the EU's strategic position was enhanced was when the context changed with the enter into force of the Lisbon Treaty, which introduced a veto actor in the EU–US negotiations and thus changed the power dynamic of the two actors.

Data protection was the main issue of conflict in the negotiations. This issue was a distributive issue where losses for one party amounted to gains for the other party. The interactions for this issue included threats and coercion, especially the threat of defection on behalf of the US. Given the above-mentioned weak EU strategic position, the EU had more need of an agreement than the US had, and the EU conceded as a result to the US demands.

The US strengthened its demands with the idea and focal point that the US and EU data protection systems offered the same protections to individuals despite the differences in these systems. This focal point supported the US interests, highlighting thus the presence of synergistic effects between the social factors of interests and knowledge.

The above suggest that knowledge and power were the prominent characteristics of the regime-formation process between the two sides. At the same time, the US too made several concessions, in order that the concluded deal would be perceived as fair and equitable by the EU.

To sum up, this chapter answered the question of how the EU and the US cooperated on internal security issues by looking at the PNR negotiations. While structural leadership and knowledge factors had a major role in influencing the two sides' interactions and regime-formation processes, these interactions and negotiations were also based on a minimum level of joint benefits for the two parties. The next chapter will provide the conclusion for this book by making a comparative analysis of the four empirical chapters.

Notes

1 Later renamed Computer Assisted Passenger Pre-Screening (CAPPS).
2 In the words of Richard Falkenrath, who at that time was head of the White House Office for Homeland Security,

> our agenda for border security is really a sort of revolutionary one, where we work with our international partners so that we can together screen out the low-risk traffic.... And then zero in on the higher-risk people and vehicles and cargos, so that those are the ones we can inspect and look at.
>
> (Federal News Service 2002)

3 The US Visa Waiver Program (VWP) was a program that lifted the visa requirement for nationals of certain countries. After the 2004 EU enlargement, the EU members that were not part of the VWP were all the new member states and Greece.

References

Agence France-Presse (2004) 'European Parliament head seeks to overturn EU–US passenger data deal', 25 June 2004.
Agence France-Presse (2006a) 'EU, US officials: New agreement will be reached on passenger data', 30 May 2006.
Agence France-Presse (2006b) 'US sends air passenger-data draft agreement to EU', 1 October 2006.
Agence France-Presse (2006c) 'EU, US Clinch air passenger data deal', 6 October 2006
Agence France-Presse (2006d) 'US likely to demand more passenger travel data', 17 October 2006.
Agence France-Presse (2007) 'EU justice chief urges European air passenger data system', 3 July 2007.
Agence France-Presse (2010) 'US seeks to persuade EU deputies to back terror data deal', 8 March 2010.
Agence France-Presse (2011) 'EU, US pen new passenger data deal to ease privacy fears', 10 November 2011.
Associated Press International (2003) 'Top EU official urges more concessions from US ahead of key talks on sharing airline passenger data', 9 September 2003.
Associated Press International (2006a) 'EU justice, interior ministers study plans to salvage trans-Atlantic passenger data deal with US', 2 June 2006.
Associated Press International (2006b) 'EU likely to close deal with Washington on new anti-terror passenger data', 27 September 2006.
Associated Press International (2007) 'EU ambassadors back deal with US on sharing air passenger data', 29 June 2007.
Aviation Daily (2006a) 'Court Scraps European Union-US Passenger Data Agreement', 31 May 2006.
Aviation Daily (2006b) 'EU, US Hope to Reach Interim Agreement On PNR Data Transfer', 27 September 2006.
Baker, S. (2010) *Skating on Stilts: Why We Aren't Stopping Tomorrow's Terrorism*. Stanford: Hoover Institution Press.
Bolkenstein, F. (2003a) 'Meeting of Parliament's LIBE Committee, Speaking note for Mr Bolkenstein on US/EU talks on PNR', 5 September 2003.
Bolkenstein, F. (2003b) 'Letter to DHS Secretary Thomas Ridge', 18 December 2003.

Bruggeman, W. (1997a) 'Policing in Europe: A New Wave?', in M. Den Boer (ed.) *The Implementation of Schengen: First the Widening, Now the Deepening*. Maastricht: European Institute of Public Administration, pp. 111–128.

Bruggeman, W. (1997b) 'The State of Cooperation between Relevant Authorities within the EU Framework', *Trends in Organized Crime* (3), pp. 57–60.

Council of the EU (2001) 'Outcome of Proceedings-Strategic Committee on Immigration, Frontiers and Asylum-Meeting with United States', 13803/01, 26 October 2001.

Council of the EU (2002) 'Plan for the management of the external borders of the Member States of the European Union', 10019/02, 14 June 2002.

Council of the EU (2003) 'Completing the provisions of article 26 of the Schengen Implementing Convention and of the Council Directive 2001/51/CE of 28 June 2001', 5174/03, 9 January 2003.

Council of the EU (2006) 'Decision on the signing, on behalf of the European Union, of an Agreement between the European Union and the United States of America on the processing and transfer of passenger name record (PNR) data by air carriers to the United States Department of Homeland Security', 13226/06, 11 October 2006.

Council of the EU (2007) 'Decision 2007/551/CFSP/JHA of 23 July 2007 on the signing, on behalf of the European Union, of an Agreement between the European Union and the United States of America on the processing and transfer of Passenger Name Record (PNR) data by air carriers to the United States Department of Homeland Security (DHS) (2007 PNR Agreement)', OJ L 204/16, 4 August 2007.

Council of the EU (2011) 'Agreement between the United States of America and the European Union on the use and transfer of passenger name records to the United States Department of Homeland Security', 17434/11, 8 December 2011.

Den Boer, M. (ed.) (1997a) *Schengen, Judicial Cooperation and Policy Coordination*. Maastricht: European Institute of Public Administration.

Den Boer, M. (ed.) (1997b) *The Implementation of Schengen: First the Widening, Now the Deepening*. Maastricht: European Institute of Public Administration.

De Busser, E. (2009) *Data Protection in EU and US Criminal Cooperation*. Antwerp: Maklu.

De Kerchove, G. (1997) 'Les progrès des groupes de travail du troisième pilier en matière de coopération judiciaire Schengen', *Judicial Cooperation and Policy Coordination*. Maastricht: European Institute of Public Administration.

Elias, B. (2010) *Airport and Aviation Security: US Policy and Strategy in the Age of Global Terrorism*. Boca Raton: Auerbach Publications.

EUobserver (2003) 'US presses European airlines on data access', 10 September 2003.

EUobserver (2004) 'EU court asked to rule on EU–US data agreement', 21 April 2004.

EUobserver (2007) 'Counter-terrorism sparks hot debate in EU parliament', 5 September 2007.

EUobserver (2008a) 'US flight security demands ruffle EU feathers', 11 February 2008.

EUobserver (2008b) 'Brussels attacks new US security demands', 14 February 2008.

EUobserver (2010a) 'MEPs look to new data protection battle with US', 7 July 2010.

EUobserver (2010b) 'Reding slams US over data privacy', 21 December 2010.

EUobserver (2011a) 'EU to collect data of international air travellers', 1 February 2011.

EUobserver (2011b) 'Unhappy MEPs to approve passenger data deal', 11 November 2011.

European Report (2003a) 'EU/US: Commission Toughens Stance in Passenger Data Transfer Row', 6 September 2003.

European Report (2003b) 'EU/United States: Air Passenger Data Transfer Deal in the Offing', 20 December 2003.

Passenger name record agreements 143

European Report (2006a) 'EU/US: Transfer of Air Passenger Data on G-8 Agenda', 14 June 2006.
European Report (2006b) 'EU/US: Passenger Name Records: European Airlines in Legal Limbo', 3 October 2006.
European Report (2006c) 'EU/US: Frattini Defends Deal on Passenger Data', 9 October 2006.
European Report (2006d) 'EU/US: New PNR Pact Leaves Questions Unanswered', 20 October 2006.
European Report (2007a) 'Justice and Home Affairs: US Pushes EU to Drop Guard on Air Data Transfers', 16 May 2007.
European Report (2007b) 'EU/US: MEPs accuse US of Undermining Fair Data Negotiations', 25 May 2007.
European Report (2007c) 'EU–US: Concerns Expressed on Airline Passenger Data Deal', 3 July 2007.
European Report (2008) 'EU/US: Ministers Fail to Find Unity on US Visa Deals', 29 February 2008.
European Commission (2002) 'Towards Integrated Management of the External Borders of the Member States of the European Union', COM (2002) 233, 7 May 2002.
European Commission (2003) 'Transfer of Air Passenger Name Record (PNR) Data: A Global EU Approach', COM (2003) 826, 16 December 2003.
European Commission (2011) 'Frequently Asked Questions: the new EU–US agreement on the transfer of Passenger Name Record (PNR) data', MEMO/11/797, 17 November 2011.
European Commission–US (2003) 'Talks on PNR Transmission Brussels, 17/18 February Joint Statement', 17–18 February 2003.
European Community–US (2004) 'Agreement between the European Community and the United States of America on the processing and transfer of PNR data by air carriers to the United States Department of Homeland Security, Bureau of Customs and Border Protection', 28 May 2004.
European Council (2001) 'Presidency Conclusions European Council meeting in Laeken 14 and 15 December 2001', 14–15 December 2001.
European Court of Justice (2006) 'Judgment of the Court (Grand Chamber) of 30 May 2006. European Parliament v Council of the European Union (C-317/04) and Commission of the European Communities (C-318/04)', European Court Reports 2006 I-04721, 30 May 2006.
European Union (1995) 'Directive 95/46/EC of the European Parliament and of the Council of 24 October 1995 on the protection of individuals with regard to the processing of personal data and on the free movement of such data', OJ L 281/31, 23 November 1995.
EU Article 29 Data Protection Working Party (2002) 'Opinion 6/2002 on transmission of Passenger Manifest Information and other data from Airlines to the United States', 11647/02/EN, WP66, 24 October 2002.
EU–US (2006) 'Agreement between the European Union and the United States of America on the processing and transfer of passenger name record (PNR) data by air carriers to the United States Department of Homeland Security', OJ L 298/29, 27 October 2006.
EU–US (2007) 'Agreement between the European Union and the United States of America on the processing and transfer of Passenger Name Record (PNR) data by air carriers to the United States Department of Homeland Security (DHS) (2007 PNR Agreement)', OJ L 204/18, 4 August 2007.

Europolitics (2009) 'EU/US: Tensions Bubble Over Planned New Data Sharing Pact', 23 October 2009.
Europolitics (2010a) 'EU/US: Crunch Time Dawns for MEPs on Data Transfer Deals', 5 January 2010.
Europolitics (2010b) 'EU/US: Counter-Terrorism Agreements: MEPs Up Pressure on Passenger Data', 8 March 2010.
Europolitics (2010c) 'EU/US: Commission Seeks Comprehensive Data Protection Agreement', 27 May 2010.
Europolitics (2011) 'EU/US: Fresh Hopes for Full Visa Reciprocity', 16 June 2011.
Federal News Service (2002) 'State Department Foreign Press Center Briefing with Richard Falkenrath, Senior Director, Office of Homeland Security', 5 September 2002.
Federal News Service (2004) 'National Press Club Luncheon with Tom Ridge, Secretary of Homeland Security. Subject: "America since 9/11: Stronger, Safer, Better"', 7 September 2004.
Federal News Service (2006) 'Hearing of the Terrorism, Technology and Homeland Security Subcommittee of the Senate Judiciary Committee, Subject: Keeping Terrorists off the Plane: Strategies for Pre-Screening International Passengers Before Takeoff', 7 September 2006.
Federal News Service (2007a) 'Remarks by Secretary Michael Chertoff, Department of Homeland Security to the Johns Hopkins Paul N. Nitze School of Advanced International Studies; Subject: Addressing Transnational Threats in the 21st Century', 3 May 2007.
Federal News Service (2007b) 'Remarks by Secretary of Homeland Security Michael Chertoff to the European Parliament (As Released by the Department of Homeland Security)', 15 May 2007.
Federal News Service (2010a) 'Hearing of the Senate Homeland Security and Governmental Affairs Committee; Subject: "Lessons and Implications of the Christmas Day Attack: Securing the Visa Process"', 21 April 2010.
Federal News Service (2010b) 'Atlantic Council of the United States (ACUS) Meeting; Subject: "Transatlantic Security, Data Sharing and Privacy Protections: A US-EU Dialogue"', 8 July 2010.
Federal News Service (2011a) 'Hearing of the Europe and Eurasia Subcommittee of the House Foreign Affairs Committee; Subject: Overview of Security in Europe and Eurasia', 5 May 2011.
Federal News Service (2011b) 'Prepared Remarks of Attorney General Eric Holder to the European Parliament's Committee On Civil Liberties, Justice, And Home Affairs Location: Brussels, Belgium', 20 September 2011.
Flynn, S. (2003) 'The False Conundrum: Continental Integration vs. Homeland Security', in P. Andreas and T. Biersteker (eds) *Rebordering of North America: Integration and Exclusion in a New Security Context*. Abingdon: Routledge, pp. 110–127.
Guardian (2011) 'Reply: Response Don't ignore the value of air passenger data in fighting crime: Our information swap with the US protects both civil liberties and human life', 10 June 2011.
Haas, P. (1992) 'Introduction: epistemic communities and international policy coordination', *International Organization*, 46(1), pp. 1–35.
Haas, P. (1993) 'Epistemic Communities and the Dynamics of International Environmental Co-Operation', in V. Rittberger (ed.) *Regime Theory and International Relations*. Oxford: Oxford University Press, pp. 168–201.
Hasbrouck, E. (2010) 'Testimony to Members of the European Parliament', 8 April 2010, https://hasbrouck.org/blog/archives/001855.html, accessed 5 April 2016.

Hasbrouck, E. (2004) 'Northwest Airlines gave NASA millions of PNRs,' 18 January 2004, https://hasbrouck.org/blog/archives/000114.html, accessed 5 April 2016.
Independent (2006) 'Court stops US getting passengers' details', 31 May 2006.
International Herald Tribune (2006a) 'EU and US plan deal to share traveller data; Wide-ranging accord expected in weeks', 1 September 2006.
International Herald Tribune (2006b) 'EU and US set accord on sharing travel data; Europe will provide passenger details only upon request', 7 October 2006.
Interview EU (2012a) Interview with EU official, 9 February 2012.
Interview EU (2012b) Interview with EU official, 16 May 2012.
Interview EU (2012c) Interview with EU official, 4 December 2012.
Interview EU (2012d) Interview with EU official, 7 December 2012.
Interview EU (2013) Interview with EU official, 14 May 2013.
Interview US (2012a) Interview with US official, 25 January 2012.
Interview US (2012b) Interview with US official, 25 January 2012.
Interview US (2012c) Interview with US official, 6 February 2012.
Interview US (2012d) Interview with US official, 7 February 2012.
Krouse, W. and Elias, B. (2009) 'Terrorist Watchlist Checks and Air Passenger Pre-screening,' Report for Congress RL33645, 30 December 2009. Congressional Research Service.
Mitsilegas, V., Monar, J. and Rees, W. (2003) *The European Union and Internal Security: Guardian of the People?* Basingstoke: Palgrave Macmillan.
New York Times (2004) 'FBI Got Records on Air Travellers', 1 May 2004.
O'Neill, M. (2010) 'The Issue of Data Protection and Data Security in the (Pre-Lisbon) EU Third Pillar', *Journal of Contemporary European Research*, 6(2), pp. 211–235.
States News Service (2007) 'Remarks by Homeland Security Secretary Michael Chertoff at Institute of European Affairs', 18 December 2007.
States News Service (2011a) 'Testimony of David Heyman, Assistant Secretary, Office of Policy, Before the House Committee on Homeland Security Subcommittee on Counterterrorism and Intelligence: "Intelligence Sharing and Terrorist Travel: How DHS Addresses the Mission of Providing Security, Facilitating Commerce and Protecting Privacy for Passengers Engaged in International Travel"', 5 October 2011.
States News Service (2011b), 'Frequently Asked Questions: The New EU–US Agreement on the Transfer of Passenger Name Record (PNR) Data', 17 November 2011.
Statewatch (2003a), 'Massive majority in European Parliament against deal with US on access to passenger data', 12 March 2003.
Statewatch (2003b), 'European Commission tells USA that demands for access to data on airline passengers breaches EU Data Protection Directive – but hints at a deal that would "fudge" the issue', 18 September 2003.
UK House of Lords (2005) 'After Madrid: The EU's Response to Terrorism,' Fifth Report, HL Paper 53, 8 March 2005.
UK House of Lords (2007) 'The EU/US Passenger Name Record (PNR) Agreement', Twenty-First Report, HL Paper 108, 5 June 2007.
UK House of Lords (2008) 'The Passenger Name Record (PNR) Framework Decision', Fifteenth Report HL Paper 106, 11 June 2008.
US Cable (2003) 'Italy's EU Presidency: US/EU Task Force Discussions', Cable #03ROME3360, 23 July 2003, http://wikileaks.redfoxcenter.org/cable/2003/07/03ROME3360.html, accessed 10 July 2016.

US Cable (2004) 'Scene-setter for June 25 visit of DHS Deputy Secretary Admiral Loy', Cable #04BRUSSELS2589, 17 June 2004, http://wikileaks.redfoxcenter.org/cable/2004/06/04BRUSSELS2589.html, accessed 10 July 2016.

US Cable (2006a) 'UK Passenger Name Recognition Contingency Planning,' Cable #06LONDON5097, 12 July 2006, http://wikileaks.redfoxcenter.org/cable/2006/07/06LONDON5097.html, accessed 10 July 2016.

US Cable (2006b) 'Czech Republic: Positive on PNR Collection', Cable #06PRAGUE804, 14 July 2006, http://wikileaks.redfoxcenter.org/cable/2006/07/06PRAGUE804.html, accessed 10 July 2016.

US Cable (2006c) 'Air France on PNR, No-Fly and CNIL', Cable #06PARIS5958, 6 September 2006, http://wikileaks.redfoxcenter.org/cable/2006/09/06PARIS5958.html, accessed 11 July 2016.

US Cable (2006d) 'DHS Counselor Rosenzweig Pushes for CT progress in Berlin', Cable #06BERLIN2654, 12 September 2006, http://wikileaks.redfoxcenter.org/cable/2006/09/06BERLIN2654.html, accessed 11 July 2016.

US Cable (2006e) 'Passenger Data Sharing Views as Old Agreement Expires', Cable #06ROME2724, 27 September 2006, http://wikileaks.redfoxcenter.org/cable/2006/09/06ROME2724.html, accessed 11 July 2016.

US Cable (2006f) 'DHS A/S Baker Engages on PNR, seeks Greater CT Info Sharing', Cable #06BERLIN3173, 31 October 2006, http://wikileaks.redfoxcenter.org/cable/2006/10/06BERLIN3173.html, accessed 11 July 2016.

US Cable (2007) 'US, European Union Conclude Negotiations on A Passenger Name Record (PNR) Agreement', Cable #07STATE97237, 12 July 2007, http://wikileaks.redfoxcenter.org/cable/2007/07/07STATE97237.html, accessed 12 July 2016.

US Cable (2010) 'DHS Sec. Napolitano Addresses EU's JHA Ministers on Aviation Security', Cable #10MADRID190, 19 February 2010, http://wikileaks.redfoxcenter.org/cable/2010/02/10MADRID190.html, accessed 12 July 2016.

US Congress (2001) 'Aviation and Transportation Security Act', 107–171, 19 November 2001.

US Congress (2002) 'Enhanced Border Security and Visa Entry Reform Act of 2002', 107–173, 14 May 2002.

US Congress (2004) 'Intelligence Reform and Terrorism Prevention Act of 2004', 108–458, 17 December 2004.

US Congress (2007) 'United States Implementing Recommendations of the 9/11 Commission Act of (2007)', 110–153, 3 August 2007.

US Customs Today (2003), February 2003.

US Department of Homeland Security (2005) 'Privacy Impact Assessment for the Advance Passenger Information System (APIS)', 21 March 2005.

US Department of Homeland Security (2006) 'National Strategy for Aviation Security', 20 June 2006.

US Fed News (2006a) 'PNR: Franco Frattini, Updates MEPS on talks with USA', 13 September 2006.

US Fed News (2006b) 'Privacy Rights Need to be Respected – Even in Police Cooperation', 27 September 2006.

US National Commission on Terrorist Attacks Upon the United States (2004) 'The 9/11 Commission Report', 2004.

US Office of Homeland Security (2002) 'National Strategy for Homeland Security', July 2002.

Washington Post (2003) 'EU Agrees to Share Airline Passenger Data', 17 December 2003.
Washington Post (2006) 'A Tool We Need to Stop the Next Airliner Plot', 29 August 2006.
Young, O. (1994) *International Governance: Protecting the Environment in a Stateless Society*. Ithaca: Cornell University Press.
Young, O. (1998) *Creating Regimes: Arctic Accords and International Governance*. Ithaca: Cornell University Press.

Conclusion

The main aim of this book is to examine how the EU and the US negotiated a number of agreements in the period after the 9/11 attacks in the area of internal security. As was shown in the introduction, the literature on EU–US counter-terrorism relations has focused predominantly on the PNR agreements. Additionally, the majority of the literature has focused on the EU and the possible influence of the US on the EU's own rules and security measures, rather than on the transatlantic relationship itself. The inclusion of three additional cases in this book, as well as the focus on the EU–US negotiations, allows a deeper understanding of the EU–US relationship in the field of internal security.

To answer the above research question, a conceptual framework based on regime theory has been employed. Theories of regime formation provide a fruitful theoretical framework for explaining how actors cooperate and establish international arrangements. The choice of this theoretical framework has also been justified by previous research, which employed theories of international regimes in the analysis of EU–US relations and global counter-terrorism cooperation.

The main finding of this book is that transatlantic regime formation in the issue-area of internal security was ultimately a negotiated process rather than an imposed process by the US. In this process, all the three social forces of power, interests, and knowledge played a role, and political context was an additional influential factor. The first part of this chapter will present the findings of this book, a comparison of the cases examined, and the implications for EU–US internal security and counter-terrorism cooperation and for EU counter-terrorism. Subsequently, suggestions for further research will be presented.

Comparison of the cases and implications for transatlantic relations and for the EU

The main research question of this book is how the EU and the US cooperated on internal security matters. From a regime-theory perspective, this question is rephrased to how the EU–US internal security regime emerged. The central finding of this research is that the transatlantic regime emerged through a process of bargaining that was shaped by the social forces of power, interests and knowledge, and by contextual factors. This section expands on the above main finding, makes a comparison of the four cases examined, and highlights the contribution of this book to the literature.

Comparison of the cases

The main finding of this book is that all cases were akin to a process of institutional bargaining on the basis of a minimum level of common interests. This result confirms previous findings that cases of mere imposition in the emergence of international regimes are rare (Young and Osherenko 1993: 247; Young 1994: 82; Levy *et al.* 1995: 282). In particular, the role of knowledge as a social factor influencing the process of regime formation was most prominent in the cases of customs security and PNR. The EU and the US shared the same customs security principles: multi-layered risk management, trade facilitation, and international cooperation. They also agreed as early as 2003 on the utility of using air passengers' data for law enforcement purposes. In accordance with the literature on regime formation (Young 1994: 84, 98, 1998: 169–170), knowledge was more important at the agenda-setting stage of these two cases, when actors faced an uncertain security environment and issues and problems were framed for discussion. The greater role of knowledge in these cases is in line with the proposition in the literature that knowledge factors are more influential in highly technical and specialised issue-areas (Haas 1993: 179).

With regard to power, this was the most important factor in the case of PNR while in the cases of Europol and customs security, power was influential along with the social factors of interests and knowledge respectively. In these cases, the US used, among others, threats in order to ensure compliance from other actors, including the EU, in a process akin to Krasner's power-based regime formation where one actor adjusts to the preferences of the other (Krasner 1991; Krasner 1993). According to Krasner, 'the actor less in need of cooperation (usually the one with the greater overall capabilities) can get his (or her) way' by threatening to defect from the negotiations (Krasner 1976: 320, 1991: 363; Hasenclever *et al.* 1997: 106). Indeed, in the PNR and Europol agreements Europol and the EU conceded to the US demands on data protection due to the costs that a US defection would occur. Structural leadership was also used by the EU officials when it started infringement procedures for the member states that signed separate customs security memorandums with the US. Such a move could have frustrated the US customs security measures and it played a role in the US change of stance.

Concerning the interest-based explanations of regime formation, they were more relevant for the MLA and extradition agreements, the negotiations for which unfolded mostly through quid-pro-quo mutual adjustment of the two actors and the use of side payments and compensations. This case highlighted also the weakness of power-based theories to account for cases where power, in the sense of material resources, cannot be translated into bargaining leverage. For example, the strategic position that an actor holds with regard to a specific

Table C.1 Comparison of the cases

Social factors	Cases				
	Customs security	Judicial cooperation (MLA and extradition agreements)	Law enforcement cooperation (Europol–US agreements)	PNR agreements
Power	Penalties for non-compliance with the US 24-hour rule		Threat of defection by the US	US sanctions for non-compliant airlines
	Legal proceedings of the EU against member states and US adaptation due to fear of costs		Distributive bargaining for data protection	Threat of defection by the US
	EU threats regarding the US 100 per cent scanning rule		EU adaptation due to fear of costs	Tactical connection of the PNR issue with the visa-waiver programme by the US
				Distributive bargaining for data protection
				EU having a weak strategic position
				EU adaptation due to fear of costs
Interests	The US CSI providing benefits to the participating states	EU highlighting the joint benefits of an EU–US agreement	The entrepreneurial efforts of Europol officials for the conclusion of agreements with third states	EU strategic position increasing with the emergence of the European Parliament as a veto power (third PNR agreement)
	EU highlighting the benefits from an EU-wide agreement	Strong strategic position of the EU	Common interests to be gained from the agreements	Common interests to be gained from the agreements
	EU competencies on customs security (first pillar) increasing EU's strategic position	Common interests to be gained from the agreements	US concessions increasing the equitability of the agreements	US concessions increasing the equitability of the agreements
	Common interests to be gained from the agreements	US concessions increasing the equitability of the agreements		

Knowledge	Concept of 'smart borders' The EU reports presented to the US Congress regarding the 100 per cent scanning rule Shared customs security principles	EU borrowing ideas from its own MLA convention The EU stance on previous data protection-related agreements shaping EU's response The US focal point regarding data protection	The US focal point regarding data protection	Concept of 'smart borders' The US focal point regarding data protection The 'persuasion' campaign in the European Parliament by the US Shared EU–US principles
Context	9/11 attacks changing threat perceptions Implementation of EU's AEO in all member states (2008) 2006 US Congress elections	9/11 attacks changing political priorities	9/11 attacks changing political priorities	9/11 attacks changing threat perceptions Negotiating the second and third PNR agreements under the third pillar after the ECJ decision Lisbon Treaty entering into force
Interaction effects	The post-9/11 security environment and threat perceptions shaping the actors' interests (knowledge-interests) The 'smart borders' concept underlying the US entrepreneurial and structural measures (power-knowledge and knowledge-interests)	The US focal point supporting the US interests (interests-knowledge)	The US focal point supporting the US interests (interests-knowledge)	The post-9/11 security environment and threat perceptions shaping the actors' interests (knowledge-interests) The 'smart borders' concept underlying the US structural measures (power-knowledge) The US focal point supporting the US interests (interests-knowledge)

issue-area can give it the ability to extract concessions from more powerful actors, and contextual factors can intervene in the exercise of structural leadership (as well of entrepreneurial and intellectual leadership) (Young and Osherenko 1993: 247–248; Young 1994: 128). This was the case in the MLA and extradition agreements, where the ability of EU member states to veto any agreement in the Council, as well as the willingness of some states, such as France, to use their veto were combined with the fact that it would be costlier for the US to leave the table of negotiations and to work directly with member states than to negotiate with the EU as a whole. Similarly, the first PNR agreement was negotiated by the EU under the framework of the first pillar, which allowed a greater role for data protection authorities. This meant that the EU warnings that if negotiations collapsed legal chaos would ensue had more credibility compared to similar warnings in the subsequent PNR negotiations. As a result of the above factors, the EU's bargaining leverage was enhanced despite the fact that, from a power-based perspective, the US was a more powerful law enforcement actor in terms of material resources.

The greater role of power in the cases of the PNR and Europol agreements is related to the fact that in these negotiations the issue of data protection was prominent. Data protection was essentially a distributive issue and this gave rise to the use of tactics such as coercion and threats, confirming thus the power-based approaches. In particular, the topic of data protection was the issue that created the most friction in the EU–US negotiations, and both the EU and the US interviewees highlighted that it was the single most important problem the two sides faced.

From a regime-theory perspective, the likelihood of success in the conclusion of agreements increases when it is difficult for the actors to determine in advance the exact costs and benefits of the various solutions of a given problem (Young 1994: 107–108). This uncertainty gives rise to integrative bargaining, where actors try to devise mutually beneficial solutions. In contrast, when it is clear from the beginning among the actors that on a given issue there will be 'winners and losers who are comparatively easy to identify' then distributive bargaining will ensue and the conclusion of a deal will be more difficult (ibid.: 108). The nature of the EU–US conflict on data protection was such that it was clear from the start of the negotiations that any European gains in the direction of data protection would harm the US preference for unhindered data exchange, use and flows and vice versa. This characteristic of the EU–US data protection conflict gave rise to distributive bargaining and it prolonged the two sides' negotiations.

With regard to the role of political context, all the cases examined in this book show that the terrorist attacks of 9/11 worked as a catalyst for the intensification of EU–US cooperation. From a regime-theory perspective, it has been noted that exogenous shocks or crises can precipitate the formation of regimes and increase the likelihood of success in institutional bargaining: global and national events (contextual factors) can 'play a major role in determining if and when international co-operation' will emerge (Young and Osherenko 1993: 251). For the knowledge-based school in particular, exogenous shocks are

Conclusion 153

important in that they 'undermine the existing order', creating an uncertain environment for policymakers (Goldstein and Keohane 1993: 17). In these circumstances, policymakers may adopt new ideas and initiate regime-formation processes (Hasenclever *et al.* 1997: 143). Exogenous shocks create the conditions in which the social factor of knowledge can play a bigger role in regime formation.

In the four cases discussed in this book, the 9/11 attacks worked as a shock changing the threat perceptions in the US and Europe. On customs security, the international supply chains in the post-9/11 period were not only perceived as vital components of transatlantic trade but also as a potential security liability. While in the pre-9/11 era the air passenger name records were used by airlines predominantly for commercial purposes, in the aftermath of the 9/11 attacks this commercial tool started being used by government authorities for security purposes. Finally, judicial and law enforcement cooperation between the EU and the US emerged at the top of the political agenda of both actors, while previously the priorities of both the EU and the US were different. The impact of the shock of the 9/11 attacks was obviously greater in the US, but the attacks had also a significant influence among both EU officials and officials from member states. For example, member states such as France that were previously objecting to the establishment of closer links with the US changed their stance.

Additionally, the cases revealed the presence of interaction effects between the social factors of power, knowledge, and interests. Knowledge can influence the way problems and issues are perceived and framed for discussion and thus shape the interests of actors (Hasenclever *et al.* 1997: 145). The conceptualisation of knowledge as a factor that shapes actors' interests has addressed previous criticisms that theories of regimes did not analyse interest formation. According to knowledge-based theories, knowledge becomes part of the causal chain that links interests and outcomes, addressing the issue of how interests were formed in the first place (ibid.: 216–217). For example, in the case of customs security, the new post-9/11 knowledge comprised of new threat perceptions regarding the international supply chains and of the 'smart borders' solution to these threats. This body of knowledge shaped US interests, and through this learning process the existent policies and measures on customs security were no longer deemed adequate.

In the above example, the role of knowledge was direct and independent of the negotiation process. In addition to this role, knowledge and ideas can be used by actors tactically in order to support their interests and positions during the bargaining process (Young 1994: 97–98). In this case, knowledge plays an indirect role supporting the other two social forces. For example, when disagreements emerged on data protection issues the principle that the US was promoting was that their own and European laws offered the same level of protection to individuals' data privacy, despite the differences between the US and the European approaches to data protection. This principle, however, apart from being highly debatable, also negated any European attempt to instil data protection provisions into the negotiated agreements. In other words, this was part of the overall US tactical plan, along with threats or side payments, to avoid making concessions on data protection issues.

An additional issue that affected the EU–US relationship was the US ambivalence towards working with the EU on internal security matters. In terms of the theories of international regimes and in accordance with Young (1994: 123), the US ambivalence and the EU efforts to showcase the importance and the benefits of having a direct bilateral link with Brussels showed that the negotiation arithmetic, or the issue of which actor would participate in the negotiations for a regime, were not neutral issues but rather part of a political process. Similar to the findings of Romaniuk (Romaniuk 2010: 5–6) concerning multilateralism and global counter-terrorism cooperation, the US behaviour was akin to forum-shopping, where the US officials calculated which avenue of cooperation would confer the biggest benefits. The fact that the EU competencies in certain areas circumscribed the US' options confirmed Young's suggestion that even powerful actors 'often have difficulty controlling the formation of the agenda and the identification of participants in the formation of international regimes' (Young 1994: 123).

To sum up, all cases showed that explanations that are based on one single factor do not have strong explanatory value and that a model based on all three social factors (power, interests, and knowledge) and on the influence of the political context, as the one employed for this research, can be more useful in explaining the negotiation and emergence of regimes (Haas 1993: 169; Young and Osherenko 1993: 247; Hasenclever et al. 1997: 216).

Implications for transatlantic relations and for the EU

On the one hand, this research has shown that the European Union could be described as a partner of the US rather than as a 'pushover', given the commonality of the two sides' interests and the shared EU–US counter-terrorism principles and approaches. On the other hand, there were several instances where the ability of the EU to extract concessions from the US and to shape the agenda of the negotiations was limited. Therefore, this book argues that the relationship between the EU and the US is more complex than what is usually presented in parts of the literature, which tend to overemphasise the reactive and passive nature of the EU in its relations with the US (Pawlak 2007, 2009a, 2009b; Argomaniz 2009), confirming the previous findings of Kaunert (2009), Occhipinti (2010) and Kaunert and Léonard (2011).

In particular, in customs security and in judicial cooperation (the MLA and extradition agreements), the EU–US relationship resembles more closely a partnership. While in the literature on transatlantic counter-terrorism the EU is usually depicted as a reactive actor (Pawlak 2007, Pawlak 2009b; Argomaniz 2009), in these two cases the EU had a proactive role: both the EU–US Mutual Recognition Agreement (for the two sides' business-to-government customs security programmes) and the mutual legal assistance agreement were EU initiatives. Regarding the case of the Europol–US agreements, both partnership and imposition were characteristics of the two actors' negotiations and agreements. Finally, the PNR agreements were closer to an imposed relationship, though the EU interests were served too through the promise of intelligence flows from the US to European countries and through several US concessions regarding data protection.

Additionally, all cases show that the US is ambivalent regarding the relationship with the EU. On the one hand, the US wanted to benefit from EU integration on internal security matters. For instance, Europol produced strategic analyses, based on information from all member states, which the US could not have access to unless it liaised with the European organisation. On the other hand, the US did not want to break long-established bilateral law enforcement relationships with the security agencies of member states. The US officials feared that cultivating closer relations with the EU in the field of internal security might undermine these bilateral links. Therefore, the US had to calculate in each case whether cooperating with the EU would provide added value to the existing arrangements.

This means that any future cooperation between the US and the EU will depend on whether the EU can show that it can provide the added value that the US seeks. For this to happen further European integration in the area of internal security is important. Otherwise, if 'hard' intergovernmentalism dominates this field then the US will not have any interest in working at the EU level. For example, the recent expansion of Europol's cyber-security activities was followed by closer Europol–US cooperation in the same area.

This ambivalent stance of the US has been largely missed in the literature, where it has been assumed that the US would automatically have an interest in working with the EU. In fact, whether the US would negotiate an agreement with the EU or not was itself a product of bargaining. For example, in the legal assistance and extradition agreements and in the mutual recognition agreement for customs the EU had to persuade the US that working with Brussels would provide the added value that Washington sought. EU officials highlighted the efficiency-related gains that the US would have by negotiating with the EU rather than separately with several member states. Additionally, the US' range of options was limited by the EU's competencies. This was the case, for instance, in the US Container Security Initiative where initially Washington sought to sideline the EU and to conclude memorandums of cooperation directly with member states. The Commission challenged the legality of these memorandums and initiated legal proceedings against the member states that had signed them.

Regarding the implications of this book for EU counter-terrorism, an important issue that emerged in the cases examined is that of EU consistency and the relationship between the Commission, the member states, and the European Parliament on counter-terrorism. In particular, two main findings have emerged. Ensuring the consistency of the EU counter-terrorism policies and measures was central to the Commission's calculations on how to showcase and increase the value of the EU to and for the Americans. Moreover, the EU's

156 Conclusion

internal consistency (or lack of it) affected its bargaining power in the negotiations with the US. Regarding the first finding, it was during the agenda-formation stage of the cases examined that the Commission made an effort to frame the problems of transnational crime and terrorism as issues that are better addressed at an EU–US level. One of the central themes that appeared in the interviews with the EU officials was the concern of these officials about how the EU could appear more credible and consequently more attractive to the US at the initial stage of agenda setting.

The initiation of legal action by the Commission against the member states that signed deals with the US on customs security was one such example of the Commission's efforts to protect its institutional prerogatives and to ensure that member states and the Commission had a common stance towards the US. In addition to this example, the EU officials feared that the generally negative stance of the European Parliament on the data protection provisions of the EU–US agreements might alienate the US and disrupt the EU's efforts to gain the trust of the US. In the case of the PNR agreements, officials from the Commission often gave speeches in the European Parliament trying to moderate the radical voices and opinions that were raised by certain members and groups of the Parliament.

The UK referendum of 23 June 2016 in which British people voted in favour of leaving the EU could potentially affect the credibility of the EU as an international security actor and, as a result, the potential for closer EU–US relations on internal security. Despite the UK's right to opt-out of Justice and Home Affairs legislation, Britain has been the driver of many counter-terrorism initiatives of the EU (Bond et al. 2016: 11). The European Arrest Warrant, for example, has been an initiative of the then Home Secretary, Jack Straw (ibid.). A UK exit from the EU would also mean that the latter would lose access to Britain's vast intelligence resources, reducing the overall capacity of the EU to conduct all-sources strategic analyses and thus the EU's importance for the US. Moreover, on the important issue of data protection and privacy, the UK has traditionally been closer to the US views on that matter and it has tried to bridge transatlantic differences (ibid.: 12). For this reason, the exit of the UK from the EU could make the US reluctant to enhance its cooperation with the EU on internal security matters, choosing instead to rely on bilateral relations with member states.

Regarding the second finding that the EU's lack of internal consistency affected its bargaining power, the PNR agreements were a case in which some of the member states were ready to conclude bilateral deals with the US. In private negotiations with the Americans several European states revealed that if negotiations failed they would not initiate legal proceedings against airlines as the EU negotiators were highlighting to their American counterparts. This stance harmed the EU's bargaining power, in an example of the negative influence of an internal 'lack of consensus among ... policymakers regarding the issues at stake' (Young 1994: 125).

The above mean that treating the EU as a single unit misses the fact that there are often different voices and perspectives among the various EU bodies and the member states. Future cooperation and agreements of the EU with the US will depend not only on the perceived common interests between the US and the Commission or Council officials but also on the behaviour and stance of other potential veto actors. For example, the EU–US 'umbrella agreement', which sets the data protection rules for transatlantic law enforcement cooperation and which was signed on 2 June 2016, has to be ratified by the European Parliament (Council of the EU 2016).

Concerning the role of contextual factors, which is discussed in this book, recent examples confirm that these factors can influence the processes of regime formation. For instance, the Snowden revelations about the US National Security Agency (NSA) surveillance activities have affected negatively the transatlantic internal security relationship (*Wall Street Journal* 2014). In light of these revelations, the European Parliament asked for the suspension of the EU–US Terrorist Finance Tracking Program (TFTP), and the EU Commissioner for Home Affairs asked the US to give more details about how the American agencies use the data shared by Europeans (*International Business Times* 2013).

Moreover, one of the arguments of this book is that exogenous shocks and events, such as the 9/11 terrorist attacks, were crucial for the start of the EU–US internal security cooperation. The importance of such exogenous shocks for transatlantic security cooperation can also be seen in the case of the terrorist attacks of January and November 2015 against France. In February 2015, the US and Europol decided to establish closer cooperation for the identification of the financing and recruitment patterns of the foreign fighters who take part in the Syrian civil war and return subsequently to Europe (Funk and Trauner 2016: 2). Regarding the November 2015 attacks, Europol and the US established a joint force for the investigation of these attacks through the use of PNR and TFTP data (ibid.). Similarly, the European migrant crisis in the second half of 2015 and the danger that terrorists may enter EU through the migrant flows concerned the US, which has tried to persuade Europeans to share their data on the identity of migrants (ibid.).

The above mean that, in the absence of any critical events or emergencies, there is the danger that transatlantic internal security cooperation might stall. A similar pattern has been observed in the case of the EU's counter-terrorism policies, which are developed sporadically and driven mostly by external crises and windows of opportunities (Argomaniz 2011).

Suggestions for further research

This book's research on four cases of transatlantic internal security cooperation has also revealed three fruitful areas on which further research could be pursued. These areas include the effectiveness of transatlantic counter-terrorism cooperation, transatlantic cooperation on establishing global security standards, and the role of private actors in transatlantic internal security.

The effectiveness of the EU–US internal security cooperation

An important question is whether the transatlantic agreements have contributed to the solution of the problem for which they were established. In other words, to what extent can the EU–US internal security relationship and transatlantic counter-terrorism cooperation be characterised as effective? The assessment of counter-terrorism strategies and measures is inherently difficult given that causal relationships between, for example, the establishment of certain security measures and the subsequent reduction of crime or terrorism are difficult to establish (Bossong 2012: 139). Often states are reluctant to release information in public regarding the successes of their specific counter-terrorism programmes.

Regarding the MLA and extradition agreements, they were framework agreements that would be followed by the ratification of bilateral instruments between member states and the US. According to both EU and US officials the effectiveness of judicial cooperation increased; the more important gain being that the procedures were simplified by the removal of the need for practitioners to go through diplomatic channels (Interview US 2012; Interview EU 2012b). The provisions on banking information are also considered a major advance. As was expected, the EU member states predominantly use the MLA channel while the US is more interested in the extradition channel. In particular, Europeans ask for cyber evidence given that the majority of data providers are located in the US (Interview US 2012; Interview EU 2012b).

Problems are not absent however, most of them stemming from the differences between the legal systems. For example, there are differences on asset confiscation and on the standards of proof. Additionally, the huge volume of requests for cyber evidence by Europeans has resulted in a clogging in the system with the result that the US tries to promote alternative means through which Europeans can access this information (for example through direct contacts between private companies and practitioners) (Interview EU 2012b). Finally, there are different interpretations of what joint investigation teams should be and how they should operate (Interview US 2012). For these reasons the EU and the US promote common seminars and conferences through which European and American practitioners can be trained on the respective legal systems and build informal contacts.

Concerning Europol, the evaluation report on the implementation of the EU–US agreements noted that for the Americans Europol had limited value given that they could not access the agency's analytical files, which were the main point of interest for the US (Council of the EU 2005). The reason for that is that member states had not yet ratified the Protocols amending the Europol Convention, which allowed, among others, third states to have access to Europol's analytical files. This confirms one of the findings of this book about the linkage between European integration and the perceived international credibility of Europeans. The total correspondence (including requests from the US to Europol as well as Europol to the US) handled by Europol's liaison office in Washington more than doubled between 2002 and 2003. But, as a result of

Europol's limited usefulness, for the first two years after the conclusion of the agreements the majority of requests for information came from Europol to the US rather than the other way around. While the 9/11 terrorist attacks worked as a catalyst for the negotiation of the agreements, only 18.6 per cent of Europol's liaison office correspondence was about terrorism (Council of the EU 2005). Rather, drugs-related requests were the most numerous, with 32.7 per cent (Council of the EU 2005).

Despite this slow progress at the start of the cooperation, in the following years, the more that Europol acquired additional powers and competencies the more the US was interested in working with the agency. This was especially the case in the area of cyber-crime, where Europol has conducted a number of successful operations, some of them in partnership with the US (Archick 2016: 8). The fight against child pornography, banking fraud, and identity theft were some of the particular areas in which Europol built expertise over the years. The recognition of the value of Europol for the US is reflected in the fact that, as of December 2015, 10 US federal agencies had 25 employees in Europol's headquarters (Europol 2015b). In 2014, Europol together with the US conducted more than 600 operations (Europol 2015a). On average, it is estimated that every year Europol supports 500 cases involving US authorities (Archick 2016: 8).

Regarding the effectiveness of the exchange of PNR data, there is less data publicly available, apart from the examples mentioned by the US officials in their lobbying campaigns in the European Parliament. In 2003, for instance, a passenger was denied entrance to the US after suspicious patterns of activity were found through his PNR data. Two years later his fingerprints were found in a truck that was detonated in Iraq killing 132 people. However, according to one of the officials interviewed, PNR data is mainly used in practice for organised crime and especially in the areas of drug trafficking and trafficking of human beings (Interview EU 2012a).

Finally, from the cases examined by this book, customs security is the area with the most intense cooperation between the EU and the US. This reflects the fact that in this field the EU has stronger competencies than in the areas of law enforcement and judicial cooperation. Products of this cooperation include the Mutual Recognition Agreement, which was covered in this book, the Joint Statement on Supply Chain Security, and the expansion of the two sides' cooperation in the area of air cargo. Similar to the other cases, measures that were taken in the context of the fight against terrorism were actually used for counter-organised crime purposes.

The above indicate that what started as the emergence of a counter-terrorism regime developed in practice into a broader homeland security or internal security regime focused not only on terrorism but also on organised crime, smuggling of drugs, human trafficking, cyber security, and other threats. The Europol–US agreements and the agreements on customs security in particular worked as a basis for the expansion of the two sides' cooperation in other areas too. In this sense, and from a functionalist point of view, they moved beyond the practical problem from which they emerged (sharing of information and the application of CSI respectively) and they worked as facilitators of cooperation in general. This facilitator role was fulfilled, among others, through the creation of customs experts' groups in the case of customs security and the establishment of liaison posts in the case of Europol.

Among the cases, customs security has reached the most advanced level, resembling a similar process of integration in transatlantic economic relations. The EU and the US share common principles, they have recognised each other's business-to-government programmes, and they started establishing common standards for customs security (for example, common criteria for the risk analysis of containers). Additionally, they have committed themselves politically into expanding these standards globally in the relevant international organisations.

It is clear from the above that further research can be done on the effectiveness and on the output of the agreements negotiated. Practical questions that could be examined could include whether the innovative rules in the legal assistance agreements made cooperation swifter, or how joint investigations teams worked in practice.

EU–US cooperation on establishing global standards

This book has argued that the cooperation between the EU and the US on internal security matters could be conceptualised as a nascent regime and has amounted to a de facto integration project between the two sides. The implications of this cooperation are broader, in the sense that the security measures and standards that the EU and the US negotiated and adopted could potentially serve as international models and be exported globally in the form of international standards. Similar processes of informal global standard-setting have been identified in the area of international intelligence liaison (Svendsen 2008, 2011). Given that the EU and the US are the biggest and most influential actors in the field of internal security and counter-terrorism they could adopt a leadership role by engaging more actively with third states and international organisations. Through the combined weight of the EU and the US laggard states could be persuaded to implement counter-terrorism instruments and measures adopted by the United Nations or other organisations. The EU–US cooperation in establishing global standards could also be important for the avoidance of having overlapping and fragmented sets of rules, which create costs and inefficiencies for companies and make international cooperation more difficult.

Indeed, in the EU–US customs security agreement it was made explicit that the two sides would coordinate their position in the World Customs Organization. Similar consultations between the EU and the US started taking place in the area of aviation security and in the context of the International Civil Aviation Organisation. Whether the EU and the US will cooperate more closely in the establishment of global standards is contingent on whether they will prioritise this aim. While the US has often expressed doubts regarding the value of multilateral solutions in counter-terrorism the EU has given it a more central place.

Conclusion 161

Therefore, further research can be done on the export of global standards by the EU and the US in the area of counter-terrorism cooperation and internal security. Questions that could be examined are to what extent the two sides cooperate and coordinate their positions in international and multilateral fora such as the World Customs Organization or the United Nations, or to what extent the EU adoption of the US rules legitimises them and makes easier their adoption by third countries.

The role of private actors

The cases of the PNR agreements and the agreements on customs security revealed a number of insights regarding the role of private actors in regime formation and in the provision of security. Despite the fact that theories of international regimes have been criticised for having a state-centric view of global politics, scholars have noted that international organisations, non-governmental organisations, and private companies and actors can indeed have a significant influence on processes of regime formation, negotiation, and operationalisation (Haufler 1993; Young 1998: 22–23). From a security governance perspective, researchers have focused on the shift from government to governance and on how states cooperate not only with other states but also with non-state actors, such as international organisations and private companies, for the provision of security (Krahmann 2005). In the case of customs, for example, the EU and the US suggested that the huge security gaps in international supply chains can be addressed by giving incentives to private companies so as that they voluntarily adopt certain security standards. These incentives took the form of the Customs-Trade Partnership Against Terrorism (C-TPAT) and the Authorised Economic Operator (AEO) programmes in the US and the EU respectively. Similarly, in the PNR case, the airlines would allow the US law enforcement authorities to access the booking information that the airlines had previously collected for commercial purposes.

However, the inclusion of private actors in the post-9/11 security measures had a number of implications for the private sector. Linkages may emerge between different regimes when the rules and regulations that are negotiated in order to address a certain issue or problem have 'unintended consequences affecting other regimes' (Young 1994: 25). The EU has often expressed concerns that the US customs security measures might amount to non-tariff trade barriers affecting the international trade regime. The new roles envisioned for the private sector were accompanied by economic costs for the private companies, which had to adapt their modes of operation and possibly invest in new infrastructure. In the case of PNR, for example, the EU was advocating in favour of a 'push system' in which the airlines themselves would filter and send passengers' data to security authorities. This meant that the airlines had to develop and pay for such computer software. Similarly, with regard to the 100 per cent scanning regulation, the managing companies of ports as well as the shippers were concerned about the economic costs that this measure would have if implemented.

A related concern for the private sector was the potential emergence globally of multiple and overlapping security standards, which would mean that companies would have to comply each time with different sets of rules. Such fragmentation of global standards could create costs and inefficiencies for companies that operate globally. The initiative of the EU for the mutual recognition of the two sides' business-to-government customs security programmes was, indeed, partly motivated by a desire to avoid the duplication of customs security standards.

The concern of both the EU and the US for the implications of security measures for the private sector and the economy was reflected in the principle of trade facilitation that the two sides have adopted. The consensus among the EU and US officials has been that security and trade facilitation should not be seen as mutually exclusive. An example that was mentioned by the EU and the US interviewees was that the security-related obligation of shippers to report the content of their cargo in advance and through electronic means has helped shippers to manage the content and inventory of containers more effectively. In the US, in parallel with the vast array of security measures adopted in the area of air travelling, the Department of Homeland Security also established four 'trusted traveller' programmes, which allowed certain frequent travellers to have, among other things, expedited processing and screening across US borders. A similar initiative for an EU Registered Traveller Programme was launched by the European Commission in 2013.

Given the above, further research could be done on the role of private actors in the area of internal security and the interaction and relationship between economic regimes and security regimes (for example, one of the early accusations in Europe about the US customs security measures were that they amount to non-tariff trade barriers).

References

Archick, K. (2016) 'US-EU Cooperation Against Terrorism', Report for Congress RS22030, 2 March 2016. Congressional Research Service.
Argomaniz, J. (2009) 'When the EU is the "Norm-taker": The Passenger Name Records Agreement and the EU's Internalization of US Border Security Norms', *Journal of European Integration*, 31(1), pp. 119–136.
Argomaniz, J. (2011) *The EU and Counter-Terrorism*. Abingdon: Routledge.
Bond, I., Besch, S., Gostyńska-Jakubowska, A., Korteweg, R., Mortera-Martinez, C. and Tilford, S. (2016) 'Europe after Brexit: Unleashed or Undone?', Centre for European Reform, April 2016.
Bossong, R. (2012) *The Evolution of EU Counter-Terrorism: European Security Policy after 9/11*. Abingdon: Routledge.
Council of the EU (2005) 'Mutual evaluation of the cooperation agreements Europol–United States', 11502/05, 27 July 2005.
Council of the EU (2016) 'Enhanced data protection rights for EU citizens in law enforcement cooperation: EU and US sign "Umbrella agreement"', press release 305/16, 2 June 2016.

Europol (2015a) 'US Ambassador to the EU Visits Europol', 7 January 2015, www.europol.europa.eu/latest_news/us-ambassador-eu-visits-europol, accessed 12 July 2016.

Europol (2015b) 'Staff Statistics', December 2015, www.europol.europa.eu/content/page/staff-statistics-159, accessed 12 July 2016.

Funk, M. and Trauner, F. (2016) 'Transatlantic counter-terrorism cooperation', European Union Institute for Security Studies, April 2016.

Goldstein, J. and Keohane, R. (1993) 'Ideas and Foreign Policy: An Analytical Framework', in J. Goldstein and R. Keohane (eds) *Ideas and Foreign Policy: Beliefs, Institutions, and Political Change*. Ithaca: Cornell University Press, pp. 3–30.

Haas, P. (1993) 'Epistemic Communities and the Dynamics of International Environmental Co-Operation', in V. Rittberger (ed.) *Regime Theory and International Relations*. Oxford: Oxford University Press, pp. 168–201.

Hasenclever, A., Mayer, P. and Rittberger, V. (1997) *Theories of international regimes*. Cambridge: Cambridge University Press.

Haufler, V. (1993) 'Crossing the Boundary between Public and Private: International Regimes and Non-State Actors', in V. Rittberger (ed.) *Regime Theory and International Relations*. Oxford: Oxford University Press, pp. 94–111.

International Business Times (2013) 'Edward Snowden NSA Scandal: EU to Suspend US Data Sharing After Swift's Interbank Messaging System Breach', 25 September 2013.

Interview EU (2012a) Interview with EU official, 4 December 2012.

Interview EU (2012b) Interview with EU official, 7 December 2012.

Interview US (2012) Interview with US official, 8 February 2012.

Kaunert, C. (2009) 'The External Dimension of EU Counter-Terrorism Relations: Competences, Interests, and Institutions', *Terrorism and Political Violence*, 22(1), pp. 41–61.

Kaunert, C. and Léonard, S. (2011) 'The external dimension of counter-terrorism cooperation', in C. Kaunert (ed.) *European Internal Security: Towards Supranational Governance in the Area of Freedom, Security and Justice*. Manchester: Manchester University Press, pp. 90–120.

Krahmann, E. (2005) 'Security Governance and Networks: New Theoretical Perspectives in Transatlantic Security', *Cambridge Review of International Affairs*, 18(1), pp. 15–30.

Krasner, S. (1991) 'Global Communications and National Power: Life on the Pareto Frontier', *World Politics*, 43(03), pp. 336–366.

Krasner, S. (1993) 'Sovereignty, Regimes, and Human Rights', in V. Rittberger (ed.) *Regime Theory and International Relations*. Oxford: Oxford University Press, pp. 139–167.

Levy, M., Young, O. and Zürn, M. (1995) 'The Study of International Regimes', *European Journal of International Relations*, 1(3), pp. 267–330.

Occhipinti, J. (2010) 'Partner or Pushover? EU Relations with the US on Internal Security', in D. Hamilton (ed.) *Shoulder to Shoulder: Forging a Strategic US–EU Partnership*. Washington, DC: Brookings Institution Press, pp. 121–138.

Pawlak, P. (2007) 'From Hierarchy to Networks: Transatlantic Governance of Homeland Security', *Journal of Global Change and Governance*, 1(1), pp. 1–22.

Pawlak, P. (2009a) 'Network Politics in Transatlantic Homeland Security Cooperation', *Perspectives on European Politics and Society*, 10(4), pp. 560–581.

Pawlak, P. (2009b) 'Made in the USA? The Influence of the US on the EU's Data Protection Regime', *Liberty and Security in Europe*. Brussels: Centre for European Policy Studies (CEPS).

Svendsen, A. (2008) 'The globalization of intelligence since 9/11: frameworks and operational parameters', *Cambridge Review of International Affairs*, 21(1), pp. 129–144.

Svendsen, A. (2011) 'On "a Continuum with Expansion"? Intelligence Co-operation in Europe in the Early Twenty-first Century', *Journal of Contemporary European Research*, 7(4), pp. 520–538.

Wall Street Journal (2014) 'NSA Flap Strains Ties with Europe', 9 February 2014.

Young, O. (1994) *International Governance: Protecting the Environment in a Stateless Society*. Ithaca: Cornell University Press.

Young, O. (1998) *Creating Regimes: Arctic Accords and International Governance*. Ithaca: Cornell University Press.

Young, O. and Osherenko, G. (1993) 'Testing Theories of Regime Formation: Findings from a Large Collaborative Research Project', in V. Rittberger (ed.) *Regime Theory and International Relations*. Oxford: Oxford University Press, pp. 223–250.

Index

9/11 Commission Act (2007), US 60, 62, 138
9/11 terrorist attacks 1, 3, 11, 16, 21, 45, 101–3, 140, 152, 159; Commission Report 46; counter-terrorism cooperation before 2, 14–15; customs security before 46–7; threat perceptions in EU and US 45, 119; US customs security measures after 49–51
24-hour rule 51–3, 55, 60, 63; Container Security Initiative and 51–2; US structural leadership for 63
100 per cent scanning rule, for custom security 59–62; consequences of 62; implementation of 60–1

Action Plan (Council of the EU) 94, 102
advance passenger information (API) 121–2
Advance Passenger Information System (APIS) 118
Air France 133
aircraft bombings 119
air-piracy 119
al-Qaeda 47, 67, 78
antitrust crimes 73
Authorised Economic Operator (AEO) programme 57–8, 161; expansion of 59; implementation of 58; with regard to EU–US mutual recognition 58
Aviation and Transportation Security Act (2001), US 121
aviation transportation system 121; Amadeus system 124; computer reservation systems (CRS) 124; Computer-Assisted Aviation Pre-screening System (CAPS) 118; PNR agreements *see* Passenger Name Records (PNR) agreements

Baker, Stewart 128–9, 132, 134–5
banking fraud 159
Bonner, Robert 50–1
border controls, problem of 117, 119
border security 10, 119–21
British Airways 133
Bruggeman, Willy 102–3
business-to-government customs security programmes 4, 16, 25, 56–7, 154, 160, 162

Canada–US PNR sharing 132
Central Intelligence Agency (CIA) 119
Charter of the Fundamental Rights of European Union (CFR) 77
child pornography 1, 5, 93, 159
Cold War 15, 93
Committee of Permanent Representatives of member states to the EU (COREPER) 99
computer reservation systems (CRS) 124
Computer-Assisted Aviation Pre-screening System (CAPS) 118
Confidence and Security-Building Measures (CSBM) 11
Container Security Initiative (CSI) 16, 25, 44, 49–50, 160; 24-hour advance vessel manifest rule (24-hour rule) 51–2; entrepreneurial 'promotion' of 53; EU–US cooperation on 56; expansion of 55; implementation of 51; memorandums 56
container traffic, between Europe and the US 44
containerised transatlantic trade 44
Council of Europe 97; Action Plan 94; Committee of Ministers Recommendation 82, 107–8; Convention on Cybercrime 82, 108;

166 Index

Council of Europe *continued*
  Convention on Human Rights 77;
  Cybercrime Convention 75; Data
  Protection Convention 80
counter-terrorism cooperation, EU–US
  relationship on 6–10, 12, 127; before
  9/11 attacks 14–15; after 9/11 attacks 70
counter-terrorism intelligence 117
counterterrorist diplomacy 2
criminal intelligence, sharing of 1, 13,
  92–4, 96
customs duties 46
customs security 153; before 9/11 attacks
  46–7; after 9/11 attacks 47–56;
  American five-pillar plan for 56; anti-
  terrorism aspect of 46; balance between
  trade facilitation and 46; border controls
  49; business-to-government 4, 16, 25,
  56–7, 154, 160, 162; cargo inspections
  46; EU–US relationship on *see* customs
  security cooperation, EU–US
  relationship on; gaps in 46; 'No-Load'
  directive 52; risk management
  techniques 54, 56, 61; smart containers,
  use of 51; social and political factors
  influencing 47
customs security cooperation, EU–US
  relationship on 10; 24-hour rule 51–2,
  60, 63; 100 per cent scanning rule
  59–62; before and after the 9/11 attacks
  45–6; agenda for cooperation 56; agenda
  formation and negotiations 52–6;
  agreement of 2004 on customs security
  49, 54–6; business-to-government
  programmes 45; Container Security
  Initiative (CSI) 49, 51–2; Council
  resolution of 2003 on 49; customs
  security programme 54; customs
  security regime, development of 57;
  declarations of understandings 53;
  emergence of 62; EU initiated customs
  reforms and projects 55–6; feasibility of
  EU–US mutual recognition 57;
  identification of high-risk shipments 56;
  industry-partnership programmes 56;
  Mutual Recognition Agreement 56–9;
  mutual recognition, process of 57; post-
  9/11 US customs security measures
  49–51; risk management techniques 54,
  56; threat perceptions and 48; threats of
  legal action 61
Customs-Trade Partnership Against
  Terrorism (C-TPAT) 50, 56, 59, 161;
  versus EU's AEO programme 59;

  mutual recognition process 59; road
  map for recognition of 59
cyber-attacks 119
cybercrime 73, 93, 159; Council of Europe
  Cybercrime Convention 75, 82, 108

data privacy 135, 153
data protection, EU–US judicial
  cooperation on 77–82, 138; data
  protection conflict, characteristic of
  152–3; Data Protection Directive and
  80, 128, 130; Europol position on 105;
  passenger name records 115; US
  position on 81
data retention, issues of 105, 107, 135–6,
  139
data sharing, Europol–US agreement on 90
death penalty, issues of 74, 77; differences
  between EU and the US on 77–8;
  protection from a case-by-case status on
  78
distributional bargaining, theory of 37, 109
drugs and drug trafficking 93, 118;
  Europol fight against 95
Dublin European Council (December
  1996) 94

East–West security regime, emergence of
  11
economic and trade relationship, between
  EU and the US 44
Eizenstat, Stuart 97
entrepreneurial leadership 31, 35, 38, 51,
  53, 55, 57, 63, 71, 72, 85, 97, 98, 107–8,
  132, 134
EU citizens, rights of 77
Eurojust 1, 13, 15
European Arrest Warrant (EAW) 15, 75,
  82–4, 156; EU–US agreement on 83;
  extradition system 83; framework
  decision on 83
European Charter of Fundamental Rights
  77
European Coal and Steel Community 3
European Community (EC) 3–4, 93;
  relation with US 11
European Convention on Human Rights
  (ECHR) 77, 79; 'Protocol No. 6' of 77;
  'Protocol No. 13' of 77
European Court of Human Rights 80
European Court of Justice 54–5, 115–16,
  130–1
European Parliament 4, 115, 129, 137,
  140, 159; EU–US PNR negotiations

128; on power balance between the EU and the US 137

European Police Office (Europol) 1, 6, 8, 13, 16, 110, 159; Action Plan (Council of the EU) 94; agreement with US on internal security *see* Europol–US agreement, on internal security; contacts between representatives, issue of 94; Convention of 93, 98, 107, 109; cooperation with third states 93; creation of 96; cyber-security activities 155; data protection rules of 98, 102, 108–9; Draft Model agreement on cooperation with Third States 94; Drugs Unit 93; effectiveness of 99–100; emergence of 92; fight against drug trafficking 95; fight against transnational organised crime 95, 98; Joint Supervisory Board (JSB) 92, 106; Lisbon Treaty (2009) 92; Maastricht Treaty (1992) 92; Memorandum of Understandings 94; Model Cooperation Agreement 98; operational powers of 92–3; origins of 93; posting of US liaison officers 90; role of 93–5; secure communications 94; Supervisory Body 107; technical arrangements 94

European Union (EU): Area of Freedom, Security and Justice 84; Authorised Economic Operator (AEO) programme 57–9; Commissioner for Home Affairs 157; credibility of 71; Data Protection Directive 122, 130; Data Protection Working Party 122; fight against terrorism 71; MLA Convention 108; proposals on mutual legal assistance 70–1, 75; Registered Traveller Programme 162; Strategic Committee on Immigration, Frontiers and Asylum 122; Treaty on European Union 76

Europol–US agreement, on internal security 25, 70; before 9/11 attacks 91; after 9/11 attacks 100–8; agenda formation for 101–4; data protection issues 105; on data sharing 90; 'exchange of letters,' formula of 108; on fight against organised crime and drug trafficking 96; internationalisation of law enforcement and 93–5; on law enforcement cooperation 90; main point of friction 104; negotiations for 92, 97–108; New Transatlantic Agenda (1995) 1, 69, 96; personal data agreement, negotiations for 104–8; political prioritisation for 91; on protection of personal data 90; regime-formation process 90, 97; relations before 2000 and 95–7; strategic agreement, conclusion of 101–4 'exchange of letters' 106, 108

extradition treaties 67, 69, 72, 149; nationality-based ban on extradition 83

Faull, Jonathan 131, 134
Federal Aviation Authority (FAA), US 118–19
Federal Aviation Reauthorization Act (1996), US 118
Federal Bureau of Investigation (FBI) 69, 94, 119
Financial Action Task Force 2
foreign policymaking, role of ideas in 32
Freeh, Louis 95

genetically modified organism (GMO) 3
Geneva Convention, for prisoners of war 78
global standards in security matters, EU–US cooperation on 160–1
Gorelick, Jamie 95
Guantanamo Bay 67, 78

Haas, P. 33, 35–7; 'modified follow-the-leader' regime pattern 33, 121
hegemonic stability, theory of 27–8
hijackings 119
human rights: European Convention on 77; EU–US judicial cooperation on 77–82
human trafficking 1, 5–6, 13, 121, 159

identity theft 159
Immigration and Naturalisation Service (INS) 118–19
institutional bargaining, theory of 28–31, 35–7, 40
integrative bargaining 28, 35, 38, 84, 100, 152
intellectual leadership 35, 38, 59, 61–2, 93, 110, 121, 132, 139, 152
Intelligence Reform and Terrorism Prevention Act (2004) 130, 134
internal security cooperation, EU–US 25, 84, 148; background of 14–15; counter-terrorism and 6–10; definition of 5–6; effectiveness of 158–60; on establishing global standards 160–1; evaluation report on 158; role of private actors in 161–2; transatlantic 6–10

168   *Index*

International Civil Aviation Organization (ICAO) 3, 160
international cooperation, idea of 1, 6, 22, 27–8, 55–6, 62, 94–5, 149, 160
international police cooperation, idea of 91, 93–4
international regimes: concept of 22–5; contextualized rationalist theory of 36; creation of 29; 'dead-letter' regime 25; definition of 22; emergence of 21; EU–US negotiations on 37–41; expansion of 22; formation of 26–37; game theory 29; Haas' 'modified follow-the-leader' regime pattern 33, 35–6; interest-based school of 28–31, 38; knowledge-based theories of 29, 31–4; multivariate model of 34–7, *40*; operationalisation of 22, 37–41; power-based school of 26–8; synthetic model of 34–7; theories of 10–12
international society, principles of 30
Interpol 6

Joint Action Plan, on EU–US judicial cooperation 69
Joint Customs Cooperation Committee (JCCC) 62
Joint Statement on Supply Chain Security 159
judicial cooperation, EU–US: before 9/11 attacks 69; after 9/11 attacks 70–3; agenda-setting phase of 72; counter-terrorism cooperation 70; Data Protection Directive 80; death penalty, issues of 74, 77; European Arrest Warrant (EAW) 82–4; Europol–US agreements 70; extradition agreement 67, 69, 72–3; extra-territorial measures to combat crimes 69; framework agreements 69; human rights and data protection issues 76, 77–82; interest-based patterns of 73, 76; intra-EU judicial cooperation 69; on issues of data protection and human rights 68; Joint Action Plan 69; legal assistance agreement 68, 73; mutual legal assistance (MLA) 67, 71–2, 75; Mutual Legal Assistance Treaties (MLATS) 69; negotiations for 71, 73–84; New Transatlantic Agenda (1995) 1, 69; partnership based on common benefits 68; 'penalty threshold' approach for 73; police and law enforcement cooperation 69; on provisions related to bank information 75; on special courts (military tribunals) 74–5; third-pillar agreements 67–8, 76, 131; variable geometry, principle of 72
judicial decisions, mutual recognition of 83
Justice and Home Affairs (JHA) 14–15, 90, 94, 102, 156

Keohane, Robert 10–11, 22–5, 28–9, 32, 39; functional theory 28
Krasner, S. 22–4, 27–8, 149

law enforcement, internationalisation of 93–5
laws and legislations, for internal security: 9/11 Commission Act (2007), US 60, 62, 138; Aviation and Transportation Security Act (2001) 121; Federal Aviation Reauthorization Act (1996) 118; Helms–Burton Act (1996) 3; Maritime Transportation Security Act (2002) 52; Safe Port Act (2006) 60; Security and Accountability for Every Port Act (2006) 56, 59
Lisbon Treaty (2009) 92, 116, 137, 140

Maastricht Treaty (1992) 14, 92
man-portable air-defence missiles (MANPADs) 119
marine transportation system, terrorist attacks against 46, 49
maritime security, EU's policy on 49
maritime transport and trade, EU–US 60
Maritime Transportation Security Act (2002), US 52
military tribunals 67, 74–5, 84; establishment of 78; Military Order of November 13, 2001 78–9
Model Cooperation Agreement (Europol) 98
'modified follow-the-leader' regime 33, 35, 121
money forgery 93
money-laundering 93
multi-layered risk management, principle of 60
mutual legal assistance (MLA) 25, 67, 71–2, 75, 149, 158; denial of 82
Mutual Legal Assistance Treaties (MLATS) 69
Mutual Recognition Agreement, EU–US (2012) 44, 56–9, 154, 159; agenda of 58; legal framework for implementation of 58

Index   169

Naples II Convention on Customs Cooperation (1997) 47
National Security Agency (NSA), US 157
national sovereignty, concept of 94
National Strategy for Homeland Security (US) 6, 48–9, 120
New Transatlantic Agenda (NTA) 1, 69, 96
Nice, Treaty of (2000) 77, 79
North Atlantic Treaty Organization (NATO) 1, 14
Nye, Joseph 11, 22, 32

organised crime, fight against 5–6, 9, 14–16, 46, 49, 68, 70, 90, 93–9, 102–3, 109, 118

Passenger Name Records (PNR) agreements 2, 9, 16–17, 25, 62, 76; agenda-formation stage 116, 117–22; airlines' reservation systems 118; Canada–US PNR sharing 132; effectiveness of the exchange of PNR data 159; EU–US relations on 121–2; features of 124; first PNR agreement 125–9; impact of the 9/11 attacks on 117–21; issues related to data protection 115; negotiations of 115, 122–5; problem associated with 117–22; second PNR agreement 129–37; for security purposes 117–18; third PNR agreement 137–9; threat of penalties 116, 129; utility of using PNR information 116
'penalty threshold' approach, for EU–US judicial cooperation 73
police and law enforcement cooperation 69
Powell, Colin 104
prisoners of war 78
purpose limitation, principle of 80, 82, 101, 104–8

Registered Traveller Programme, EU 162
Richard, Mark 81
risk management, customs security model of 61
Roadmap towards Mutual Recognition of Trade Partnership Programs (2008) 58

Safe Port Act (2006), US 60
Schengen Area 118, 120
Schengen Convention (1995) 118
Secure Freight Initiative (SFI) 59
Security and Accountability for Every Port Act (2006), US 56, 59

smart borders 153; concept of 49, 53, 63, 116, 120, 139; and idea of screening people and goods 120; US plan for the establishment of 50
state power, importance of 27
Storbeck, Jürgen 93–4, 98, 103
Strategy to Combat Transnational Organized Crime (US) 6
Straw, Jack 156
supply chains, international 153; Joint Statement on Supply Chain Security 159; security controls in transatlantic 63; security problem 53; terrorist exploitation of 47

Taliban 67, 78, 85n2
Tampere European Council 82
Task Force for the Fight against Terrorism 102
terrorist attacks: 9/11 attacks *see* 9/11 terrorist attacks; exploitation of supply chains for 47; against marine transportation system 46; sea containers, use of 48; and US fight against terrorism 102
Terrorist Finance Tracking Program (TFTP), US 9, 157
terrorist financing 2
third-pillar framework, EU–US negotiations on 67–8, 76, 131
trade relations, US–EC 21
trade wars 3
transatlantic relations, EU–US: comparison of the cases 149–54; European Union and 154–7; implications for 148–57
trans-boundary externalities 10–11
transnational organised crime 93, 109; Europol fight against 95, 98; international cooperation for combating 95
Transport Security Cooperation Group 62
Treaty on European Union (TEU) 76, 79
TREVI group 93

US Coast Guard 50; Maritime Strategy for Homeland Security 48
US Customs and Border Protection Unit (CBP) 50, 59; Advance Passenger Information System (APIS) 118; on expansion of C-TPAT to exporters 59; five pillars of customs security 50; mission and activities 50
US Customs Service 50, 94, 118

US Department of Homeland Security (DHS) 48, 120, 128, 162; 100 per cent rule 61–2; on feasibility of scanning all US-bound containers 59; Secure Freight Initiative (SFI) 59
US Helms–Burton Act 3
US Immigration and Naturalisation Service 118–19
US law enforcement agencies, internationalisation of 95
US National Strategy for Global Supply Chain Security (2012) 62
US Secret Service 98
US–Soviet security relationship 11

variable geometry, principle of 72
veto power 30, 74, 76, 78, 128, 137

Visa Waiver Program (VWP), US 124, 138, 141n3

war on terror 74, 78
World Customs Organization (WCO) 3, 57, 61, 160; SAFE Framework of Standards to Secure and Facilitate Global Trade (2005) 57; views on 100 per cent rule 61
World Trade Organisation (WTO) 61, 63

Young, Oran 29–30, 129, 135, 154; institutional bargaining, theory of 28, 40; model of regime establishment 30–1; on role of knowledge in agenda formation 35; on stages of regime-formation process 35